Table o

Preface

This is the story of my life in aviation. You have heard people say, "You should write a book!" I'm a firm believer that everyone has an interesting story to tell. The problem is getting one to sit down and write it. As time is running out, I will give it a go. They say that when you are over the hill you pick up speed. How true!

I will get my AK story out of the way right off the bat. When "hangar flying,"or reminiscing, all pilots have their AK stories, as in Almost Killed!

My AK story happened October 22, 1947, and it is still vivid in my mind after all these years.

Burke, my copilot, and I departed Charleston about 4 PM in an old war surplus DC-3 with twenty-eight Bahamian farm laborers for Nassau. It was about a 3¾ hour flight. Our little airline, Nationwide Air Transport, had the contract to bring farm laborers into the United States for the picking and field work. The passengers sat in the military bucket seats on each side of the bare cabin.

This was before the days of radar or good weather reporting. We knew there was a weather front over the ocean between Charleston and Nassau, but it didn't seem too serious. Forty minutes out, we could see a line of dark green boiling weather stretching from horizon to horizon, so there was no chance for an end run. It was too high to go over, so we elected to go under it. We let down to 1,500 feet. It was a solid wall, but we figured it wouldn't be too wide. So, we cinched down the seat belts – no shoulder straps back then – took the bird off auto pilot, and entered this mass of ugly stuff.

As soon as we entered, I knew we were in trouble. We were in a roll cloud, flying through a waterfall. The noise was deafening as it pounded on the windshield and aluminum. The water was so dense, I had the feeling both engines would quit due to the lack of air. But they hung in there.

And then the violent turbulence hit. It tossed our DC-3 around like a chip in a tornado. One minute we were going up with the rate-of-climb instrument pegged and the next moment plunging down with rate-of-descent pegged. This with full prop rpms and full throttle. There was no stopping it. I saw 300 feet on the altimeter and I thought it was going to smash us into the ocean. I learned later that, under those conditions, the pressure altimeters are highly inaccurate, so there's no telling how low we really went.

So there we were going up and down like a yo-yo with the instrument panel shaking so bad the instruments were just a blur. It was like a dog shaking a rag. At that point, I had the feeling the plane was tumbling and that we were inverted. I yelled to Burke, "Take it! I have vertigo." I didn't know our attitude.

He yelled back, 'Hell, no – you keep it!"

That DC-3 had two turn-and-bank instruments (needle and ball). They were worthless in the turbulence as the needles and balls were banging both side limits of the instruments.

But for instrument flying the main gauge to watch is the artificial horizon. This is a gyro instrument that shows the pilot the attitude of the plane in relation to the earth's horizon. We had three artificial horizons: one on the Captain's side, one on the copilot's side, and one for the autopilot. The turbulence was so violent that two of the three gyro horizons tumbled and spun crazily. The third one hung in there, and had it tumbled also there is no doubt in my mind we would have disappeared in the Bermuda Triangle.

Along with all this severe turbulence something was happening that I had never experienced before. One second the rudder pedals would stand me up in the cockpit. They would go full to the stops. All my strength would not budge them. The next second there would be no pressure on the rudder pedals at all. Obviously no air was passing by the rudder. If we were in fact tumbling, the fuselage must have blocked out the airflow to the rudder. I have yet to talk to any pilot who has experienced the phenomenon. Possibly they didn't live to tell about it.

After what seemed ages, we popped or were thrown out of the backside of this squall line. Burke and I looked at each other, and we both knew that from here on out we were living on borrowed time.

When my heart and pulse got back to normal, I went back in the cabin to check on our passengers. There sat twenty-eight huge black British laborers grinning from ear to ear. They thought that was the best ride they ever had. Not one got airsick. What great passengers! Of course they didn't know they also had an AK story to tell. It was close.

I knew then that I wasn't immortal, and that night I made out my first will.

Thinking back, the question is “Was I scared?” There wasn't time to be. I was too desperate and busy trying to keep the plane flying and right side up.

That's it folks. No more AK stories.

PART I:

MY LIFE IN AVIATION

The War & Before

I'll begin at the beginning, with my first airplane experience. I was about ten years old and staying with my grandparents in the small town of Waterbury, Conneticut. That was 1930 and, yes, I am now eighty-six. No, I can't believe it either.

A barn stormer in a bi-wing fabric-covered open-cockpit plane flew low over town and landed in a farmer's field. Naturally, the town folks headed out to the farm to see the action.

The barn stormer was hopping passengers, so my grandpa paid for my sister and me to have a flight. We both climbed into the front open cockpit with the pilot in the rear open cockpit. We took off, and what a great view. There was no sensation of height. It was a smooth flight. It probably only lasted ten minutes, but it was an unforgettable experience for a young kid.

Eleven years later, I was twenty-one, and it was 1941. Pearl Harbor had been bombed, and we were at war. I had a very low draft number. I was about to be called up. I suddenly realized I didn't want to be a foot soldier, so I had better get off my butt and do something.

I was living in a suburb of Philadelphia. I headed downtown to the courthouse to enlist in the Army Air Corps. They required two years of college, which I had. They wanted to see college credentials. Since I didn't have them with me, they said, “Tough, kid. Guess the draft board has you.”

Discouraged, I left and saw a sign in front of the courthouse: “Join the Navy Air Corps.” So I went back to the second floor and went through the same routine. They notified the draft board that they were holding me pending approval of college credentials.

With the proper paperwork, I was approved for the Navy physical. We were stripped down to our shorts, not knowing what to do. After the exam, I was told I was disqualified because I only weighed 80 pounds. I actually weighed about 137. I said, “Look at me. The chart is wrong.” But no luck. I spotted an officer with a lot of stripes. I had no idea of his rank, but I told him my story and pleaded to just put me on a scale and correct this error on the records. He did. He shook his head and changed the item.

Then another seaman second said I was disqualified because I had a cap between my two front teeth. He said I wouldn't be able to hold an oxygen tube in my mouth, that it would slip out and I would pass out from lack of oxygen. So I went back to the many striped officer. He sighed and came to my rescue. The war had just started, and the Navy needed bodies – fast. So I passed the physical.

I started ground school and flight training at the Philadelphia Navy Yard. The hardest part of ground school was learning Morse code. It seems to me we practiced four hours a day. To pass, we were required to copy and send twelve words a minute. We were told that in combat we only had about three minutes to live and had to get the message out in less time than that. I'm not sure we all made the grade, but everyone passed. As I say, the Navy needed recruits.

At the Navy yard, I had about ten hours of flight instruction in a Navy M-3. It is similar to a Stearman. Two open cockpits, fabric-covered bi-wing, tail wheel, no radio. We used Camden airport in New Jersey for the training, a huge grass field with no runways.

We shuttled from the barracks in the Navy yard over to Camden in a station wagon. I did a lot of the driving. The old station wagon had a poor carburetor, so I had to goose the engine all the time to keep it from stalling. On one drive over, I heard one instructor say to my instructor, "I hope he doesn't fly a plane the way he drives a car."

My Navy instructor was Lieutenant Stewart, who was a calm, low-key man. Thank the Lord. I should have been washed out because I was getting airsick.

Lt. Stewart said, "Why don't you quit?"

I told him, "I can't quit. I have a girlfriend, boy friends, parents."

At that point the Navy needed pilots, so he said, "Okay."

I got over it and soloed after ten hours. Every pilot can remember his first solo flight. What a blast. My dad was outside the fence taking pictures of these training planes. The Navy saw him and took his film – for security, you know.

Then it was on to Jacksonville Naval Air Station in Florida for the advanced training in the first part of 1942.

What a change from the cold winter weather of Philadelphia to the wonderful warm climate of Jacksonville. Hog heaven.

I won't bore you with all the ground school details. Eight hours a day of power plants, navigation, celestial navigation, Morse code, semaphore code, theory of flight, and radio procedure, plus physical drills.

I went right into the Stearman flight training. Spot landings in a circle; slips to landing in the circle; acrobatics, including spins, loops, snap rolls, slow rolls, Immelmanns, inverted flight, and wing overs.

The communication in these planes was unusual. There were no radios. Communication was with a Gosport tube – a hollow, flexible metal tube that started at the instructor's mouth with a canvas cup strapped around his helmet. This tube fed back to the student and split to each ear in his helmet. So it was a one-way deal. The instructor could talk to the students, but the students could not talk to the instructor.

The student always had the rear cockpit, so the plane would not be nose heavy when he soloed. The instructor in front had a mirror on the top wing to see the student behind him. So he was always looking back and saying, "Do you understand?" And the student would most often nod his head yes, even if he didn't.

With this picture in mind, I'll relate an incident in night flying. There were about twenty planes at this one field practicing night landing in pitch black darkness. On the final turning, I happened to turn and look over my shoulder and there was a plane letting down right on top of us. I grabbed the stick and turned rather violently out of the way. The instructor yelled at me, “WHAT THE HELL ARE YOU DOING?” I pointed at the plane he had not seen that was now in the spot we had just vacated. The instructor said, “Guess I owe you an apology. Nice work, kid.”

Next, I checked out in the SNJ. This is a larger, heavier single-engine plane with retractable landing gear, flaps, radio, and enclosed cockpit. Quite a step up. I thought I was really hot stuff flying this plane. I had about thirty hours in it.

The only exciting episode was on one solo takeoff over the St. Johns River. I had just reached the shoreline and was about a hundred feet in the air when the engine quit. I thought for sure I would have to ditch, but a moment later the engine came back to life and I breathed a huge sigh of relief.

Due to the Navy's need, or maybe because they figured I wasn't fighter pilot material, they put me in PBY training. This is a twin-engine plane with a boat hull for water landings. It is designed for patrol scouting and bombing. It is big and slow, but it can stay in the air for thirty hours. In the fleet there was a club called “The Two Sun Club.” To qualify, the pilot would take off in the dark, see the sun come up, fly all day and night and see the sun come up the second time.

The big difference between landing on land and landing on water is that if the water is smooth it is like a mirror and thus makes it impossible to judge one's height above the water. So the procedure in this case was to set up a rate of descent and hold it, without flaring, until the hull hit the water and then retard the throttles. Of course, out in the Pacific this was never a problem, as the water is seldom crystal smooth.

In this plane, I was trained to use the Nordon Bombsight. Back then, it was a highly guarded secret. I made about five practice runs and received an okay score. Then we were trained to shoot the fifty-caliber machine guns out the waist hatches at a target sleeve towed by another PBY. Each student had different color-coated bullets, so we could count the number of hits on the target later. The only exciting episode was when one student started shooting at the target sleeve just as it was being let out. Since it was close to the towing plane, there were a few holes in their tail section. Needless to say, there were some unhappy instructors. I flew about sixty-two hours in that big old bird.

It seemed I was hard luck on roommates. I had three washouts. Two couldn't make the grade, and Steve failed on purpose. He was in love and thought flying was too dangerous.

There were thousands of flights daily and this base alone averaged one fatality a day while I was there. I read later that more pilots were killed in training accidents than were lost in war zones. The thinking was, had the training not been so thorough, more would have been lost in combat.

I passed all my tests and received my navy wings August 3, 1942. I was a mighty green ensign. Having completed my training and received my commission, I wished to be ordered to a PBY squadron. But at this period of time the Navy was trying to expand and needed instructors. So I was ordered to Stearman instructor's school, still at Jacksonville.

Back to acrobatics and getting airsick again.

I got an appointment to see the base commander. A nervous green ensign facing a grizzled, old, full Navy Captain. I stated I would be a better asset to the Navy in a PBY outfit, as I was getting air sick in the Stearmans. He took one hard look and said, "If you can't cut it, son, turn in your wings. Dismissed." With a quick salute, I beat a hasty exit.

Fortunately, I got over the air sickness and learned how to instruct all the acrobatic maneuvers. It was a matter of standardization. The Navy wanted all maneuvers and landings to be taught the same way.

A month later I successfully passed this course and waited for an assignment to a training base.

In the fall of 1942 I received orders to report to a new training base being built at Norman, Oklahoma. If you are in the Navy, you can't get any farther away from the ocean. The base was so new, the barracks had not been built, so I had to find a room in town for a few months.

Flying in open cockpits through the winters of 1942 and 1943 was a bit brisk. No, it was downright bone-chilling cold. I had fur-lined gloves, helmet, jacket, boots, and even fur-lined leather pants. These proved to be too cumbersome. It was a problem to climb on the wing and into the cockpit with them on, so we didn't use those pants.

Then there was the wind. It seemed one day Kansas would blow down to Texas, and then Texas would blow back to Kansas. These training planes had a stalling speed of only 40 mph, so if the wind was blowing above that, we could hang the bird on the prop in the air and remain in front of the tower, stating it was time to put up the recall flag.

Another fun thing to do in the strong wind was to make a wheel landing with the tail up and, as you rolled to a stop, gradually add brakes and power so the plane would come to a stop with the tail still up and parallel with the ground. It took a fine touch. Anything to relieve the boredom of hours of instructing.

When giving check rides in the wind, the student could seldom hit the spot landing circle. So, I would say, "Take me back to the base." The poor kid knew he had busted his check ride. He didn't know I had a huge hangover and just wanted to be on the ground. On returning to base, I would tell the student that due to the wind, I wasn't going to give him a down check, that I would give him an incomplete mark. He would be so grateful that it was embarrassing. In the cadet ranks, I got the reputation as one of the good guys; it was not deserved.

I trained a huge number of cadets to fly and had only one who couldn't solo. It was ironic. He was in the first group of five assigned to me. He just couldn't get the hang of it. He was reassigned twice to two other, more experienced instructors, and they couldn't pull him through either. So I didn't feel like I had failed. Later, he sent me a letter saying he was happy in his new job and appreciated my patience and spending so much extra time with him. It showed class.

The learning curve is hell. No one had prepared me for what happened on one flight. We had been doing stunts and were flying inverted – upside-down, hanging on our seat belts. Usually, one would roll out to level flight. This time I lowered the nose and started a half loop out. What I didn't realize was we had way too much speed and now were going straight down with me pulling hard on the stick. I was afraid the wings would buckle or that we would hit the ground. We didn't exactly go through the tree tops, but it was close. I looked in the mirror and the student was laughing. He didn't know I had just made a very stupid error. Fate is the hunter.

On one flight en route to an outlying area, I cut the engine. The student was to find a field, glide down, and make an approach. Just off the ground, I would add power and climb out. This time, as I added power – BAM! – we hit something. I took over the controls and couldn't move the ailerons. Through the Gosport tube, I told the student I had it: "Take your hands off the stick." I looked in the mirror and saw he had both hands in the air. Seems we did not see a pole and it had ripped through the left wing and aileron. No big deal. Back to the base to get another bird.

At an outlying field, I was sitting on the ground while my student was solo shooting landings to a circle. Another instructor saw me and thought it would be good sport to buzz me. He dropped down on me, and as I dove down flat, I tossed my Gosport tube up in his prop. He knew he had hit something, so I lay there not moving, pretending I had been hit. He made a quick short circuit, landed, jumped out of his plane and ran to me. I let him turn me over then winked at him. He exploded and swore at me for scaring him so bad. I feel sure that was his last buzz job.

We would work ten and two. Ten days on and two off. On days off we could take a plane and go anywhere we wanted. Since Oklahoma was a dry state, it was off to Dallas or Kansas City for a booze run. One weekend sticks out in my mind. I flew up to Des Moines. A thousand WACs were stationed there and desperate for company. When I left early Sunday, the airport was entirely covered fence to fence with military planes that had flown in for this action.

I know we drank far too much, and, too often, we flew with splitting hangovers. Oklahoma City was only twenty minutes away and had a club where we could party and dance. And it had lockers for our booze. It was no trouble at all to get to town. At one point, the squadron commander had enough and posted a memo: “No more dress blues on the flight line.” Pilots had been going directly from a party to their flights without changing to the work uniform. We were told we were bad examples for the cadets.

Occasionally, we were assigned the duty of officer of the day. About two o’clock one morning, I was driving the patrol car around the base perimeter to check on the guards. Way out on the back fence, I found a seaman sound asleep. I took his rifle and put it in the wagon and then woke him up. I asked him if he had been issued a rifle when he came on duty. The poor kid was terrified, looking under twigs and leaves. I said, "Did you fall asleep and let some civilian jump the fence and steal your rifle?" I left him and returned back about one hour later. I handed him his rifle, saying, "Okay, I'm not going to say or write anything about this, and I don't want you to tell anyone. Chalk this up to experience and move on." He was a mighty relieved kid. Thinking back, I don't know if it was a cruel thing to do. But I couldn't see ruining his career with a possible court-martial.

It wasn't all one-sided. Every six months or so, the senior instructor from the Jacksonville instructor's school would come to our base and fly with us to make sure we were doing the job correctly. I never heard of a base instructor getting washed out, but it was still a check ride.

At one point, the Navy came up with a stupid idea. We had to instruct inverted spins at night. After gaining some altitude, you rolled the plane upside-down, kicked the rudder, and thus started to spin down with centrifugal force trying to throw you out. You're hanging on your seat belt. Of course, this centrifugal force is throwing everything that is loose out of the plane. Goggles, Gosports, clipboards, fire extinguishers, flashlights, etc. This only lasted a few weeks before the Navy came to its senses and cancelled the order.

By the end of this duty, I was a senior instructor and mostly did check rides with students. I ended up with over one thousand hours in the training plane.

While I was teaching new pilots in Oklahoma, my older sister, Barbara, was driving a huge Red Cross clubmobile in England. A few days after the Normandy invasion, she drove it off a landing craft, through the surf, up the beach and followed the troops across Europe. She would park it behind a stone building, if possible, for protection.

It didn't seem right that I was in the Navy, in Oklahoma. And to have a sister writing home about the war. Another embarrassment is that I was in the Navy five years and never aboard a ship. Fate is interesting.

Transport Pilots in Fort Worth, Texas, 1944

In June of 1944 the navy had plenty of pilots. What to do with all these instructors? First, they tried to make carrier pilots out of them, but it didn't work out. The old instructors were used to thinking for themselves and would not follow the orders of the landing signal officer. So the Navy decided to make transport pilots out of us. The Navy had a contract with American Airlines for training. I reported to the Fort Worth American Airlines School. They had American Captains as instructors.

My first flight in the DC-3 was a disaster. I was in the left seat flying, and this grouchy old Captain in the right seat barked at me to follow the river. We were only at 500 feet, and as a sharp bend in the river came up, I slid out over land. The Captain grabbed the yoke, stood it up on the wing and shouted, “I told you to stay over the river!” Man, what an introduction. Fortunately, that Captain went back on the line, and I got a new instructor who was a dream. Calm, patient, funny. What a great guy. After completing the course, we took the Captain and his wife out to a great party to show our appreciation.

So now I was a DC-3 transport qualified Captain. It felt good to be finally out of the light trainers. There was no slot open in a DC-3 squadron, so I was assigned to a flying boat outfit in Alameda, California.

I reported in and was told no slot was available, to check back in two weeks. The Navy had more pilots than they knew what to do with. I found an apartment in town and partied for two weeks. It was three weeks before my first flight in the flying boat.

The PB2Y-3R is a four-engine flying boat with retractable wing floats and two decks assigned to carry passengers and cargo. It had no wheels, but after landing in the water and being attached to a buoy, wheels could be floated out and attached to the fuselage, and then the plane could be towed by a tug up a ramp to a hangar. This usually took about an hour. After a fourteen hour flight in the Pacific, you waited, sweating, in a humid, hot plane for another hour before stepping on dry land.

The plane carried four pilots, and I was number four. Being new, I was at the bottom of the barrel. My main job was to guard the mail sacks. I strapped on a 45 revolver that I didn't know how to shoot, signed forms for mail sacks and off we went. Then I was told if we had to ditch and were sinking to make sure the mail sank.

The takeoffs from Oakland Bay were not easy. If the water was smooth, the plane did not have enough power to break the water suction on the hull. So crash boats would come out and roar around making white caps and waves so we could lift off. Then we were so heavy we couldn't climb fast enough to clear the Oakland Bay Bridge, so we had to circle some twenty minutes before we could head west for Honolulu. With four pilots and long flights, I got very few takeoffs or landings.

The planes were so heavy and underpowered we had to step-climb to altitude. We cruised for three hours at 2,000 feet until we burned enough gas to allow us to climb to 4,000 feet. Our final altitude was 8,000 feet, as the plane was not pressurized.

The two main destinations were Saipan and Auckland, New Zealand. Oakland to Honolulu is fourteen hours; to Johnson Island is five and a half hours; to Kwajalein is ten hours; to Saipan ten hours. In total, it's a seventy-nine hour round trip. The other route is Oakland to Honolulu in fourteen hours; six and a half hours to Palmyra Island; five and a half hours to Canton Island; five hours to Suva; five hours to Noumaya; and seven hours to Auckland. In total, it's a ninety hour round trip.

This plane had a six bunk compartment with sheets and blankets and no windows, so it was dark and we could sleep. However, anytime an engine so much as missed a beat, anyone sleeping was instantly awake. I never found that sleeping at altitude rested a person. It just made the time go faster.

This plane had a kitchen and a cook. On the way to Saipan, we ate high on the hog. On the return flight, we ate Spam. The cook would trade whatever goodies he had left for war souvenirs.

Auckland was a great layover. Most local men were off to war, and here comes new American talent. The remaining men didn't seem to like us, but the gals didn't hesitate. It was a great party town.

The bay at Auckland was crowded with moving boats. Our Captain would be waiting for an open lane. There never was one, so he would pour on the power, get the bird up on the step and weave in and out down the bay, just missing the boats. We had a thrill, and I'm sure some of the boats did also.

Takeoffs and landings on the open ocean were more than interesting. Sometimes the water would come up over the cockpit. The corrosion must have been horrible from that salt water. I have seen landings so violent they would knock rivets out of the hull. Then a seaman would poke a pencil in the hull to keep the water from squirting in. I spent seven months in this squadron and flew 572 hours in these boats.

A Coronado PB2Y-3R. I flew 572 hours in this plane from September 27, 1944 to May 23, 1945.

PBY Flying Boat taking off from Canton Island

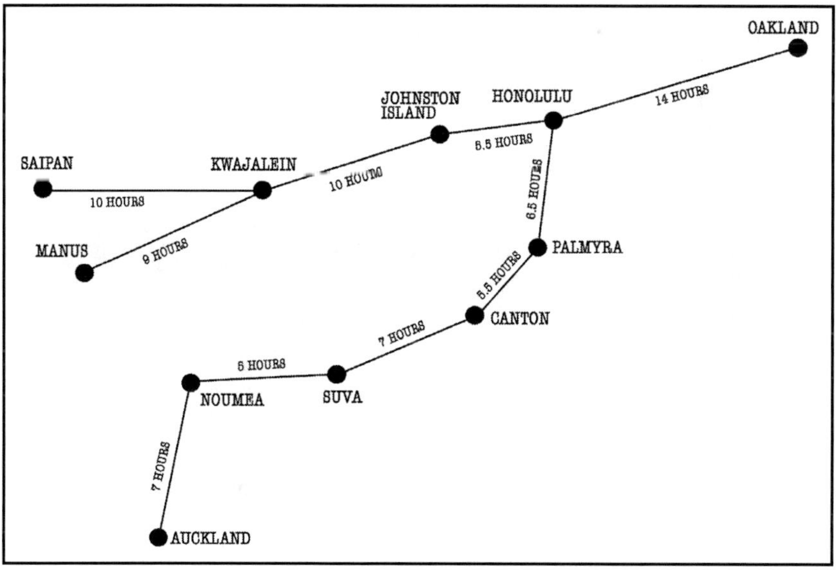

Flying Boat Routes in the Pacific, 1944-1945

Navy men pulling a PBY Flying Boat to the dock

PB2Y-3R at Canton Island

Quarters on Manus Island

Quarters on Ebeye Island

I wrote the following letters while I was in the boat squadron.

December 14, 1944.

Well now,

It's about time something more was written from this neck of the country than "still sitting around waiting for work". At long last there is something to write about that at least a few more than myself might be interested in.

Our schedule crew met Friday night, Dec. 1st, were briefed, picked up the confidential and secret mail, and boarded the already loaded, waiting, four engined flying boat. The size of the darned thing always amazes me every time I get in it. Up forward there are two decks with standing room on both. At any rate we started the engines, were lowered down the ramp into the water by the tractors, called the tower for a clearance.....and so were off for Pearl Harbor about 2300 miles away. The plane was so heavily loaded with cargo and gas it seemed as if it would never leave the water but it finally staggered clumsily into the air amid roaring motors, flying spray, and sweating pilots.

As we gained altitude from Alameda we first crossed the eight mile Oakland-Frisco Bridge. The cars and trains were streaming across, as I had done so many times in the last few months. Being fairly low we could almost see the people in them, laughing and heading out for the evening sport. Still slowly gaining altitude we passed over Alcatraz and could look off to the left and see all the beautiful blazing lights of Frisco. It certainly is a wonderful sight to see a city at night with the millions of lights forming unthought of patterns and the carlights chasing around as if trying to change that pattern. Crossing over the Golden Gate Bridge is the last radio contact for the VR-2 squadron radio but the lights up and down the coast take a long time to fade back into the night.

After gaining our altitude, the plane is flown by hand for a while and then put on the gyro pilot. From then on it is just a matter of twisting knobs to keep the plane at the right altitude and in the right direction.

Once in the air one of the men has nothing to do except see that all the crew is well fed.....which isn't much trouble because of his equipment and stores.Back in the center of the ship he has a stove, icebox, and table with benches. I probably shouldn't mention what there is to eat aboard.....it makes the job seem too soft.....but at any rate.....there are steaks, shrimp, soups, ham, cookies, cake and all sorts of fruit juices. How about that now? Almost forgot the ever present bacon and eggs.

So here we have the picture of the cockpit. The engineer sitting in front of all his dials, gages, levers, and cruising charts, watching the engines for the first sign of trouble or waste of the ever precious gas. The radio man sitting among all his receivers and transmitters, earphones hung on, guarding a couple of frequencies for emergency messages and sending in an hourly report as to where we are.....or where we think we are.....all this is coded of course. The navigator is at his table with his charts and

-2-

and every once in a while takes a sun or star sight, watches the drift and then plots in our latest test position. And lastly we come to the pilots, sitting up front, feet propped up on the panel, half asleep, working the gyro pilot and lazily watching the miles and miles of ocean slide by underneath.

Up front at night the pilots have a curtain behind them to keep the light glare off the windows, the dials and instruments are all coated with illuminous paint, with fluerescent light shining on them which makes them show up in sharp green producing no glare. The roaring engines can be seen right over our shoulders with the large whirling propellors.....the exhaust stacks red hot spurting a bright pink flame. By watching the color of the exhaust we can tell to what degree the gas mixture is leaned out.

All the way over to Pearl we could hear the dance bands and programs from the States.....a great help in staying awake. But just let any one of these four motors miss once and our eyes race over the instruments.....all thoughts of sleep completely vanish.....at least for a time.

Dawn the next morning was a beautiful sight.....the sun first hitting the tops of the clouds making them a brilliant white with a dull gray bottom.....and gradually the whiteness crept lower and lower until it looked like huge puffs of cotton floating around in the sky. A short time later the sun hit the water which was an amazing sight. The dark clear blueness of the color with the scattered white caps here and there was a new and beautiful sight to me.

Finally, after over fourteen hours in the air we saw Pearl Harbor creeping up over the horizon.....seemed like we would never get there but finally circled in for a landing and the first leg of the journey was over.

There we had a day lay over to rest up and took another ship out the next afternoon heading for Ebeye in the Marshall Islands. About five hours out of Pearl we landed at Johnson Island to leave off a little mail but mainly to gas up. An hour before reaching this island it started raining with visibility about half a mile.....strictly instrument conditions.....and being at night it made it that much harder.....all our radio direction finding-equipment showed the island to be straight ahead but it was half an hour before it suddenly loomed up out of the darkness. The skipper put down the landing lights, wheeled the plane around and came in for the landing. The lights shown down on the water producing another new sight for me. The water was a very light bluish green, probably because of the shallow white coral bottom. It was just like coming in for a landing in an immense indoor swimming pool. Our landing lights reflecting off the coral bottom gave the effect of having the whole lagoon lighted with underwater lights..... like one might see at an aquacade.

Johnson itself is a very small atoll.....not more than a few hundred yards wide and about three quarters of a mile long .....just large enough for a landing strip and buildings. After refueling and getting a bite to eat we were off again for the Marshall Islands.

-3-

After another all night flight, about seven hours later, Kwajalein and Ebeye came into the picture.....a welcome sight after all those hours in the air. The water was rough enough to have whitecaps and sure made for a hard landing. The skipper bounced it once.....thought the bottom was going to cave in but he informed me I hadn't seen anything yet.....can't say as I want to see a landing made on any rougher a sea.

The Atoll of Ebeye is very small and at no place more than five feet above the water.....a hurricane would wipe it off the map. There were a few old Jap airraid shelters to prove we hadn't always had that island. Both here and at Pearl, there was an outdoor movie, the seats were made out of pieces of steel landing strips set up on logs......really made a good set up.

There in the Marshalls is an island called Wotji still held by the Japs. I can't understand the set up. We had to alter our course so as not to fly over it (they still seem to have antiaircraft guns) but they never bother the Americans on the other Atolls and the Americans completely ignore them. Where they get their supplies I don't know but it seems funny to have Japs on a neighboring island.

So the next morning, what ever day that was (we passed through so many time zones in such a short space of time that I got tired of changing my watch and just used Greenwich Civil time) (also passing over the international date line confused me on the days) we took off for Saipan. About eight hours out of the Marshalls we had to feather one of the propellors due to an oil leak and went in on three engines for two hours. Having seventeen passengers aboard besides the crew, the skipper got a few more gray hairs. Landed O.K. and saw the sights of the bloody battles of Saipan. All the old timers outdid themselves telling gruesome stories, one among them was the fact they had killed forty eight Japs the night before. Seems there are still lots of Japs hidden up in the hills but the Americans work night and day on the landing fields for the big superfortresses.

About four o'clock in the morning I saw my first shots fired in all this time I've been in the Navy. There was an airraid by the Japs so we all tore outside to see the fireworks. They were aiming for the superforts on the other side of the island and must have gotten a couple of hits because of explosions we heard. Our anti air~~xxxx gxxx~~ craft guns were going a mile a minute and did a good job. We heard one Jap plane start a power dive from which he never pulled out.....he crashed about half a mile away. We saw another go down in flames which must have scared a third Jap pilot because he unloaded all his bombs at once on our side of the island. The whole string of bombs hit on a hill about two hundred yards from our tent with a terrific roar. Maybe that primary instructing wasn't so bad after all!!

The funniest thing of all though was seeing two jeeps roaring down a pathway towards each other, completely blacked out of course. Thought sure they were going to hit head on but at the last minute they saw each other and both shot off into the weeds. The raid lasted two hours which meant practically no sleep at all

-4-

that night. Talked with a marine the next day, who had been on the radar screen and he said there were about twenty Jap planes milling around up there. We shot down four of them and one of the marines gave me a piece of metal from one that had crashed.

When we took off a few hours later I certainly felt sorry for the fellows left on the island. You could just see in their faces that they wished they could also be heading back to the States.

So all in all our crew flew about 12,200 miles in about sixty five hours of actual flying time in the last eleven days.

That's about it for now.

Frank

February ? 1945.

For laughs!!!

From Alameda to Pearl there wasn't much in the way of excitement..... outside of the fact we were about three hours behind forecast, due to unexpected headwinds; consequently we were getting darned low in the gas department. It took us 18 hours of flying time, which is plenty long in the air for one stretch .

From Pearl we had a lot of luck....... we're the one crew assigned to go to the South Pacific that week. First hit Pylmyra south of Honolulu for gas, then on to Canton in the Phoenix Islands. Canton is just a small atoll, with nothing there but a landing strip, a few buildings, and a bit of sand or coral. Spent the night there and then roared on South to the Fiji Islands, about a thousand miles Southwest or about seven hours flying time. At this stage of the game, it was the first time I had been below the equator. Fellows tried to tell me there was a big purple line across the ocean, showing the equator, which, of course, I pretended to believe. At any rate, we roared into the Bay of Suva, which is a town on the Island of Nita Levi in the Fiji Group. After landing and making the dock, we were given a car to go into town to our hotel. The Kid here drove in and almost forced three cars into the ditch before I realized the island was English and the people drive on the left hand side of the road. Had to really concentrade to stay where we belonged.

The first thing of interest were all the Fiji islanders. Big black men with an enormous mop of fuzzy hair and all wearing skirts instead of pants. Passed the Governor's palace on the way in, a really beautiful, large, rambling estate, with huge flashily dressed Fiji guards holding chrome plated rifles. Looked exactly like all these postcards that drift up state-side. Arrived at the hotel that before the War was a well-known tourist spot. Large old building with all the rooms opening into the hall and also on to the verandah. The waiters and bell-boys all were barefoot and most of them wore the Fiji skirts. The Fiji policemen are a really interesting sight. Dressed in black with a big red sash, sandals, and the usual skirt, of course, and that ever present fuzzy hair.

The climate there was hot and muggy about the worst we have hit so far.

From there we roared on over to New Caledonia in the Loyalty Islands. I certainly am brushing up on my geography, before this all these islands were just names, but now it actually means something. We were too tired to go into the town of Noumea, heard there wasn't anything there of much interest anyway, so hitthe sack for a long awaited rest.

1.

-2-

The actual work of flying isn't tiring at all......due to the fact there is nothing much to do, but the long hours of less oxygen, due to high altitude, the constant vibration, and that ever steady loud drone of the engines, all combine to sap our strength. One doesn't actually notice the noise but to talk to someone, we have to either shout or talk right in his ear.......that's not using the inter-communication system, of course. It seems the less we do in these long hours of flying the lazier we get, just don't seem to have any ambition to do much else besides read or play cards.

The next day we headed still further South, hitting the high point of the trip. Went down to Auckland xxaxN in New Zealand. After all these islands it was a beautiful sight to see green pastures, sheep grazing, and towns or cities aroundthe country side. As we came in over the city of Auckland the first thing that met the eye was the fact that <u>all</u> the rooftops were of red tile. The red tile company there must have had a monoply on the roofing business. We were given a station wagon to use that night for recreational purposes, (it said) and headed in for the hotel. Here, as in Suva, I had trouble with the units of English money. Never did bother to figure it out, so don't know whether I paid more or less than things should have cost.

The high point of the evening were the New Zealand dollies, of course. I had a number I had picked up in Honolulu, so called her and she got a big party cooking for the officers and the crew Those New Zealand totsies are really sharp and without a doubt the Americans go over in a big way. Can see now why the Australian men hate the Americans so. The dollies would and do leave them in a second to be with an American. The majority of the New Zealand and Australian men seem to be drab, shy, and a bit stuffy, while Americans seem to be full of life, forward, and plenty sharp. It amazed me that the dollies were plenty on the ball, and I know they could hold their own, even in 'Frisco. The ones I danced with were by far better dancers than the average American totsie. All these girls when brought right down to it, admit they want to marry an American and head state-side. Their accent and manner of speech is so different and unexpected it was amusing. Many things were "bloody" this and "bloody" that. Fine way to do some sociable swearing?!!! There are very few Americans now stationed in New Zealand and the ones that are there now love it. It is <u>now</u> believable that there is a lot of complaining when the Overseas Relief arrives and the men are sent back to the States for a rest. The men don't want to go back States-side, as I wouldn't either for at least a little while. Man, that is really a town!

The next day we tried to find something wrong with the plane so we could lay over another day...... but with no luck. Having about 22 passengers aboard made our conscience hurt a bit, so we didn't look so very hard for a plane "squawk." The take-off out of Auckland was good for lots of laughs.

2.

It is rather a narrow harbor with the usual ferry boats shuttling between the shores and other steamers heading into piers or docks. We taxied down the harbor as far as possible, headed into the wind and looked for a clear stretch of water from which to take off. With all these boats plodding around neither of us pilots saw an opening, and after waiting for some minutes, there was still no opening, so shrugging our shpulders, we poured the "coal" to the four big screaming engines and ~~x~~ the huge Coranda slowly picked up speed, lumbered up on the step, and went roaring down toward the boats with spray flying and navigators praying.......I heard later. As we slowly gained the necessary speed to leave the water, ~~the~~ we shot by the stern of one boat, passed one going in the same direction, and ducked by the bow of the third. By this time, the harbor was in a bit of an uproar, with startled passengers looking amazed at those crazy Yanks, boat captains swearing at those bloody Yanks, - and of course, we were having a big time! We managed to leave the water and just about had sufficient flying speed when we found ourselves bearing down upon two ferries, going in the opposite directions across our path.....with us in the middle! I could see some passengers nervously eying the rapidly closing distance and begin to wonder.....as a matter of fact I was doing the same thing myself, but one ferry swerved to give us room to get through and shouted something as we roared by......can't in the least imagine what he said.....and the other ferry tried to run us down .....or he didn't see us.....I'm not sure which.....at any rate it was an exit from New Zealand that will be a topic of conversation for at least a few hours.

And so started the long trek back to Pearl. Arrived there a few days later, tired and not too happy.....due to the fact we had to head West again instead of going Stateside. All in all we had been out of the States eight days and had flown about 84 hours or an average of over eight hours a day. Since we had a day "lay-over" in Pearl on the way out we actually only flew seven days which makes an average of twelve hours per day of flying.... plenty in any man's league. So in these seven days we covered approximately thirteen thousand miles which is what the average automobile drives in a year.

On the next trip west from Pearl we flew down to in the Admiralty Islands. It is right north of New Guinea and about the hottest darn place I've ever seen. Actually I do feel sorry for Larry being stationed down in that neck of the Pacific. Coming back to Pearl our automatic pilot went out so we had to fly about 17 hours by hand. Never realized how important that gyro pilot was and how much better a job of flying it can do than we pilots. I was flying a long ~~flying speed when we found ourselves bearing down~~ stretch through the night and got pretty tired so let one of the navigators take over for while. A little rough on the controls as was to be expected, but the funny part was the bad time he gave the sleeping passengers and crew when he suddenly saw he was gaining altitude; he would push the nose over sharply and consequently centrifugal force would lift the sleeping people about three or four inches out of their bunks

3.

-4-

or chairs and then set them down with an awakening crash. At the end of the trip I certainly got in the wrong end of some mighty dirty looks from many of the passengers..... I, strongly suspected I was doing it on purpose. It reminded me of the time I started to step on to the five foot ladder going up to the flight deck at the same time the plane hit an unusually strong down draft very hard, slid right up the railing, the body floated up in mid-air and I was able to step right on to to the top flight deck, but never touched a rung in the ladder..... Sort of sport, these planes!

And so at the moment we are almost to Frisco after having been out for three weeks and flying 150 hours or about 24,000 miles. That night life is going to look mighty good to these kids..... that's for sure.

As ever,
Frank.

April 7 1945

Once again!!!

These kids certainly are hitting the weather this trip ..... or maybe the weather is hitting us ..... at any rate it is definitely not on the good side. Between Honolulu and Johnson Island, aerology told us there was a small cold front that probably was very mild so there was nothing to worry about. Well about two thirds of the way across, the clouds started building up, rain falling more continuously, and flashes of lightning in the distance. Didn't think a thing about it because we had flown through many a storm before and always seemed to make out O.K. Pretty soon we were entirely on instruments at about eight thousand feet with the air getting rougher all the time. Being at night made the sky seem a whole lot blacker and much more ominous. The rain was driving onto the windshield at a rate I had never seen before ..... as if the very weight and quantity of it would overcome the resistance of the panes of glass.

The most startling effect was to put down the landing lights and see the beam try to bore through the rain and darkness but only reaching a short distance and ending in an oval of dim light. Due to our speed the rain roared through this light beam in a horizontal stream ..... reminded me of driving on a snowy winter night and watching the snow rush up at the car, seemingly magnified by the headlights.

The turbulance by this time was increasing to an alarming state ..... there was no turning back of course due to the gas department ..... so we kept bouncing on. Pretty soon the plane was tumbling and jumping so fast the instrument board was a blur at times ..... and every once in a while the flashes of lightning would momentarily blind us.

A bit later we were caught in a swift strong updraft and the plane was carried up and up as if a giant hand were pulling a small toy on a piece of string. With each sudden jolt of air current the wings would of course take a terrific strain ..... the safest thing to do would be to slow to a minimum air speed, but the engines were running cool, making it unwise to decrease power. As this updraft continued to carry us even higher I pushed the nose over to hold our assigned altitude, looked at the "rate of climb" indicator and it showed we were descending about five hundred feet per minute but yet the altimeter showed we were gaining altitude ..... fine state of affairs ..... and before we knew it we had gained a couple of thousand feet. The mechanics were a bit worried about the wings snapping off ..... I was a bit worried myself ..... and lord only knows what the passengers were thinking. Back at Norman we did thousands of violent maneuvers but never gave it a thought because if anything happened to the plane we could just step out and come swishing down in that silk umbrella ..... but here we have no parachutes and even if we did it wouldn't do any good in the middle of the Pacific ..... rather a helpless and futile feeling.

But we gradually pulled through the front and landed at Johnson every bit of alright. Understand they cancelled a few flights when they received our weather report ..... but that's the way it goes ..... some days you can't make a hundred dollars!

May 1st 1945
7000 ft.
Alameda bound from Saipan.

Dear Folks!!!!

There sure is a difference in the atitude of this crew depending on whether we are heading East or West. Going West we don't particularly care if we get out on time ..... or if something goes wrong with the plane in the air we'd just as soon return to base ..... back to the party town ..... and I think we'd keep going even if we had to taxi to the next Island ..... that is if we were heading East.

This is just like living two lives ..... both of them good ..... work from about ten to fourteen days ..... and then land in Frisco or Oakland for a seven day vacation ..... a never ending good time ..... hitting the States so often ..... getting clean clothes, picking up a stack of mail ..... a few hours rest ..... and then roaring into town to see what's new ..... and there's always something new!!!!

Our outfit is going into the Philippines now so the trips will be a little longer ..... but still a good deal.

Ran into a fellow out in Saipan that I knew up at F. & A. ..... and old Norman buddies are always calling up the apartment ..... so naturally the kid here has to line up the "dollies" and get a party cooking. If this keeps up I may have to take the phone out. I lined up a deal over in Frisco ..... a whole floor of an apartment building .....six bedrooms, living room and kitchen ..... for $180.00 a month ..... that makes $30.00 apiece for six fellows ..... five of my buddies have already moved in and I haven't decided whether to move in or not. Haven't seen the place yet because I left the day I fixed the deal up over the phone. Fellows coming out from the States later told me about the whole place so it sounds O.K. Fine state of affairs ..... having too many apartments!!!

Seems funny but I gain a lot of weight on these trips, but lose it back in the States. Out in the Islands the life is about as heathful as can be ..... lots of sun ..... tennis ..... swimming ..... sleep ..... and plenty of food ..... while back Stateside we seem to be running around here and there all the time and don't bother much with the food department. The kid here is getting a bit of a tan ..... and getting a lot better with the tennis racket .....

May 4th Oakland

Got in yesterday and received your letter this morning. Yes Alameda is right next to Oakland across from Frisco ..... would just as soon have mail come out to this apartment ..... looked at the deal over in Frisco and it isn't half as nice as mine so I'll keep this one ..... got a bang up letter from Bobby ..... man she is sure having a time ..... went over to Frisco last night and saw a lot of the delegates in the Conference ..... saw Anthony Eden up in the Mark Hotel and lots of these Arabian men ..... lots of sport.

Lots of love,
Frank.

In the cockpit of our PB2Y-3R

In 1945, with the European War over and the Japanese War winding down, many pilots were being discharged. Suddenly, the Navy was short of DC-3 transport pilots. I received rush orders to a DC-3 squadron for recurrent training, route checks, and scheduling as plane commander. After a few weeks of copilot, I was flying the line as Captain. That felt mighty good after flying fourth pilot on the boats. The navy had an airline system called NATS, Naval Air Transport System. The DC-3 route was coast to coast with one flight a day each direction. This was for passengers only, no cargo. I was based at Alameda, flying the western section: Oakland, Los Angeles, San Diego, Phoenix, and Winslow. I would lay over twelve hours and pick up the return flight to Oakland. This type of flying was most enjoyable. We were all instrument rated, so we flew a regular schedule like the airlines on an IFR (Instrument Flight Rule) clearance.

A short time later, the Navy needed plane commanders out of Miami. This also was a DC-3 squadron flying south to Panama or southeast to Trinidad on the north coast of South America.

The route to Panama was Miami to Vernon Field in Jamaica, then to Coco Solo in Panama. It was a little over seven hours of flying one way. The route to Trinidad was Miami to Guantanamo Bay in Cuba, then on to San Juan, Trinidad. This was a ten or eleven hour flight depending on winds. We were scheduled to depart Miami at three in the morning so as to arrive at our destination in daylight. Trinidad had mountains near the airport, and Panama often had heavy rain and low visibility, so a daylight arrival was desired.

The schedule was a dream. We would fly two days a week: fly down one day and layover one night, then fly back the next day. Then you had five days off. So there was lots of time for tennis, horse racing, clubs and the ocean. What a life.

On one flight to Panama a very strange situation happened. We took off from Miami about two in the morning and passed over the beacon at Camaguey, Cuba right on schedule. We were sitting there on autopilot without a worry in the world – but not for long. The copilot was asleep. This was normal due to such early departures. The next homing beacon for our ADF (Automatic Directory Finder) was Vernon Field in Jamaica. I tuned in the frequency. Nothing! We were flying in the moonlight above a cloud deck, so I could not see the surface. It came time to be over Vernon Field and there was still no beacon. Now I was really worried. Sometime previous there was a small break in the cloud deck, and I could see a tip of land with a fire burning and smoke streaming in our direction. Was there a strong, unforecasted tailwind? But the huge question was whether the tip of land was Jamaica or part of Cuba. Another twenty minutes of no beacon and then came decision time. If we keep going south and Jamaica was not ahead, we would run out of gas. So the only smart thing to do was to turn back. The worst thing that could happen is we would land in Cuba and be the laughing stock of the squadron. But with a plane full of passengers, we would be alive.

Sometime later, we picked up the Vernon Field beacon, homed in and landed. We had overflown the island. The base stated the beacon had been in full operation. Why we couldn't pick it up, I'll never know.

On a return flight from Panama, we had a daylight landing at the same Vernon Navy Base. I had an experienced copilot, so we had switched seats. He was flying in the left Captain's seat. There was a strong crosswind and the DC-3 tends to weather cock into the wind on landing. He touched down okay, and as the plane slowed, it started off the runway. He had not adjusted his rudders so with full rudder, he could not reach the brake. I had not adjusted mine either, so I couldn't reach my brake either. What a stupid error. So we both grabbed the upwind throttle to bring us back on the runway. We plowed through some bushes and got back on the runway. It was a wild ride. At the ramp with the cockpit door closed, I suggested we sit still and let the passengers deplane. Ten minutes later, we left the cockpit and found all twenty passengers waiting to hoot and howl at us. It was most embarrassing. Fortunately, there was no damage to the plane – only to our egos.

While stationed in Miami, I met a most beautiful lady by the name of GG. My roommate, Tom Quinn, had been over at Miami Beach swimming and struck up a conversation with some bathing beauties. The next day, he asked if I was interested in a blind date. I said sure, and the rest is history. We seemed to hit it off and like each other. From then on, I guess the expression is we were an "item." It must have been the uniform, the wings, the flyboy attitude. I was one lucky guy.

It was 1946, and the war with Japan was over, so more pilots were getting out of the service. The Navy was short of DC-4 commanders, so I got sent to Moffett Field in California for DC-4 Captain school. On graduation, I was assigned to Patuxent River Navy Base in Maryland to fly NATS routes.

One route was north to Argentia, Newfoundland. There was one flight that sticks out in my mind. Our DC-4 arrived over Argentia with a full load of passengers at about ten at night. The field was socked in. We made two attempts at instrument approaches but couldn't spot the runway, so we pulled back up and headed back to Sydney in Nova Scotia. In range, the tower said we had better hurry as the fog was rolling in. We added power, made a short approach, and could see about one half of the runway clear of fog. As we touched down, the fog rolled over the cockpit and we had trouble finding the ramp. It was a huge relief to be on the ground, as we were a bit low on fuel. I put the passengers up in a hotel and convinced management that the Navy would pay the bill. The next morning on preflight, we found a broken exhaust stack. We took it off and went into town and had it welded. It probably was not up to air worthy code, but it got us on our way with our flight back to Argentia.

The copilot had never flown into that airport before. When he saw the two hills we had come down between on our low approaches the night before, he was flabbergasted. The pilots loved this base. At the officers' club, whiskey sold for twelve dollars a case or a dollar a bottle. We never left there without a few cases.

The route south out of Patuxent River was via Charleston and Jacksonville, with a layover in Miami. One trip was unforgettable. Tom Quinn was a Captain, but he wanted to see Mary in Miami, so he flew with me as co-Captain. We arrived in Miami about two in the afternoon and were due to depart for Trinidad at three the next morning. Mary, GG, Tom, and I partied until 1 a.m. Since it was a cargo only flight, why not take the gals to Trinidad? We would be back in Miami the next day. We were all feeling no pain, so the gals thought it was a great idea.

We smuggled them on the Navy base and Tom took them out to the plane, while I went to Base Ops to file a flight plan. A Lt. Commander introduced himself and said he was going to give Tom and me a route check on this flight. Big trouble. I said, “Just a minute, sir, I'll be right back.” I got ahold of Tom and told him to get the girls off the plane and back home.

We took off headed for San Juan. I was in the left seat, Tom's was in the right seat, and the check pilot was in the jump seat between us. Thirty minutes out, Tom climbed out of his seat and headed for the bunk compartment AFT. The check pilot asked, "Where are you going?"

You have to know Tom to know that he can say anything to anybody. Tom replied, "You don't expect me to fly in this condition, do you?"

So the check pilot moved to the right seat. A short time later, he tapped me on the shoulder and said, "You better hit the sack also." I guess the alcohol fumes were getting to be too much. Had it been wartime, we probably would have been grounded. At this late date, the Navy needed transport pilots. After two days we were buddies with the check pilot. Thankfully, he was one of the good guys.

Now the two wars have been over for some time, and Navy life has drastically changed. In wartime, the attitude was, the hell with regulations – let's get the job done. The peacetime Navy went back to strictly by-the-book inspections, shore duties, never getting out of the line. It wasn't much fun anymore, so Tom and I put in for discharge.

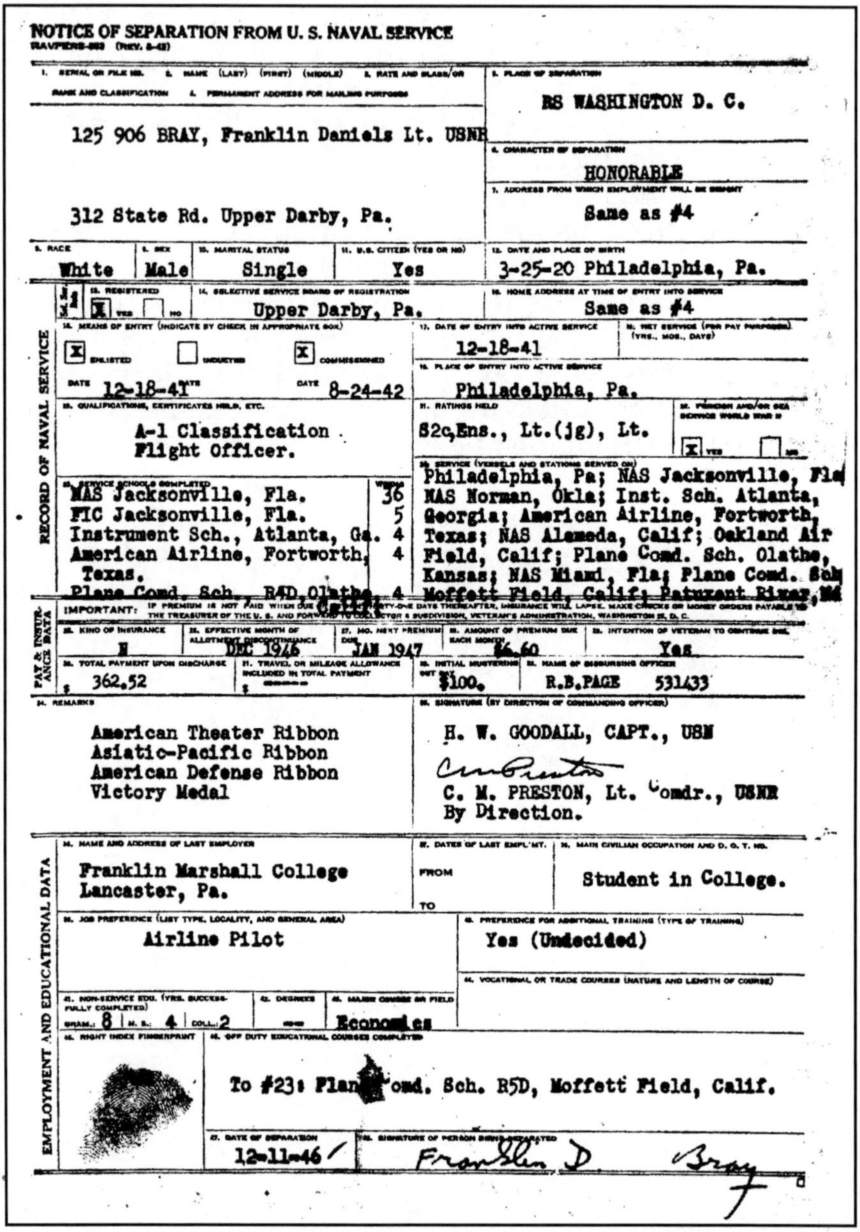

NOTICE OF SEPARATION FROM U. S. NAVAL SERVICE

125 906 BRAY, Franklin Daniels Lt. USNR

312 State Rd. Upper Darby, Pa.

RS WASHINGTON D. C.

HONORABLE

Same as #4

Race	Sex	Marital status	U.S. citizen	Date and place of birth
White	Male	Single	Yes	3-25-20 Philadelphia, Pa.

Registered: [X] Yes — Selective service board of registration: Upper Darby, Pa. — Home address at time of entry into service: Same as #4

RECORD OF NAVAL SERVICE

Means of entry: [X] Enlisted, [X] Commissioned — Date 12-18-41 — Date 8-24-42

Date of entry into active service: 12-18-41

Place of entry into active service: Philadelphia, Pa.

Qualifications, certificates held, etc.: A-1 Classification Flight Officer.

Ratings held: S2c, Ens., Lt.(jg), Lt.

Foreign and/or sea service World War II: [X] Yes

Service schools completed (weeks):
NAS Jacksonville, Fla. 36
FIC Jacksonville, Fla. 5
Instrument Sch., Atlanta, Ga. 4
American Airline, Fortworth, Texas. 4
Plane Comd. Sch., R4D, Olathe, 4

Service (vessels and stations served on): Philadelphia, Pa; NAS Jacksonville, Fla; NAS Norman, Okla; Inst. Sch. Atlanta, Georgia; American Airline, Fortworth, Texas; NAS Alameda, Calif; Oakland Air Field, Calif; Plane Comd. Sch. Olathe, Kansas; NAS Miami, Fla; Plane Comd. Sch. Moffett Field, Calif; Patuxent River, Md.

PAY & INSURANCE DATA

IMPORTANT: IF PREMIUM IS NOT PAID WHEN DUE OR WITHIN THIRTY-ONE DAYS THEREAFTER, INSURANCE WILL LAPSE. MAKE CHECKS OR MONEY ORDERS PAYABLE TO THE TREASURER OF THE U. S. AND FORWARD TO COLLECTOR & SUBDIVISION, VETERAN'S ADMINISTRATION, WASHINGTON 25, D. C.

Kind of insurance	Effective month of allotment discontinuance	Mo. next premium due	Amount of premium due each month	Intention of veteran to continue ins.
N	DEC 1946	JAN 1947	$6.60	Yes

Total payment upon discharge	Travel or mileage allowance included in total payment	Initial mustering out pay	Name of disbursing officer
$ 362.52	$ ------	$100.	R.B.PAGE 531433

Remarks:
American Theater Ribbon
Asiatic-Pacific Ribbon
American Defense Ribbon
Victory Medal

Signature (by direction of commanding officer):
H. W. GOODALL, CAPT., USN
C. M. PRESTON, Lt. Comdr., USNR
By Direction.

EMPLOYMENT AND EDUCATIONAL DATA

Name and address of last employer: Franklin Marshall College Lancaster, Pa.

Main civilian occupation: Student in College.

Job preference: Airline Pilot

Preference for additional training: Yes (Undecided)

Non-service educ.: Gram. 8 H.S. 4 Coll. 2 — Degrees: ---- — Major course or field: Economics

Off duty educational courses completed: To #23: Plane Comd. Sch. R5D, Moffett Field, Calif.

Date of separation: 12-11-46

Signature of person being separated: Franklin D. Bray

Honorable Discharge from the US Navy, 1946

Non-Scheduled Airline Flying 1946 - 1949

It was mid 1946, and Tom and I were now civilians. We drove to Miami to be with GG and Mary and to look for a flying job. Airlines were hiring, and Miami had at least ten small non-scheduled airlines cranking up with war surplus planes. Ex-fighter pilots were a dime a dozen, but experienced transport pilots had a big edge. We turned down a number of offers.

We wandered into a little office of Nationwide Air Transport Service. They had six DC-3s and were owned by a Paul Weesner, a former navy NATS pilot. Thus the close name of the airline. Also with this outfit were Benny Goodman, Bud Dyess, and Bob Sheker, all ex-NATS pilots. They welcomed us with open arms. It was old home week. Paul said, "One of you is going to take the flight into New York tonight – you can toss for it."

Tom lost and took the flight. He turned to me and said, "You see? I told we should have spent a few weeks playing before looking for a job." That was vintage Tom Quinn. We were both hired as Captains.

Nonscheduled airlines are vastly different from scheduled airlines. They operate on a shoestring. No dispatches, no weather service. Once you leave Miami, no

With fellow nonsked pilot, Jim Savage

support of any kind. No vacation pay, no medical coverage, no training, no base pay – nothing.

Captains were paid five cents a mile and copilots three cents a mile, only if you flew – and there were no guarantees. Scheduled airlines at that time were starting copilots at $250 a month. So even at five cents a mile, non-scheduled Captains were averaging $500 a month. A good sum of money those days.

So we were off and running at a hectic pace. The first three months, I flew 112 hours, 120 hours, and 136 hours, which was not legal. Scheduled pilots fly a max of 80 hours.

It seemed the entire island of Puerto Rico was moving to New York, so our little fleet flew night and day between San Juan and New York with a crew change at Miami. Full loads northbound and very few southbound. The Puerto Ricans were poor passengers. They tended to get airsick with any small amount of turbulence. We had to remove the floor carpets so we could wash out the planes. Yes, we pilots did it all: loaded baggage, dumped the honey bucket, did minor maintenance. Speaking of maintenance, it was terrible. The planes were falling apart. As a fix, the boss put a mechanic on every flight. It was amazing how rapidly the maintenance improved.

As civilians, we had converted our Navy pilots' licenses to FAA commercial pilots' licenses. Now FAA said non-scheduled Captains must upgrade to an ATR (Airline Transport Rating), the highest rating there is. The boss said, "Okay, guys, you are on you own. I'll furnish the plane, but you have to put in your own gas." Can you imagine an American or Delta Airline saying this? The ones with drive passed the written test and took an hour of practice in steep turns, stalls, cut engines – things we hadn't done with passengers. Then we took a flight check with an FAA inspector – a stepping stone upward.

You may or may not have heard of the famous Bermuda Triangle. This is a space in the Atlantic Ocean that ships have disappeared in without a trace for many years. Airplanes have also disappeared in this area. The most publicized case was the five Navy torpedo bomber planes that took off from Florida on a training mission and disappeared over the ocean. The Navy sent out a patrol plane to try to spot survivors or wreckage, and it also disappeared with no distress call.

Well, that old Bermuda Triangle almost got me in 1946. I had flown the direct route from Miami to San Juan, Puerto Rico dozens of times. It is over 1,000 miles, about a six-hour flight in the old DC-3. This night I departed Miami about ten at night with twenty-eight passengers, climbed to a cruising altitude of 9,000 feet, set the autopilot and sat back to enjoy the flight. The compass heading does not change the entire trip. I checked by Nassau right on schedule. The next checkpoint was over South Caicos Island. It had a homing beacon, so we homed in and flew directly over the island, still on the predicted time. From South Caicos to San Juan there are about 450 miles over water and out of sight of any land. It was a clear, moonlit night with smooth air. Sometimes you could pick up a beam from Santo Domingo in the Dominican Republic for a ground speed cross check.

I wasn't concerned when I couldn't tune it in. The next checkpoint was a beam from the west tip of Puerto Rico where the military had a homing beacon. On this direct route, if you couldn't pick up the beacon, you could maybe see a glow in the sky. But there was nothing. At this point, we were still out of sight of land. We pressed on, assuming we were on schedule, but when we couldn't pick up the San Juan beacon to home in on, the pucker factor started to kick in. When our ETA (Estimated Time of Arrival) over San Juan came up we could see nothing but ocean. Just what the hell was going on? It couldn't be happening. With twenty-eight passengers behind me and no land in sight, the pucker factor was going full blast. Since there is no land north of San Juan, I turned due south. If we didn't spot Puerto Rico, maybe we could sight one of the Virgin Islands. All I could think of was those Navy planes disappearing. After about twenty minutes of flying, the San Juan beacon very faintly came in. What a sigh of relief when the lights of the city came in view. How did we possibly end up so far out in the ocean when we had never changed direction?

I told this incident to my fellow pilots, and they looked at me like I was crazy. They said, “You just fell asleep.” I couldn't possibly have fallen asleep; I was too worried about running out of fuel. Then they said, “You put your clipboard on the glare shield and it pulled your compass off.” My clipboard was aluminum, so that couldn't be. So they passed it off as, “You screwed up.” If so, I wish I knew how. That night is still very vivid in my memory. I wish I had a logical explanation for that very weird flight.

In 1946 San Juan had a very small terminal building with only two gates in front. I was parked in one and another plane was in the other gate. We loaded baggage and twenty-eight passengers for New York. I climbed in the cockpit to start engines when Pan Am drove one of their gas trucks right in front of us and left it, blocking us in. Juan Tripp of Pan Am did not much like the non-skeds flying his passengers. Can't say as I blame him, as his airline had pioneered the routes. I left the plane to try to locate the airport manager. Pan Am controlled the terminal. A customs officer saw what was happening, took me aside, and said, "Just relax, Pan Am has a flight due in ten minutes and they need your spot." Sure enough. So I got back in the plane. The Pan Am flight landed, taxied in, and the gas truck drove off. We fired up and away we went. All in the life of a non-sked pilot.

Ninety-nine percent of flights are routine, some even boring. But once in a while one will jump up and grab you, like that trip through the Bermuda triangle. One such flight happened on a trip with passengers from Miami to Newark. By the time we passed over Philadelphia, the whole eastern seaboard suddenly fogged in with not a reachable alternate available. Way back in 1946, it is hard to believe that we were the only plane in the air at 3 a.m. Air traffic control called us with the dreaded words, "What are your intentions?" Hari-kari came to mind, but that was no option. I declared an emergency. I requested the Navy at Floyd Bennet Field wake up a GCA (Ground Controlled Approach) crew and warm up their equipment. In the Navy, I had used this radar approach to very low minimums and even though the weather was 0/0, I felt it was doable.

I relayed that I would make one pass at Newark, and, if we couldn't see the runway, we would proceed to Floyd Bennet. This old war surplus plane didn't have ILS landing equipment. All we had was the old range approach equipment with a minimum of 500 feet.

I had flown into the Newark Airport many times and I knew there were no high obstructions on the approach. I really concentrated to nail the range leg. I went down to 100 feet and saw the high intensity approach lights flashing in sequence toward the runway slightly off to the front left. I wheeled it over and plunked it down on the runway. Man, what a relief. Those strobe approach lights saved us. I had the Newark Tower thank the Navy GCA crew and offer our apologies for getting them out of bed.

We found the terminal in the fog, but since it was 4 a.m. and they were not expecting any flights, it was dark and locked up. It took thirty minutes to find someone to open it up so our passengers could get to the street. In this day and age, it's hard to believe.

By 1947, the Puerto Rican traffic had slowed down to the point that our airline needed another source of revenue. The boss found one in recruiting farm workers in the islands and flying them all over the United States for the corporations and growers. The islands were starving and the workers jumped at the chance to work in the U.S. We recruited in Nassau, Jamaica, Barbados, Antigua, St. Kitts and Martinique. So we did a lot of flying in the Caribbean area. We used the very bare war surplus DC-3s. No headliner or carpet. Bare walls. Fourteen bucket seats down each side. At the beginning of the growing season, we all flew night and day. In June, I flew the most hours in one month ever: 203 hours. In one two-day period, I flew 33 hours: Miami to Nassau to West Palm to Jacksonville to St. Louis to Cheyenne to Butte to Walla Walla, Washington. This was a load of farm workers to pick apples. Then I flew back empty, Walla Walla to Cheyenne to St. Louis to Miami. The big problem was trying to stay awake.

On one flight somewhere in Missouri at about two in the morning, we ran toward a squall line of weather. Lightning went from cloud to cloud and from cloud to ground. It was very ugly stuff. We stuck our nose in it, but it seemed a repeat of my AK story. So I did a hard 180° turn and flew back out into the clear dark night. But this violent storm had apparently knocked out all the electricity in the whole area, because there were no town lights, farm lights – nothing. Only a very few car lights on country roads. We had absolutely no idea of our location. By this time the gas gauges were showing about empty. It's bad enough to run out of gas in a car, but in a plane it is horrifying. Airports have generators to kick in if they lose power. So I was frantically looking for an airport's revolving green light. Finally, I spotted one on this dark night and prayed we wouldn't run out of gas before we reached it. Oh, man. Gray hair time. The two main tanks hold 400 gallons, and I think we put in 420 gallons. That was too close for comfort.

On one of these labor flights a funny thing happened. I stopped in Lumberton, South Carolina for fuel and went in the terminal to file a flight plan and pay for the gas. I returned to the plane and there sitting in a bucket seat, back to the wall, with twenty-six big black farm workers was a business man in a suit, tie, hat, and a briefcase on his lap. I said, "Sir, I think you are on the wrong airplane." He replied, "Isn't this Eastern flight 242 to Newark?" I couldn't believe it. He failed the intelligence test.

A funny thing happened on another flight, too, but maybe it wasn't so funny. I had a load of farm workers to deliver to this little town in Wisconsin. The weather was lousy with rain and a low ceiling. I let down, got under the cloud deck, cancelled my IFR clearance, and, through the rain-soaked windshield, I spotted the airport shown on my map. It was a grass field and looked awfully small. But these DC-3s don't need much room to land in. So I got way back, flew just above a stall, hanging it on the props, and set it down just over the fence. Because of the rain, the grass and mud was slick, so the brakes had little effect. Whoa, Nellie! This sucker wasn't going to stop. I saw it wasn't going to stop before going through the far fence, so I unlocked the tail wheel and kicked full rudder, hoping to ground loop and stop. So there we were, sliding sideways down the dirt strip. I ended up with the wing over the fence but not touching a thing. I taxied back to the small terminal and called the grower to bring trucks for his workers. He said his trucks were waiting at the airport. Seems this town had built a brand new airport with 5,000 foot concrete runways. With the rain, low visibility and my out-of-date chart, I hadn't seen it. He requested I fly the workers over to the new airport. I explained with the mud, short runway and heavy load I could not do it. So he had to bring the trucks back to the old airport. The learning curve is hell.

Here is another crazy flight in the DC-3. I had a flight from Miami to Kingston, Jamaica to take a load of farm workers home. There happened to be a huge shortage of tomatoes in Florida, so rather than flying back to Miami empty, the boss arranged for a full cabinload of tomatoes. So at Kingston we folded the bucket seats against the wall and loaded a huge amount of crated tomatoes. Accelerating down the runway at Kingston, the tail of the old DC-3 wouldn't come up. Man, those tomatoes were heavy. I kept rolling the trim tab. I couldn't believe how tail-heavy we were, but the plane flew even with this tail-heavy situation.

I used extra speed for a wheel landing in Miami, but the tail plunked down at once. There was no way to ease it down. This was 1947, and you parked the plane right outside the window of the custom office. I took the paperwork in, and the officer said, “Well, look at that.” In the doorway of my plane was a huge, 250 pound black Jamaican farm worker – a stowaway. He jumped out and started running. The custom officer called security to pick him up. Then he said, “Let's go out to your plane and see if there are any more.” So we went back out. In the rear of the plane there is a little compartment that has the honey bucket (or toilet, if you will). On the rear wall of this compartment is a very small door that goes to the very rear of the plane. We opened that door, and there was another huge stowaway. The two of them had squeezed back there among the control cables. It's a wonder the bird flew at all being that tail-heavy.

If we had a starter conk out, we would hand-prop it to get started. On a small engine, a single person could pull it through to start the engine. The larger engines on the DC-3 had too much compression, so we used a three-person chain. The copilot would grab the prop, a farm worker would take the copilot's other hand and the second farm worker would hold hands with the first worker. People on the ramp would watch this odd operation and have a look of amazement when there was just enough pull, snap, for the engine to kick in. With no ground support, non-scheduled pilots had to improvise.

Farm workers boarding the airplane

One day I had a load of farm workers for Jamaica. I was scheduled to drop them off and return to Miami with an empty plane. It was GG's day off, so she went along on the flight. On the way back to Miami – BLAM! A piston on the left engine had let go and come through the cylinder head. We were right over Camaguey, Cuba at 8,000 feet. I throttled way back as it was still developing some power and started a descent to land at Camaguey. I didn't know it, but we were trailing a long, thick stream of oil smoke. The people in town saw this and by the time we landed, there were hundreds of spectators watching this crippled bird arrive. They were probably disappointed it was a routine landing.

We checked into a little Cuban hotel with no baggage, toothbrush, nothing. We had expected to be back in Miami. The office said it would be two days before they could send a plane with a replacement engine. GG called her boss and said she was stuck in Cuba. The boss thought that an unlikely story, but GG convinced him.

The hotel had no air conditioning and lots of mosquitoes. The bed had a big frame over it with a mosquito net. It was like crawling into a tent to get in bed. GG, the copilot, and I went out to a little bar/restaurant. In those days it was rum and coke. The bartender put a bottle of rum on the table with a pencil mark on the label to show the level. Most interesting.

Two days later a plane arrived with a replacement engine. We pulled it out and then sent GG and my copilot back to Miami. I stayed to help our two mechanics change the engine. I was the gopher and put to work cleaning parts in gas.

Finally, we got the engine changed and put the removed engine aboard. The two mechanics and I cleaned up in this little Camaguey terminal. While I filed a flight plan, the two mechanics bought six bottles of liquor at a little stand there. Most any plane can be flown with a single pilot, so there was no problem with a non-pilot in the right seat. The mechanics hid the booze in the plane so they wouldn't have to declare it. I was so tired and not thinking straight that I let them do it.

At Miami, customs came out to the plane, which was unusual, and asked, “Are you sure you are taking everything off the plane?” They were trying to give us a break as a Pan Am station agent at the Camaguey terminal had wired to Miami about the purchase.

Customs found the booze and put us in a room and told us what the penalty for smuggling could be. They let us stew for some time and then came in and said the mechanics could pay duty on the lot and they would let us go. One of the mechanics spoke up and said he was allowed to bring in so much and would pay duty on the rest. I could see the custom officer was about to blow his stack, so I jumped up, grabbed the front of the mechanic's shirt and got right in his face, telling him to shut the hell up, that the customs officer was giving us all a huge break. It calmed customs down and saved the day.

Nothing's easy. I explained later to my mechanic about the system and when to keep still. I hope there were no hard feelings.

In 1947 I had a flight from Chicago to Miami. There I met GG's young pretty daughter, Janice, for the first time.

With GG, 1947

She sat in the cockpit jump seat. I had anticipated we could get to know each other on the flight but she kept her concentration on her comic books. I appeared to not have impressed her at all. Years later, she told me she was not uninterested. She was terrified! It was her first flight. How I wish I had been more discerning and realized her mindset! In spite of this very poor start, we have a great relationship. Janice grew into a beautiful person just like her mother.

This little item has nothing to do with aviation, but hopefully it will bring a smile. When GG's and my days off coincided, we would head for Miami Beach and check into an oceanfront hotel for a couple of days of sun and surf. I checked us in as "Mr. and Mrs. Frank Bray" with my Philadelphia address as I had ID for it.

It seems GG left one of her lacy nightgowns in the room. The hotel found it and sent it to Mrs. Bray, my mother. Sometime later, I received a package with the gown in it but no note – nothing. I guess us unmarried sons shouldn't be doing these things to their mothers.

I was living a wonderful life back in 1947. I had a job that I loved flying transports, I was going steady with a pretty young lady, and I was based in Miami, one of the best playgrounds in the world. Talk about being fat, dumb, and happy. So it was a bit of a shock to get a wake-up call one night. GG said, "Frank, if you aren't serious about our future, I'm moving on." It didn't take long for the light to come on. I passed the intelligence test. I came up with the three magic words. I wasn't about to lose that special person.

All the pilots in town came to the wedding. The airline was small, and GG knew them all. It was like a family or club. The camaraderie was great. For a wedding present, the boss furnished a plane for a sightseeing tour for the wedding party. It was one of the perks of a small airline, but I had to put in the gas. So I flew a tour over Miami, Miami Beach, and the Everglades. That marriage lasted 57 years. I was one lucky guy.

In 1947, a war surplus DC-3 sold for $5,000. Later, the war surplus Curtis Commando C-46 came on the market for $1,500; the boss bought two. Later still, we had twelve C-46s. These planes had been pickled in storage and stored at Bush Fields in Augusta, Georgia. At a pilot's meeting, the boss, Paul Weesner, asked if anyone had C-46 flying time. Smokey Lee said he had checked out in it. So Paul said, "You and Frank go up to Augusta and bring the first one back to Miami." I found Smokey down in the hangar looking at a C-46 manual. He had never been in one before.

We flew it back to Miami, and a week later the second bird was ready. Smokey was out of town, so with just a few hours in the right seat and having never touched the controls, I was now the expert. Go figure. Now it was my turn to study the manual. I flew it back to Miami okay. There is an old saying that if a pilot checks himself out in an airplane, he has a fool for an instructor, but that's the non-sked business. So now Smokey and I were the experts, and we checked out the rest of the Captains. The airlines loved the C-46, because it could carry twice the load of the DC-3 at one and a half times the cost, and thus was more profitable.

Flying farm workers was seasonal, so our airline found another source of revenue: flying shrimp out of Mexico. The shrimp were fished out from the Atlantic and the Gulf ports. A man by the name of Eccles discovered a new and fabulous shrimping ground off Carmen, Mexico in Campeche Bay. He had shrimp boats, but no way to get the shrimp to market. Paul, our boss, contracted to provide this service. We took a DC-3, stripped the cabin bare, and built a bin to carry the fresh shrimp, which were shipped in burlap bags that were stacked with layers of crushed ice between them. We used 2"x6" lumber to build a rectangular bin six inches high, and we lined the bin with metal and sealed all the joints to try to make it waterproof. The plane sat tail low, so a drain pipe was installed in each low corner. This went down to the fuselage and overboard. Of course, some of the shrimp juice leaked into the belly on its way out. This smell never left the plane.

Carmen is located about 850 miles southwest of Miami, about five hours flying time. You flew over the Gulf of Mexico, over the Mexican Yucatan peninsula, then let down into Carmen. We also carried shrimp up to Brownsville, Texas, some 500 miles. There was no communication between Miami and Carmen. At first, it was only through a Ham operator. The airport was great, but empty, with a boarded up terminal and an empty tower. There was no fuel at Carmen, and the planes could not carry enough for the round trip. So we would load six 55 gallon drums of gas. Also, the ice plant couldn't produce enough ice, so we loaded six 300 pound blocks of ice.

Gassing these DC-3s in Carmen was an interesting operation. Just imagine it: there's this airplane sitting on the ramp with 55 gallon drums of gas in the cabin. How do you get the gas into the wing tanks? There are only two ways. One is to run a hose from the barrel of gas out a window hatch and, standing on the wing, take the end of the hose and suck as hard as you can, trying to get the air out and get a suction going so that it will siphon the gas from the barrel to the wing. It's a tough situation, because you either can't get it to flow or you get a mouthful of gas. That's not very practical, so obviously the only other way to do it is to carry a hand pump. You take the cap off the barrel of gas, insert the pipe, take the rubber hose from the pump to the wing, and start pumping. Here we were on a hot ramp in Mexico. It was humid, 120° inside the cabin of the airplane. So we stripped down to our shorts – perspiration was running freely – and we started pumping. I don't know how many turns it was to take 300 gallons from those barrels into the wings, but it was plenty.

Remember, we were flying for five cents a mile. We were not being paid for all of this. Can you possibly imagine a TWA Captain doing this just to keep his job? We must have loved this type of operation to put up with this kind of stuff, but for a non-sked pilot, it was a way of life.

When we first got word that there was a load of shrimp ready for us in Carmen, Mexico, Paul and I took the plane down, landed, and found out they expected to have a load but did not actually have one yet. After a day, it didn't look like they would have one for another four days, so Paul left me with the airplane. I had nothing to do, so I went out on the shrimp boats and helped get a load of shrimp. It was an interesting operation. The shrimp boat went out in the bay and sent down a little trial net, dragging it on the bottom for thirty minutes, then hauled it up and had a count of the shrimp. If there was a good number of shrimp, they circled that area and put down a huge net. They dragged this net for at least an hour, and when they winched the huge net up over the deck and pulled the drawstring, this whole load of everything you could imagine dropped down onto the deck. There were shrimp, clams, eels, octopus, fish, jellyfish, starfish – I can't even think of it all. At this point, the crew and I went to work. We all had a little wooden paddle, and, sitting on a box we'd flip overboard everything that was not a shrimp. When we came to a shrimp, we'd flip the shrimp down into this open hatch, and it would land on a layer of ice. To sort out this big pile of debris would take maybe forty-five minutes, but it passed the time.

A week later, the first load was ready, and we loaded up the airplane. There was the American fisherman who wanted a ride back to Miami, so I stuck him in the right seat. As I mentioned before, these airplanes can be flown by a single pilot. Since there was no communication, there was no such thing as filing a flight plan. As a matter of fact, there was no Mexican customs there. As soon as the shrimp bags were loaded, we closed the door, fired the engines, and got up to altitude as soon as possible to decrease the amount of time in the hot weather that would melt the ice. The next communication would be when we were approaching Miami. We'd call the tower and tell them we were in range. They'd give us landing instructions, and we'd go from there.

I brought that first load of shrimp into Miami, and, because of the shrimp juice draining out of the DC-3, I parked the plane on the grass between the ramp and the taxi way. Customs insisted I bring the plane up to their building. I tried to explain, but he was ready to explode. So I fired it up and taxied up to the spot he wanted, right in front of the terminal. Well, that shrimp juice hit that hot asphalt on the ramp in the hot Florida sun, and did it ever stink. Oh, it was terrible! A week later, I brought the second load into Miami and pulled up to the customs spot on the ramp. Before I could shut down, the customs officer came running out of his office, waving his arms wildly and pointing at the grass and shouting: "On the grass, on the grass!" I could read his lips. Ah, the old learning curve!

Speaking of smell, when I'd arrive home after a trip my clothes reeked of this shrimp. We had a washer in the garage, so when I arrived home, GG made me undress in the garage, put the clothes in the washer, and head immediately for the shower. If we had to lay over in Brownsville, we checked into a hotel, and if anyone

Refueling in Carmen

Shrimpers hauling up the net

Preparing to unload the catch onto the deck

Sorting out the shrimp

happened to get into the elevator with us at the same time, you could imagine the looks we got. They'd look and wonder, "What in the world is that odor?"

The other thing that is really amazing is that on every trip at least one burlap sack would split open. I don't know how that was possible, but we had more shrimp than we could eat for two years. As hard as it is to believe, after a while, we finally got tired of eating shrimp, but, oh, it was so wonderful.

Paul was adding a room to his house, and he wanted us to bring in mahogany from Mexico. At that time it was illegal to bring raw mahogany wood into the States. So he contracted with some folks down in Carmen, and before they loaded the shrimp, we'd put a layer of 3-inch thick mahogany planks down into the bin we'd built and then put the shrimp bags on top of the mahogany. When we came into Miami, customs would come out and they'd count the bags of shrimp, but they didn't realize that there was a layer of pure Mahogany wood under the shrimp. You could imagine the weight that we were carrying. With that mahogany lumber plus the shrimp, we were a bit heavy, and I often wondered if Paul ever got the shrimp juice smell out of that mahogany. Sitting there for five hours, all that juice must have impregnated those boards.

On one flight from Brownsville to Carmen I had some fun. Tom, my buddy, had taken off about twenty minutes ahead of me. After I took off, I guess my plane was a bit faster then his. I saw him up ahead of me, and I was catching up to him. The procedure was first in, first out of Carmen, so whoever landed first, got the first load and departed. I flew the plane just behind and under him so he couldn't see me. As he was landing, I landed on the taxiway right by the ramp, so I'd be on the ramp before him and be first out. I'd never seen another airplane in Carmen, Mexico, but sitting at the end of the taxi strip was a little single engine airplane waiting to take off. I didn't see it until the last moment, and I figured, "Ah, what the heck. I'll just hop over the top of him and plunk it down a little bit farther down the taxiway and hit the ramp," which I did. I can just imagine that poor guy seeing this

DC-3 almost flopping down on top of him. It was a stupid thing to do, but there was an empty airport and no one around. I ended up parked on the ramp when Tom taxied in. I told Tom, "I guess I'm first out." I knew he was unhappy, so I said, "I'm just kidding. You're first out." The only repercussion was that the Mexican pilot complained to someone, so we pleaded engine trouble and paid a little *mordita.* That was the end of that.

We started this shrimp run with one plane. Two years later we had four DC-3s and one C-46 with shrimp bins. At the end, we were flying over ninety tons of shrimp a month. When we started, Carmen had two shrimp boats and one ice plant. Two years later, there were ten ice plants and 150 shrimp boats. By that time, a huge freezer boat had arrived, and this, plus the bay getting shrimped out, ended our operation there.

Flier Watches Shark Snatch Pal's Body

BROWNSVILLE, Tex., Feb. 21. (AP)—Rescued by a banana boat after drifting nine days in the Gulf of Mexico, a flier related yesterday that sharks snatched the body of his companion from their raft after their plane had crashed into the sea.

Esteban De Leon of Matamoros, Mexico, in a weakened condition, was picked up about 47 miles off the coast from Frontera, Mexico, yesterday afternoon by the Pan-American banana boat Roatan. A radio message received at Brownsville said De Leon would recover. The boat is due here today.

De Leon said his companion, Neil Womack of Brownsville, died three days after the plane went down only 15 miles short of its destination, Carmen, State of Campeche, Mexico.

The two-engine cargo plane, which took off from Brownsville on Feb. 10, crashed after the right engine caught fire, De Leon said.

The plane was being used to fly fresh seafood from Yucatan Peninsula to Texas and New Orleans.

Womack was injured. De Leon got him on the rubber raft the plane carried. When Womack died three days later, De Leon placed the body on the edge of the raft. According to the radio message, the surviving flier saw a shark grab Womack's body from the raft.

Womack was a graduate of Carsen Newman College of Jefferson City, Tenn., and served during the war as a Navy pilot in the Pacific.

He was the pilot of the plane that crashed, and De Leon the co-pilot.

Womack's brother, Jerre Womack of Watertown, Tenn., came to Brownsville to help in the search for the fliers. Both American and Mexican planes participated in the hunt.

Womack is survived by his wife and baby son.

That sad incident happened only fifteen miles from Carmen after our airline had pulled out. The consequences of a possible ditching were always in the back of our minds.

Can you imagine the shark frenzy with three tons of fresh shrimp chumming the sea? A little life raft wouldn't last long in that turmoil. .

I call this the Vegetable Fiasco. We had a C-46 flight scheduled down to Aruba. Aruba is a small island off the north coast of South America. Standard Oil had a tanker that had come in, and there was a crew change. We were to go down there to pick up these sailors and take them to San Francisco. As it was an empty flight down there, the boss decided to send a load of vegetables. So we contracted with an agent down there, and by the time I got to the airport, the airplane was already loaded with all these vegetables. Like everything else, it was "hurry hurry." They gave me the clipboard, and I filed a flight plan and checked the gas. I climbed into the airplane, and from the floor to the ceiling there were just crates and crates of vegetables. It was just jammed. There was a little narrow aisle where we could go from the rear door to the cockpit, but the airplane was completely filled with vegetables.

After a routine flight to Aruba, we landed there, and customs came out. I gave them the manifest and debriefed the airplane. The customs folks came up to me, and they were very perturbed. The vegetables they offloaded didn't match the manifest. This was too big of a problem for them. So we all went downtown to the courthouse and went up to the second floor where the big customs officers were. These customs officers had all the braids and the epaulets, and the situation was explained to them. Why didn't the offload agree with the manifest? Well, I didn't know anything about carrying vegetables. It was the first load of vegetables I'd ever had. I tried to explain that possibly fifty bushels of corn in fifty boxes was the same as fifty bushels of corn in sixty boxes. It was fifty bushels of corn. Well, it didn't make any sense to me either. They hemmed and hawed and put me in a car back to the airport.

I had a night's sleep at the hotel, came out the next morning, and we pre-flighted the airplane, waiting for our passengers to come out. I opened the baggage bins in the belly, and, lo and behold, they're full of vegetables. No wonder the manifest didn't agree with the offload. No one told me they had put vegetables in the belly bins – I thought it was just in the cabin. The customs people at the airport couldn't handle this problem either, so back in the car we went, back downtown, back into the courthouse, back up to second floor to the big wigs there.

They asked me, "What are you going to do?"

I said, "The airplane's already been cleared in. Let's just donate these vegetables from the belly bin to a hospital or charity."

They thought it over for a while and said, "No, we can't let you do that."“

I said, "Well, okay. I think I'll just close up the bins and leave them there. I'll put the baggage in the cabin, and we'll take the vegetables back to Miami."

They thought that over. "No, we can't let you do that."

"Well," I said, "I'll tell you what I'm going to do then. I'm going to take all the veggies out of the belly, and I'm going to put them in the cabin. I'm going to fly over the ocean, and I'm going to kick them out of the door. Then I'm going to come back and load up the baggage."

"No. No way is that an option."

"Well, okay. I think I know what the best bet really is: why don't I give you some money to hire some trucks so we can donate to this hospital?" Now that money was mentioned I had their attention, and they determined that was the solution. So that's what we did. I have no idea if those veggies were ever donated to anybody, but that's the end to the veggie story.

This is a little story about watching a pilot's pilot. My little company bought two DC-4s from National Airlines. Part of the deal was that National would train two crewmembers, get them type-rated with the FAA, and get the designation on their license. So our chief pilot, Phil Brown, and I were the ones who elected to receive this training. For me, it was more or less a refresher training, because I had flown the DC-4s in the Navy. I did my homework and so forth. It came time for the flight check with FAA. Phil Brown and I reported to the airport and met with the check pilot for National, Skeeter Royal.

I've got to give you a little background here. A year previous, business had been slow and National had gone on strike. Phil Brown had gone to National as a strike-breaker – you could say relief pilot, but he was a scab, a strike-breaker, and flew the line as Captain for National. When the strike was over, they released these strike breakers, and Phil came back to our company. Skeeter, the chief pilot for National, knew this ex-strike breaker, and he was going to bust him.

We reported to the airport, and I took my flight check first and passed it okay. Now it was Phil Brown's turn. So he climbed in the left seat with Skeeter Royal in the right. The FAA agent was in the jump seat, and I was standing behind the FAA inspector watching this whole operation. Skeeter was really trying to bust Phil, and Phil was handling everything nonchalantly, no problems. Phil was under the hood, and the hood was up in front of him. He couldn't see the ground. All he could see were the instruments, and back then the ILS was very simple. You had two needles: one needle for the glide slope and one needle for the localizer. The object was to keep them centered. Later, it was integrated and you had a computer to help you, but back in those days, it was really tough to keep those needles centered.

Can you picture the flight? Phil Brown was flying an instrument and approaching the outer marker. The check pilot was giving him hydraulic failure, electrical failure, simulated fire, and pulling circuit breakers. Phil was handling all this calmly. Next, Skeeter shut down the #4 engine. Over the outer marker, Skeeter shut down the #3 engine. Two engines out on one side is tough to handle. While taking care of all these simulated emergencies, Phil had the glide slope and localizer needles nailed.

Nonchalantly, he reached into his pocket, took out an unwrapped cigar, and put it in his mouth. He turned to Skeeter Royal, the guy who's trying to bust him, and said, "Hey, buddy, you got a match?"

It was just an unbelievable feat of flying. I couldn't possibly have done it. I looked at the FAA inspector, and he was grinning. He knew he was seeing a pilot of the same caliber as Chuck Yeager, Bob Hoover, or the like. There was just no way to bust that guy. He was just too good. I guess the old expression is, "He wasn't flying the airplane, he was wearing that airplane."

From then on, anytime a pilot was in a tight situation or nervous, to appear nonchalant the expression was "Hey, buddy, you got a match?" It just went through the outfit like wildfire.

I had a scheduled DC-4 flight to take the plane from Miami to Toronto and pick up a load of breeding cattle and fly them over to Bermuda. It was a routine flight to Toronto. I got up there late in the afternoon, and as they were loading the cattle an extreme blizzard blew in. It was snowing so hard that they couldn't keep the runway open, and they closed the airport. They predicted the airport would be closed till nine o'clock the following morning.

They had already loaded the cattle, so I went up to the trainer and said, "Well the airport is closed; we can't take off before nine tomorrow morning. I guess you'll have to take the cattle back to the barn."

He said, "Son, you don't know much about cattle do you? You just go up to the hotel and come out in the morning, and everything will be fine." I thought those darn cows would freeze to death.

I came out the next morning and entered the airplane. That airplane was as warm as toast. Those cattle could give out that amount of heat. There was snow on the wings but none on the fuselage. It had all melted. So, no, I didn't know anything about cattle.

We had a C-46 flight with cargo that flew down to Managua, Nicaragua, and while it was there, the dictator General Somoza saw this C-46. He liked it. He needed it. He took it! He confiscated it. There was nothing the crew could do. The crew took a commercial flight home. The boss, Paul Weesner, went to the State Department and tried to get it released, but the State Department was helpless.

About a year later, one of our crew members spotted our old aircraft parked at the Miami airport. It had a different paint job, but they recognized it was our old C-46 that the General had confiscated. I was out of town at the time, otherwise I'm sure I would have been in on it. About two o'clock in the morning, Phil Peters and Paul Weesner went out there. It was pitch dark. They got a fuel truck and put fuel in it. Then Phil Peters fired it up – no lights on, no radio contact – and he taxied it out and took off. Of course the tower could see an airplane leaving, and they alerted security. But by the time anyone could do anything, the airplane was gone.

Our company had an outfit over in Brownsville called Frontier Air Motive, a maintenance outfit. Phil flew the plane from Miami to Brownsville, and Paul alerted the mechanics over there. The airplane landed, and they immediately wheeled it into the hangar, and within thirty minutes both engines were off that airplane. There was no way that anybody could fly it back to Nicaragua.

Well, of course, there was a huge cry about a stolen airplane. The FAA tried to nail the boss for hijacking and stealing an airplane. Paul was an ex-lawyer from Washington, and he would have no part of that. His statement was, "I didn't steal that airplane; I repossessed it." And he had all the paperwork to prove it. So that was the end of that. Obviously, we took no more flights down to Nicaragua.

I call this story Little Deliveries. Our little company sold two DC-3s. We were based in Miami, and we were to deliver these two DC-3s to Van Nuys, California. They were in pretty bad shape, but to save money the boss determined that, "Hey, you don't need copilots. Two guys, two airplanes, that's all you need. Take it over there."

Okay, that was no problem. One of the airplanes did not have communication, but it did have an ADF for navigating. The other airplane had the communication. I forget who the other pilot was, but I got in one airplane, and the other pilot got in the other airplane with no copilots. We flew a very loose formation, with one airplane doing the navigation and the other doing the communication. We flew directly from Miami to our outfit in Brownsville, Frontier Air Motive, and fueled up. From there, we flew out to Van Nuys. It had the usual soup out there, but the other pilot was navigating, and I flew wing on him. We came in and landed. They parked us out in the boondocks. We parked side by side, and we got our gear and closed up the airplanes. A jeep came out to pick us up to take us back to the terminal. The other pilot and I climbed into the jeep, and we sat there and waited and waited.

Finally, I said to the driver, "What are we waiting for?"

Well, he was a young kid. He said, "We're waiting for the other two pilots."

I said, "There are no other two pilots. It's just us." He wasn't used to the non-sked business and how non-skeds cut corners and operate on a shoestring. It was a learning curve for him.

I had a flight from Miami to Chicago in a C-46 and had a brand new copilot who'd never been in a C-46 before. As I pre-flighted the airplane, I noticed the left auxiliary tank showed empty, and the right auxiliary tank showed full. The fuel gauges in these old airplanes were highly unreliable. They could be empty and say full; they could be full and say empty. They could be fluctuating and showing the wrong number. They were very unreliable. The only sure way to know how much fuel you had was to stick the tanks. The Curtis Company must have known this, because they furnished a five foot stick graduated with numbers on one side for the main tank and graduated on the other side for the auxiliary tanks. The procedure was to take the cap off and stick the stick in the tank, and the wet part told you how much fuel you had in that tank.

I was busy, and I explained this procedure to the copilot. I said, "I've got to file a flight plan. I want you to climb on both wings, and I want you to stick all four tanks and make sure you know what we've got." He said, "Okay." I came back, and I said, "Did you stick all four tanks?"

"Yeah."

"Okay, so the aux tanks are empty?"

"Yeah."

So we proceeded to Chicago, made a fuel stop, and landed at Chicago. Slick Airways was doing our maintenance up there, and we were laying overnight, so I wrote in the log book, "Right aux tank shows full when it's empty."

I came out the next morning and found a note written in big letters that read, "RIGHT AUX TANK SHOWS FULL BECAUSE IT IS FULL."

We'd gone from Miami to Chicago and stopped for fuel when we had a tank full of fuel. Well, naturally, I was pretty unhappy. I got the copilot, and I said "Hey, you told me you stuck all four tanks in Miami, was that correct?"

He said, "Yes I did; I stuck all four tanks."

I showed him the log book, and I asked, "Well, then, how's it possible that you stuck the right aux? You told me it was empty, but it's full."

He then admitted that he'd stuck the left wing and assumed the right wing was the same. You see, stupid errors kill people. One of those things.

We had a C-46 and got it contracted to fly cattle. So we built stalls inside the airplane, covered the deck in about 8 inches of sawdust, and picked up the breeding cattle. The route from Miami to Santiago was Miami down to Panama, then to Guayaquil in Ecuador, to Lima, Peru, then on to Antofagasta, Chile, and finally to Santiago, Chile. It was about twenty-six hours of flying time. I don't remember laying over anyplace, but we must have. That's a two day trip. The interesting part is that on each fuel stop they'd feed about fifty gallons of water to the livestock in the airplane. At the time I didn't realize they were doing that. Consequently, the airplane was getting heavier and heavier, because the wet sawdust was not going overboard. By the time we got to Santiago, we were really staggering.

In South America it was so hot and humid that at each stop, we'd pull the hatches off the windows to give the cattle some air. The cattle could naturally feel this little cooler air so they'd stick their heads out the window. Passengers sitting in these airports in South America would look out and see this airplane with cattle sticking their heads out the window. Pretty soon, the newspapers came down and took pictures.

An interesting thing about Guayaquil, Ecuador, is that the airport was controlled by Pan American. Pan Am pioneered the routes in the twenties and thirties down into South America. As a result, the airport manager was Pan American, and Pan Am controlled the airport. I went in and talked to the manager to see if I could get the weather down the line. He showed me a letter from Juan Tripp stating that any Pan American employee giving help to an unscheduled airline pilot was subject to immediate dismissal. I told him, "Don't do anything to jeopardize your job. I understand. It's not a problem." We discussed other things and were friendly and so forth. I saw him take some papers, and he put them face down on his desk. He looked at his watch and said, "Oh, I have to go out and take a weather observation. It will take about ten minutes, and I'll be back." So he left.

Well, I had a hunch. I went to his desk, turned the papers over, and, sure enough, there was the present weather and the forecast down the line. I got what I needed. I turned the papers back over and sat back down. He came back, and we discussed some more things. He was very friendly, and I didn't say anything about the weather. I gave him my card and said, "If you're ever in Miami, give me a call. We'll go out and have a lobster dinner. Be sure to call me." And that was that. What a great person!

I talked to another pilot about the situation in South America. One time a non-sked pilot was behind schedule and arrived at a Pan Am-controlled airport after dark. Pan Am turned off the runway lights and turned off the beacon. The poor pilot knew where the airport was in relation to the town, but he couldn't find it in the dark. He

Unloading cattle in Santiago, Chile

made a couple of passes and finally a Texaco employee felt sorry for him and sent a couple of fuel trucks down to the end of the runway. They pointed their headlights down the runway to give this pilot a fighting chance.

We finally arrived in Santiago and delivered our load of cattle. We didn't have any return load, so we spent six days in Santiago while the company tried to locate a load. They never did; so after six days, we ferried back to Miami.

I flew a second load of cattle down there in May of 1949, and it was the same route: Panama, Guayaquil, Lima, Antofagasta, Santiago. We had a return load of race horses, so the next day we hopped over the Andes to Buenos Aires to meet the owner. We were going to be there two days. The next day was Sunday, and he invited us out to the race track to watch his horses run. On one race he took us aside and said "Hey, we've got a darned good chance to make some money this race. I can't guarantee it, but if you want to put some money on it, you've got a better than fifty percent chance." It sounded good enough to us, so we placed a sizable bet. When that race came up, he was watching the start through his field glasses. As the horses made the first turn, he turned to us and said, "We have won." I don't know what he saw or what he was looking for, but it was pretty interesting: "We have won."

The next day, we loaded these race horses to take them up to Los Angeles. We had originally planned to go Santiago, Antofagasto, Lima, Guayaquil, Panama and up. But there wasn't a cloud in the sky, and we figured we could cut the corner and eliminate a fuel stop. Instead of going from Buenos Aires to Santiago, we'd go from Buenos Aires to Antofagasto. The only problem with that route was that the Andes were considerably high, and we didn't have any oxygen in the airplane. Inasmuch as there weren't any clouds covering the mountains, we said "Okay, let's give it a go." We kept climbing and climbing and climbing, and finally we got up to about 18,000 feet. We were just hanging on there, because we didn't have any oxygen. I don't know how those horses made out, but I was gasping for air. When we could look down through a pass and see the other side of the hills, it was a tremendous relief.

We landed at Antofagasto, Lima, Guayaquil, and finally at Panama. From Buenos Aires to Panama is twenty-one hours of flying. The old airport in Panama had a mountain at the end of the runway, and they didn't allow any night takeoffs. It was dusk, and the owner was pleading with me to take off to get in the air where it was cooler because the horses would die on the ground that was hot and humid. He just pleaded with me to leave. We didn't have any clearance to land anywhere in Central America, and I could not see taking off with Pan Am controlling all the airports in Central America. I would have no place to land; I couldn't take off. By this time, the airport was closed and the decision was taken out of our hands. The copilot and I rented a truck, went down to the ice house, and got 6,300 pounds of block ice. We took it out to the airport and put it in the airplane with the horses. I don't remember now how we got the ice into the airplane, but I know we did. By this time, it was probably eleven o'clock at night, so we went in and got a few hours sleep. We were back at the airport at dawn and checked the airplane. The horses were just as good as gold. That ice did the trick. It kept the airplane relatively cool so the horses weren't harmed.

We made one fuel stop in Central America, at Belize, and then on into Brownsville to Frontier Air Motive, where we were going to have a crew change who would take it into Los Angeles. A government inspector met the plane and said, "You have to burn all that sawdust." We had arranged to have that done in California, not in Brownsville. The government inspector was drunk with power and said those horses had to come off and the sawdust had to burned there. The flight was grounded. This was a C-46 with a high door, and there was no ramp to get these horses off. It seemed to me like an impossible thing to do. Fortunately, Buzz Renicker, a jack of all trades and head of maintenance there at Frontier Air Motive said, "Ah hell, I'll take care of it." He called up a trucking company and told them to send out the longest flat bed trailer-truck they had. They came out to the airport, backed it up to the airplane, and unhitched it so it wasn't fastened to the tractor. Then they pushed the tail of the airplane towards the high end. Buzz put two huge hydraulic jacks under it and jacked the back of this trailer up. Now we had about a 35° slope, and the top end was even with the door. Buzz took some 2"x4"s and put cleats across the bed of the truck. He built a couple of temporary railings and just walked those horses off that thing as sweet as you please. That's what you call non-scheduled ingenuity.

I think this next incident happened in 1947, shortly after the war. I was a passenger on a Braniff flight, I believe it was a Convair, and I noticed on the front bulkhead the name of the Captain. It was a buddy of mine I'd flown with in the Naval Air Transport. I sent my card with my name up, and immediately he sent word back to come up to the cockpit. I went up to the cockpit and sat in the jump seat, and it was Old Home Week. We landed at an intermediate stop and the passengers deplaned. My buddy got out of the left seat and said, "You fly the next leg."

I said, "Bill, you're out of your feeble mind. I'm not going to jeopardize your job by flying the next leg." Can you imagine in this day and age an airline Captain offering a passenger the opportunity to climb in the left seat and fly the next leg? It just shows you the attitude back in those days. Talk about relaxed! That was falling apart.

Scheduled Airline Flying 1949 - 1961

We had an opportunity to become a scheduled airline, something that we always looked forward to. Rosco Turner, up in Indianapolis, had a government certificate to run an airline but he didn't have any equipment. We had a lot of airplane pilots but not much business, so it was a fit. Rosco Turner was one of the old famous barn stormers and air racers. He was one of the first to put on a military uniform. He had a Sam Browne belt, puttees, visored cap, huge wings. He had a waxed mustached and he was flying as a public relations man for Gilmore Oil Company. His gimmick was he carried a little lion cub with him on his flights and his lion's name was Gilmore.

So we moved the airline lock, stock and barrel from Miami to Indianapolis. Now was the opportunity to fly a scheduled route. Rosco said, "Hey, guys, I want you all to have the same uniform that I've got."

Well, of course, we were horrified. The Sam Browne belt... God, you'd look like a freak. We told him, "Okay we'll wear the uniform exactly like you have but we have to have a lion cub." That put the end to that.

The other funny thing was that his wings were so long. He had diamonds in his wings. He said, "Anyone that's flying for me ten years from now, I'm going to put diamonds in your wings." But these wings were so darn long you'd pin them on, and as your left arm went back

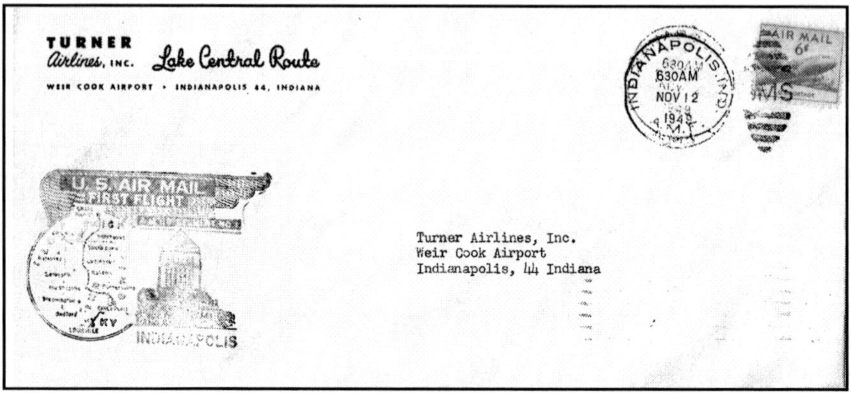

First Flight envelopes from Turner Airlines, 1949 - 1950

I worked for Turner Airlines from 1949 to 1951

and forth the wing would wear a hole in your uniform. It was sort of ridiculous, but interesting.

This Rosco Turner was a real character. One Sunday I went out to the Indianopolis airport with not much to do, and Rosco was hopping passengers to go sight-seeing in an old twin-engine fabric airplane. He saw me and said, "Hey, climb in the right seat and go with me." I had nothing to do, so I climbed in and we took off. Just as we were breaking ground, Rosco turned to me and said, "Oh, hell, I forgot to take the elevator control lock off." This is an external lock to keep the elevators from banging around. The elevators would not move. He said, "These passengers paid for a ride, might as well give 'em a ride." We flew for thirty minutes, and he was using the trim tab to control the airplane. He was nonchalant. He gave the people a full ride and came back in, and I didn't know what the landing was going to be like. He was one of those expert pilots. He was a stunt pilot. He'd flown in the Bendix air races. As a matter of fact he flew in the small GB airplane, a stubby little airplane that killed an awful lot of pilots because it was so sensitive. He'd flown in the Cleveland air races so he was totally qualified. It was an interesting flight with him.

Johnny Horn was number one on the seniority list and I was number two. Before flying a route, we had to take a check flight with an FAA inspector. Johnny and I went flying with this FAA inspector. We had an old DC-3 with a very complicated electrical system, and it failed in flight. I was very fortunate; I knew that airplane well and Johnny didn't. Johnny was trying to fix it but couldn't. Finally I got up out of the seat and fixed it. We completed the flight. I heard later that the FAA went in to the president of our company and said, "Hey, you've got the wrong guy as chief pilot. It ought to be Frank Bray." I thought that was a compliment.

The routes when we started were Indianapolis, Kokomo, South Bend, Kalamazoo, Grand Rapids, back and forth, back and forth. Later we added another route: Indianopolis, Lafayette, Chicago, Richmond, Cincinnati. You'd make a landing every twenty minutes, and there was no way you couldn't get sharp.

The wintertime was interesting. Weather-wise, you had the lake effect coming in off Lake Michigan from the westerly winds. It would blow across the lake and pick up all this moisture. Of course it affected Grand Rapids, Kalamazoo, and South Bend. The tops of the cloud deck might be only 2,000 feet. Perfectly clear above. Then there'd be snow and maybe a three to four hundred foot ceiling. There'd be a lot of instrument approaches into Grand Rapids, Kalamazoo, and South Bend. It made life interesting.

The airline was getting paid to carry mail. If there was no mail, then there was no pay for that leg of the flight. The station agent at each stop had stamped letters ready to mail all the time. If no mail came in, he'd take the mail bag with one stamped envelope and put it in the airplane and away we'd go. So we'd get mail pay for that leg of the trip. I heard previous airlines were paid by weight. If they didn't have enough weight, the station agents would put telephone books, lead, or anything heavy in the mail bag so that they could try to make a profit for that segment.

Another thing was really a conflict of interest. The station agent took the weather report, and as we approached the field we'd call and ask for the weather. If he didn't have any passengers, he'd give us the true weather report, but if he had passengers he'd always give us at least minimum ceiling even though it wasn't there. For instance, if we came into Kokomo and made an approach and didn't see anything, we would climb back up and call the station agent and ask, "What's the weather down there?" He'd say, "500 feet; I've got six passengers." So, you 'd go back and make another approach going lower, desperate to get in because we were desperate for passengers.

Talk about a conflict of interests!

We carried male stewards. A charter came up from Indy to Las Vegas, and they requested a female stewardess. My wife, GG, had been a stewardess and had traveled with me before, so she went along. I introduced her to the copilot as just GG. He had never met her. We flew to Las Vegas, and when GG and I moved into the hotel room together the copilot thought, "Oh, man, this pilot's really fast. First trip and he's shacking up with the stewardess." So that was sort of fun.

It was 1949. We had a black man on board It was embarrassing when we checked into this hotel in Las Vegas. They wouldn't let him register. He had to go to another hotel. Fortunately, I was not in charge of the passengers – it was the responsibility of the person who booked the charter. It was an embarrassing situation and hard to believe. But that's the way it was at that time.

We had one charter trip from Indy to Springfield, Massachusetts. It was a hockey team. The Indianapolis hockey team was playing over in Springfield, and they had a game Saturday night in Springfield and another game Sunday night back in Indianaopolis. I flew them into Springfield, routine. We were supposed to leave right after the game for Indianapolis. A blizzard came along. It was just snowing so hard they closed the airport. I got ahold of the manager of the hockey team and told him it would be impossible to leave. If we could leave by about ten or twelve the next day, then we could get back in time for the hockey game Sunday night. He was really put out and desperate. He checked the buses. He checked the trains. But there was no way to get back in time for the game Sunday night. Fortunately, the weather did clear the next morning, and we loaded up at ten and flew back to Indy in time for the game. So that turned out okay.

This type of scheduled flying became very boring. Up and down the same routes, day after day, week after week, month after month. You got to know every house on the route; you got to know when the cattle had calves. You got to know when the ladies put their wash on the lines. I just couldn't believe how boring it was. I always thought scheduled airline flying would be fun. But after non-scheduled airline flying it was a drag. About 1951 I had an opportunity to return to the original outfit that was still operating. They had four-engine equipment and naturally I'd rather fly four-engine equipment than two-engine equipment. I left the airline and went back to the original one. The other thing that made my decision easier was that we were carrying so few passengers that we were operating at a loss, and I couldn't conceive that the airline would profit and make it. I thought they would fold. But of course I was wrong. Later they changed the name from Turner Airlines to Lake Central, merged with Allegheny airline, then there was maybe one other merger, and now it's part of US Air.

Another small point was that neither GG nor I much cared for Indy. The chance to leave was too tempting, so we jumped at it.

Without a moment's regret, we moved from Indianapolis to San Antonio. This was wintertime, and San Antonio was nice and warm. We didn't miss the snow and ice at all. It looked like we were going to be in San Antonio for a while, so we bought a house. The main business out at San Antonio was flying CAMs, which stands for Civilian Air Movement. These were military contracts. We were flying military personnel from base to base, but the main business was meeting the ships that came in from Oakland and Seattle, where they had thousands of troops coming back from the Korean War, and taking them to the various bases around the country. To take care of this business, we had ten C-46s and four DC-4s plushed up.

I had one interesting flight. I think the CIA had some secret mission over in Europe, and needed an unidentified DC-4. They contacted our company, and I think they chartered the airplane for a thousand dollars a day. Doug Bell, who was chief pilot, and I flew the airplane from San Antonio over to Frankfurt, Germany, and left it there. The next day we got on Pan Am and flew home.

A month later we got a call telling us to come get the airplane, that they couldn't use it. So Doug and I got back on Pan Am and flew back over to Frankfurt. We found that they'd resealed the fuel tanks. When we delivered the airplane over there it was not leaking a single drop of fuel. I don't know why they took the planks off and resealed it. I'm not sure what it was all about I don't know what the mission was. But they took the planks off and resealed the tanks, and then to hurry up the thing, they put heat lamps in there to dry it up quicker. Then they put fuel in, and it leaked like a sieve. They never did use the airplane, but they finally got the leaks stopped. Doug and I picked up the airplane to fly it back to the United States.

The operations officer there said, "Sorry, we can't release you. You don't have a navigator."

We looked at each other and thought, "My God, we fly all over the world without a navigator." So we said, "Ok, we're not going to the States. We're just going up to Paris, so I guess we won't need a navigator."

He said, "Ok." We filed a flight plan for Paris, and as soon as we got in the air we refiled for Keflavik in Iceland.

We landed at Keflavik and loaded up with fuel for our next leg. We were going over to Newfoundland and then down to San Antonio. Doug and I had been switching legs, and it was my leg to fly. I took off, and we just got off the ground when we lost one of the engines. I feathered the sucker. We should have dumped fuel because we were way over maximum landing weight, but, being non-sked pilots, we couldn't afford to dump fuel. So I brought it in fast, and I really greased it on. I could hardly feel the landing, but, with all that weight in the wings, it was just enough to flex them a little bit. When we pulled up to the ramp, one of the aux tanks was pouring gas out onto the ramp. So we immediately called for a fuel truck, and the truck came over and defueled that tank.

The company shipped up a new cylinder for the engine and we had it installed. We were there for about four days. When we were ready to leave, we filed a flight plan and had everything all set. We filled up the good tanks first, and at the last moment we filled up this leaking auxiliary tank. Well, it leaked on the ramp. Personnel there looked at us:

Feathered Engine #4

"Hey, what's going on here?" But as soon as that tank was full we started the engines, taxied out, took off, and were on the way to the States. As soon as we got up to 1,000 feet, through the crossfeed systems in the airplane we fed all four engines off that leaking tank to take out the gasoline before too much of it leaked overboard. But once we got down near empty we put three engines back on their main tanks and left one engine on that aux tank until it was dry. That's the way non-skeds operate.

A month later I was in a C-46, and I had a flight from Cheyenne to Chicago. We had four airplanes in Cheyenne. We'd delivered troops, and we were to ferry them to Chicago. It was about ten o'clock at night, and there was a huge squall line between Cheyenne and Chicago with the usual lightning – cloud to cloud, cloud to ground. You have to remember, back then the planes had no radar, and there was no radar on the ground to vector you around these cells. We were all on an instrument flight plan, and the only thing to do was to blunder through it.

Well, three of us made it. One of our airplanes didn't. He must have hit a tornado or violent turbulence, because when they found the airplane, the wings had bent down. I can imagine wings bending up from turbulence, but not wings bending down, particularly considering that on the C-46 the wingspar was built like a girder. It was unbelievably strong. It's just hard to believe that it could fail. But we lost the airplane and three crew members, a captain, copilot, and stewardess. We all knew the families of the crew. What a sad time.

I have to tell this story about one of our pilots in a thunderstorm. Anybody that's not scared of a thunderstorm is just absolutely stupid. They've never been in one or they've failed the intelligence test, because obviously thunderstorms can tear an airplane apart. Well, Woody Woodward was not scared of thunderstorms. He laughed at people who wouldn't fly through them. His copilot told me about this one trip. There was a thunderstorm ahead, and, rather than go on around it, Woody decided he'd just plow right through it. The turbulence was violent. He was carrying a jet engine in the back, and it was chained to the deck. But the turbulence tore this jet engine loose, and half of it went out through the side of the fuselage. Then something happened with Woody's seat. The seat could be adjusted up and down, and there were two pins that held the adjustment. The turbulence was so violent that it broke these two pins, and Woody was going up and down the seat tracks like a yo-yo, screaming. He was thinking that the airplane was coming apart because of the seat going against the stops up and down. The copilot told me, "If we hadn't been so darned scared, I would have died laughing." There's an old saying in aviation, and that is, "Never fly in the same cockpit with someone braver than you." And that's a great saying.

We had a contract with the immigration service. They would round up Mexicans who had come in illegally, and we'd fly them to Mexico. I talked to some of these Mexican passengers, and it was very interesting. Most of them laughed. They said, "Well, at the end of the growing season we want to go home for a visit, so we arrange to be picked up by the immigration. You guys fly us down there for free, we see our family, and we stay there until next growing season." It seemed like a no-win situation for immigration.

The home outfit in San Antonio was now called Resort Airlines. Nationwide Air Transport service, the original airline, had merged with Resort Airlines. So I was flying for Resort Airlines. Actually, it was the same management, same president, and same director of operations. But Resort Airlines ran tours down through the Caribbean area. They'd pick up passengers in New York, Philadelphia, Washington, Miami, and fly tours down to Havana, Cuba, Haiti, San Juan, Barbados, Nassau, and back. It was never entirely successful because the majority of the trips, there were 80 percent women and very few men. I think the women were going down there for the romance, and there just weren't enough men to go around. Anyway it never did seem to pan out.

I have to tell you this little story. As I say, we were living in San Antonio, and GG and I went over to Miami on one of our vacations, where they were running these tours. We were just there on vacation, and for something to do I stopped in our local office and met my old buddies. They said, "Oh, man, you're a life saver. Our crew over in Nassau has extreme food poisoning, they're in the hospital, and we have no way to get them home. We want you to hop on Pan Am and fly over to Nassau and pick them up and fly them home."

I said, "Well, ok."

I flew over to Nassau, and the crew came out. I forget whether they came in an ambulance or what, but they were definitely out of it. They got in the airplane, and I flew it back to Miami.

Then the office said, "Hey, this crew is out, so you've got to take this DC-3 on the next tour."

I said, "I'm down here on vacation. I can't take that tour. I've got my wife with me."

He said, "No problem, take your wife along. All expenses paid. We'll call your outfit over in San Antonio and square it with them, but we've got to have you take this flight out as captain."

I talked it over with GG and she said, "Sure, why not?"

I hadn't been in a DC-3 for a couple of years, but it was like riding a bicycle. You don't forget. So I flew it down to Havana. It was an interesting place. We put the airplane to bed, and the four of us, GG and I and the stewardess and the copilot, went into the hotel and checked in. We met down at the bar before dinner. We were sitting in the bar and the gals said, "Hey, let's have some of these banana daiquiris."

So we all ordered banana daiquiris, and the girls complained, "There's just nothing in this stuff."

We had quite a few of them, and then it came time for dinner. The stewardess excused herself and said, "I'll be right back."

She didn't come back, and she didn't come back, so I said to GG, "You'd better go up and see what the deal is with our stewardess."

GG went up, and she didn't come back. And she didn't come back. So the copilot went up to the rooms, and there were the two gals in their beds, sound asleep. Nothing in those banana daiquiris.

The copilot and I went out and had a nice evening. First we went out to dinner. Then we went out to a night club. The next morning, GG was real unhappy because she'd missed out on the night club. But from then on: “Oh there's just nothing in those banana daiquiris.”

Resort Airlines’ C-46

Resort Airlines’ DC-4

Fellow Resort Airlines Pilots

Taking in the view from my office window

A year later, in 1954, the company got a contract with the government to fly a program called Log Air. They moved a bunch of us from San Antonio to Oklahoma City. The theory was that there was no need for all the military bases having a huge inventory. With two flights a day arriving at their base, they could get any part within twenty-four hours.

I was assigned the first flight on this Log Air program. The airplane was at the Oklahoma City International Airport, and I was to ferry it over to Tinker Air Force Base on the other side of the city. It was only twenty miles. It was ten o'clock at night, and as usual the weather was bad. I had a brand new copilot who'd never been in a DC-4 before. It was a model with a strange radio system that I wasn't familiar with. There was about a 2000 foot ceiling, so I figured I could fly from the Oklahoma City Airport over to Tinker under this ceiling. I took off from Oklahoma City, and Tinker said they wouldn't accept us underneath, that I had to climb up and get into the stack, take my turn and make an instrument approach. I was handling the radio, flying, doing the navigation, and I was busier than a one-armed paperhanger because the copilot was no help.

Anyway, we climbed up and got into the stack. By the time it came our turn to land at Tinker, they'd fogged in, 0/0. So I got clearance back to the Oklahoma City Airport, and of course had to climb back up and get into the stack over Oklahoma City. When it was my turn for approach, Oklahoma City was fogged in, 0/0. Well, I guess the company had been following us, because through the approach control they sent me a message to go to Tulsa. I figured, this stuff is moving east and I don't want to go east, I want to go west and get behind this problem. So I requested the Guthrie weather and that was good, so I headed up to Guthrie and we landed there. We had been flying 2½ hours to go twenty miles and never reached our destination. On the next day, of course, the fog burned off, and we fired up from Guthrie, flew back to Tinker, picked up our load of cargo, and headed out. But what a fiasco for the first flight.

We had two flights a day: one going eastbound and one going westbound, counter-clockwise. With layovers it took us ten days to get back to home base. The problem with all this flying was that we as pilots were out of town so much. It was ten out, ten in, ten out, ten in, so we were gone 50 percent of the time. I asked GG if she was happy with this situation, and she said, yeah, she was happy half the time. The only problem was, she never said which half.

We had twelve DC-4s on this Log Air program. They were all different models, so the cockpit configurations were different. They had a trap in the airplane that got me one stormy night. I don't know why it's always dark, stormy nights when these things happen. When we landed at intermediate stops, we always moved the fuel selectors to the off position, so that one tank wouldn't leak to another through the cross-feed. Before start-up, we'd move the fuel tank selectors back to the main tanks. Well, one model had the main tanks' fuel selectors all the way down and the auxes halfway down, and the other model had the fuel tank selectors for the mains halfway down and the auxes all the way down, just the opposite of each other.

This one night, I had ptomaine poisoning or something, and I just wasn't thinking. After they'd loaded the cargo I came out and did the preflight checklist and went out on the runway. As I say, it was a dark, stormy night. We took off, and one of the engines quit. Oh boy, but no big deal; we had three other engines operating, so I just told the tower that we'd like to come back and land. I contacted a mechanic to see if he could find out what was wrong. I hit the restroom, threw up and had a little diarrhea. I was feeling miserable, but as I sat there, I said, "Oh, sugar. We had the fuel selectors in the wrong position, and that one engine didn't get any fuel!" I thought about it and went back out to the plane and, sure enough, I'd been trapped. I was just lucky that all four engines didn't quit. That's what they call, "I gotcha!" But it wasn't fatal.

I have to repeat that 99 percent of all flights are routine. It might even be more, so I'm just recounting that other 1 percent. Here's a 1 percent story. I was a check pilot for the organization, and one of my duties was to check out new copilots. Well, the company had hired this elderly pilot – which is what I became later. But anyway he just didn't seem to be aware of the situation, and I recommended that the company terminate him before his probation period ended. His name was Pappy Daniels.

On a flight with Pappy, we landed at the military field in Sacramento, McClellan Air Force Base. As I landed this dark night, the tower said to expedite. They had an airplane waiting to take off. To speed up the airplane, I called for the flaps to be retracted. In the dark cockpit Pappy reached his left hand down and pulled up the landing gear. Oh, what a deal. Fortunately only the nose wheel came up. The main gear did not come up, so we were sliding down the runway on our nose. The batteries were up in the nose compartment, and they shorted out. So now the airplane was dark, and we couldn't call the tower to tell them we were stuck in the center of the runway, nose down. We couldn't move because we had no electricity.

Luckily, the airplane that was waiting to take off was one of our own airplanes. They watched us land and watched us start to roll down the runway. Then all they saw was this big flash of fire, and then silence. They couldn't see anything either, but they knew something had happened. When the nose wheel came up, the sparks fired off the hydraulic fluid, and that's the flash they saw. My buddy in the other airplane called the tower, and said, "Hey, you guys better send the crash crew out – something's happened out there. They're in the middle of the runway, and they're quiet."

Well, here's another trap that was designed into the airplane. The flap handle and the gear handle were identical, side by side. They did have a little guard between them, but the big protection was a sensor switch on the gear strut. When you have weight on the airplane, the sensor switch sends a signal to a solenoid pin that crosses the gear handle so if everything's working properly, the pin's across the landing gear handle, and

Our plane on the runway at McClellan Air Force Base, after the copilot pulled the wrong handle

you can't pull up the gear. Being an older airplane, the pin had frozen. It had not come across the landing gear handle. So that's the thing that saved me from getting reamed out by the company. They found that the pin had not come across the landing gear handle. It's ironic. I'd recommended that they release Pappy because he was going to get somebody in trouble. I ended up being the guy in trouble.

On later airplanes they designed this trap out of the airplane. They designed it so that they had the landing gear handle on one side of the cockpit. The handle was shaped like a wheel, so even if you weren't looking at it, you felt it. On the other side of the cockpit they put a handle to operate the flaps. And it looked like a flap, it felt like a flap, and the handles weren't side by side.

The military field at Harrisburg was interesting. It was built along the river there, and there was a large dike to keep the river water out. At the end of the runway was this twenty foot high dike. On the side of this dike was a huge sign that said, "Cut your engines." If the runway was slick with ice or snow and you couldn't stop, cut your engines.

At the same Harrisburg airport I had a funny thing happen. We were to lay over there in Harrisburg so I taxied in and we parked with the hangar right in front of the airplane. So when I looked out the windshield, I was looking right into the hangar. I had my face down filling out the logbook, and I felt this little jolt. "What was that?" I looked up and saw nothing but blue sky. For an instant I thought, "What's going on? What happened to the hangar?"

Well what had happened was they had forgotten to put the tail stand on our DC-4. We had a heavy jet engine that we were carrying, and when they moved it to the rear of the cabin the weight was way off. Without the stand under the tail, the airplane pivoted on the main gear and landed on the tail. I was looking up at the sky. Just for an instant it was a mighty weird feeling.

There are just so many AK stories, but this was an interesting one. We were in a DC-4 westbound from Biloxi into Kelly Field in San Antonio. We were on an instrument flight plan. There was a layer of clouds. The top of this layer was about 7000 feet, clear above. The base of this layer was 3000 feet, clear below. So just a little layer of clouds. We were cleared to let down into San Antonio, and we started the letdown. We're in the soup, and radar reported that we had traffic at twelve o'clock, fifteen miles out.

Back then the radar couldn't tell the altitude of any traffic. All they could tell was their position on Earth. So we didn't think anything of it, and pretty soon the radar said, "You've got traffic at twelve o'clock seven miles out." We were letting down in the soup, and we figured he was either below the overcast or above the overcast. We still didn't think anything of it.

Then the radar said, "You have traffic at twelve o'clock, three miles out." Ok, so he's below us or above us, no problem.

Then... it was unbelievable. The belly of this airplane filled our windshield just for a blink of a second. All I could see was aluminum. We must have just missed him by ten or twenty feet. We were letting down legally on an instrument flight plan, and he was climbing up through this overcast illegally because he didn't have an instrument clearance. It was just the luck of the draw. Obviously, from that point on, anytime radar control gave us traffic at twelve o'clock approaching us, we asked for a vector around it. I still can't believe how close that was.

Another time on the same route, I happened to have one of those men who wears gloves in the cockpit for a copilot. He was drunk with power, and he was the local god. To keep morale up, every other leg we'd switch seats. So this particular leg it was his turn to fly. He was in the left seat, the captain's seat, and I was in the right seat acting as copilot. We were letting down into Kelly Field in San Antonio, and it was a perfectly clear day. We were maybe ten miles east, and he said, "run the checklist."

"Yes, sir."

I ran the checklist. We were approaching, and he said, "Flaps, quarter," so I gave him flaps a quarter.

Well, I could see he was lined up for San Antonio Municipal Airport and not Kelly Field. So I let him go, and we were getting close to the airport. He called for flaps a half. So I give him flaps a half.

"Call the tower," so I called the tower.

He called for gear down, so I gave him gear down. By this time he was down to 500 feet, about to land at San Antonio Airport instead of Kelly. I looked at him and said, "Hey, I'm just curious. Are you going to carry all this cargo from San Antonio Municipal over to Kelly?"

He looked at me and saw that he had the wrong airport, and he said, "You son of a bitch, you let me get this low!" He poured the coal to it and went on. It was sort of amusing. I think he learned a lesson: let's have cockpit management, let's communicate here. It's not all a one-pilot deal.

About 1955, the little airline got a contract to fly cargo from California to Tokyo. They decided to move the whole operation from Oklahoma City to Oakland and do our maintenance out there. Continue the Log Air program, but also do the program to fly cargo to Tokyo. To keep both operations going, one by one they moved crews from Oklahoma City to Oakland. Everybody wanted to move. No one much cared for Oklahoma City. We cared for Oklahoma City even less than Indianapolis. When GG and I got word that it was our turn to move, we immediately disconnected the telephone so the dispatcher couldn't call us and change his mind. We wanted out of there. So we drove over to Oakland.

Those flights to Tokyo out of Oakland were interesting. We were based in Oakland. We did all our maintenance in Oakland. We ferried the DC-4 up to Travis Air Force Base, which was outside of Sacramento, and then we flew with a full load of cargo to Honolulu. Back in those days it was about fourteen and a half hours, a long flight. We'd lay over a day, and pick up the next day's flight and take it to Wake Island. That's another thirteen hours. Lay over a day and take it to Tokyo, an eleven hour flight. Lay over a day and pick up the next day's flight back to Wake, nine hours now we've got a tailwind. Lay over a day and then to Honolulu, ten hours. Lay over a day. Then back to Travis Air Force Base, unload the cargo, and take the plane down to Oakland for maintenance. So round-trip it was seventy-two hours. This took about thirteen days, and then we'd have thirteen days off. So we were back to the old deal: I was out half the time and in half the time.

I have to tell you a little thing that happened on the way out to Tokyo. Here again I had a copilot who had never been out in the Pacific. When we landed at Honolulu, we had a day off waiting for the flight the next day to Wake. He knew Wake Island had this gorgeous, beautiful, clear water, and he wanted to go snorkeling. So while we were in Honolulu he went and bought all the gear: the flippers, the goggles, the snorkeling gear. Of course he had his bathing suit. He was all set for Wake Island.

The next day, the flight came in, and we picked it up and flew over to Wake. We had a full day there waiting for the next day's flight. So he put on his gear and went out in the lagoon, and it was hog heaven. He dove down and was exploring the underwater when this huge moray eel came out to investigate what this strange thing was. Well, the pilot saw the Moray eel coming at him with all these teeth. If you've ever seen a man walk on water, he came out of that water, roared up the beach, and gave all his equipment to the first local guy he saw. He said, "That's the last time I'm ever going in that water." God, we all just sat there howling. It was hilarious.

One other time I was on Wake waiting for the airplane to come in from Tokyo, and a gentleman came up and introduced himself. He said he was an FAA inspector, and he was going to give us a route check from Wake Island to Honolulu. I said, "Hey, that's great, no problem, glad to have you aboard." When the incoming crew came in, they said the left mag on the #2 engine was out. Of course that's a no-go item, but there's no maintenance there on Wake. I'm an old non-sked pilot so, "Hey, no problem."

RESORT AIRLINES, INC.
Oakland International Airport
Oakland, California

INFORMATION BULLETIN

TO: All Pilots DATE: July 1, 1959

FROM: Vice-President Operations

The following is the official Resort Airlines Pilot's Seniority List as of July 1, 1959, in accordance with Section 21 of the ALPA Contract.

	NAME	DATE OF HIRE		NAME	DATE OF HIRE
1.	Poteet, L. W.	8-17-46	35.	L'Hommedieu, J. S.	7-9-51
2.	Bray, F. D.	9-1-46	36.	Ising, W. S.	10-7-51
3.	Day, D. L.	10-18-46	37.	Peetz, R. J.	12-22-51
4.	Warner, E. S.	11-15-46	38.	Menge, W. S.	6-2-52
5.	Evans, C. T.	12-16-46	39.	Jessup, R. M.	6-2-52
6.	Tripp, E. A.	6-30-48	40.	DesJardin, H. J.	7-21-52
7.	Haddad, A.	11-18-48	41.	McGinn, R. E.	10-24-52
8.	Walker, T. E.	12-1-48	42.	Uffe, S.	10-30-52
9.	Peters, C. P.	3-10-49	43.	Mainenti, R. N.	11-3-52
10.	Archer, F. O.	6-1-49	44.	Hill, R. D.	11-5-52
11.	Paris, F.	2-5-50	45.	Rutherford, W. A.	7-8-54
12.	Witmer, N. D.	6-15-50	46.	Merrill, C. W.	6-1-55
13.	MacDonald, A. W.	7-10-50	47.	Brayton, J. D.	1-16-56
14.	Neidig, W. M.	8-19-50	48.	Guerra, R. J.	2-1-56
15.	Thelen, E. T.	9-21-50	49.	Sullivan, T. W.	2-7-56
16.	McKendree, L. C. L.O.A.	10-30-50	50.	Yeater, D. A.	2-15-56
17.	Brown, F. A.	12-13-50	51.	Savage, J. M.	3-1-56
18.	Wiggins, A. C.	12-16-50	52.	Bridges, A. L.	3-19-56
19.	Stahl, C. R.	12-27-50	53.	Neal, D. J.	3-19-56
20.	Mudgett, L. A.	1-10-51	54.	Becker, R. E.	3-24-56
21.	Deardorff, R. O.	1-10-51	55.	Vogan, J. O.	3-28-56
22.	Marks, H. P.	1-10-51	56.	Shwaiko, J.	4-7-56
23.	Bayliss, R. T.	1-16-51	57.	Zimmer, R. L.	5-25-56
24.	Cremer, H.	2-2-51	58.	Oberg, H.	6-19-56
25.	Kahmann, D. E.	2-9-51	59.	Marston, C.	8-1-56
26.	Baker, E. K.	2-20-51	60.	Pacheco, J. G.	10-4-56
27.	Jossey, C. J.	2-25-51	61.	Chastain, K. L.	10-7-56
28.	Sanders, C. P.	2-25-51	62.	Ellis, J. R.	10-19-56
29.	Lovell, W. S.	3-5-51	63.	McDonald, F. E.	10-26-56
30.	Bobo, H. P.	3-7-51	64.	Stokes, H. Q.	11-1-56
31.	Callahan, W. M.	3-12-51	65.	Reynolds, J. L.	11-9-56
32.	Woodward, G. A.	4-16-51	66.	Bybee, W. C.	12-23-56
33.	Rideout, P.	6-11-51	67.	Edinger, C. E.	1-11-57
34.	Alexakos, T. N.	6-19-51	68.	Robinson, L. M.	1-12-57
			69.	Neumeister, H. P.	3-15-57

DPL:rvj

Resort Airlines Pilot Seniority List, 1959

After we fueled up and filed our flight plan, we got in the cockpit, ran our preflight check, started the engines, and taxied out to the end of the runway. Well, at the end of the runway you checked your mags to see if they're all working. I was in the left seat, the check pilot was in the jump seat, and the copilot was in the right seat. I had told the copilot, "Just keep quiet, no problem."

When it came time to check that engine, the procedure was to increase the power and move your hand to the mag switches. You switched both to right and watched the drop in the rpms, then both back to the left and watched the drop in the rpms, and finally back to both. So you checked both mags. Well, I knew the left mag was out, so with my other hand I put my finger on the RPM gauge to draw the FAA inspector's eyes there, so he would watch the gauge to see what the drop was. I went both to right, watched the drop, and back to both. Then I said left, but I put the mag switch on right. I did it both times on the good mag. Back to both. He never realized that the left mag was out. It's an old non-sked procedure, but it wasn't anything dangerous. That's why all engines have two mags, in case one goes out. The worst thing that could happen was if the other mag went out then, ok, you didn't have that engine, but you still had three engines.

Around this time our little company bought two spanking new Lockheed 10-49 Constellations. We'd been flying war surplus junk all these years, and now we had beautiful, brand new transports. We figured, maybe our airline has finally arrived. I was one of the senior captains, so I was in line to get type-rated.

I was assigned to flight training to check out in this Constellation. I went to a week and a half of ground school and then started flight training. The controls of the Constellation were hydraulically boosted to assist the pressures on the controls. To demonstrate that you could land the airplane without that hydraulic assist, the check instructor would turn off the hydraulic boost, so we were actually landing the airplane with locked controls. They would barely move. I thought this was ridiculous. It was a brand new airplane, and we were jeopardizing our airline by actually landing with locked controls. I thought that wasn't a simulated emergency; it was a real emergency. Of course, later on they had simulators to do this type of thing. However, I completed the training and took a ride with an FAA inspector and got my type rating in the Constellation as Captain.

The first trip out, George Merrill, who was director of operations and also our flight instructor, and I – of course he was the captain, so I rode copilot for him – took this Conny up to Seattle to pick up a load of passengers for Tokyo. These airplanes were not for cargo. They were just passenger airplanes. We loaded up a planeful of troops and took off.

We were only about forty minutes out in this brand new airplane when we had an engine problem. We had to shut down one engine. We'd just departed Seattle, but the people doing our maintenance were Pan Am down in San Francisco. We figured we couldn't get any maintenance up in Seattle, so George Merrill decided we'd just go down to San Francisco, get our maintenance, and then proceed to Tokyo. We'd notified air traffic control that we'd had an engine shut down, and they said, "We'll send the Coast Guard out to escort you down to San Francisco." The only problem was that we could fly faster on three engines than the Coast Guard could fly with all their engines. So we left him in the dust. We flew into the San Francisco area still way over our maximum allowable landing weight. We had to go out over the ocean and dump fuel to get down to a legal landing weight, then came in and landed. We put our passengers up in some barracks at one of our local bases, got our maintenance and the next day went on our way to Tokyo.

I had two more trips to Tokyo before disaster struck. We had new management. The airline people who started this airline sold out to a management group, and they were money people, not airline people. All they cared about was the bottom line. Here we had two spanking new airplanes, and the scheduled airlines were short of airplanes. Our airline could sell these two and make a

AIR MATERIEL COMMAND

Certificate of Merit

THE COMMANDER OF THE
AIR MATERIEL COMMAND
AWARDS TO

FRANK D. BRAY

This certificate in recognition of outstanding professional skill, proficiency and alertness in the service of LOGAIR. *By this certificate, be it known that he has logged over 3,000 hours flying time for* LOGAIR. *The sincere appreciation of this Command is extended for this accomplishment towards the growth and success of* LOGAIR *in its contribution to the national defense effort.*

25 January 1961
AF-WP-O-JAN 61 300 DATE

I received this certificate for participating in the LogAir program.

tremendous profit. So they sold them. We made four trips to Tokyo, and then the airplanes were gone.

We were still operating the Log Air contracts. The contracts ran on a fiscal year of July to July, and they were coming up. Inasmuch as the management were not airline people, well, the pilots had a disagreement, and we joined ALPA, Airline Pilots Association. So we were unionized. We could see that to meet competition we would have to take a cut in salary. All of us wanted to take a cut so we could stay in business and keep our jobs. We went to the union and said, to be competitive, we as pilots want to take a cut in salary. The union refused. They said no way. Consequently we lost both contracts, to Tokyo and the Log Air contract. The management group decided there was no future here. The airline folded. Kaput. Out of business. Gone. Seventeen years and it's out of business.

World Airways was awarded our Log Air contract, so most of our pilots went over to World. They were flying the same routes, the same airplanes, and management had gone over to World as well. Maintenance went over to World, so they had the same maintenance, too. The only thing that changed was they had different colored uniforms and 75 percent of the pay. But they were working.

I decided I'd test the waters for corporate aviation, so I put out hundreds of feelers and talked to everybody that I knew and made phone calls. I wrote resumes, and the bottom line was, I was overqualified. By this time I had over 16,000 hours flight time. Various flight departments didn't want this guy stepping in with all this experience. At the end of the month, being out of work, I swallowed my pride and went out to the airport and walked in George Merrill's office. He was now general manager for World Airways. I asked him if he had a slot for me. He said, "Frank, what kept you so long? Of course we need you. You're going out as Captain. No problem." So here I was, same deal, flying the same airplanes, same routes, new uniform, and less pay. But at least I was working.

I only flew the DC-4s for World Airways for about six months. I was flying the same old routes, and, being gone so much, I was really getting tired of being away from home. I'd talked to corporate pilots. They had glowing reports of how much time they had off. They were always home, they had beautiful equipment, they were well-paid, and they had a pension, which I'd never had. It sounded attractive.

One of my buddies was an aircraft broker. He was also chief pilot for an insurance company. He sold this Twin Beech to an insurance company down in Texas. They had an office there in Los Angeles, and they needed a pilot. So my buddy recommended me. On one of my days off I went down for an interview, and we sort of hit it off. I was talking to the President of this insurance company, and it seemed like a good opportunity to get a job where I could be home more. I gave my two-weeks notice to World, left them, and started in on my corporate career.

So ended my airline flying. Most of it was enjoyable, but it was not without its tragedies. In the fifteen years and thousands of flights, we lost four airplanes. The first was a DC-3 flight from Miami to New York. Bob Sheker was scheduled as captain. He wasn't feeling too hot, so I offered to take the flight. Since we got paid only if we flew, he took it. That night the weather was forming faster than the plane could fly. There were all kinds of planes declaring emergencies due to low fuel. Bob's luck ran out in New Jersey. He crash-landed. The copilot and some of the passengers were killed.

Of interest, that same night an American Airlines DC-3 scheduled flight became trapped in this same weather. He flew out over the ocean, let down to the wavetops, and then turned toward the beach. He bellied it in on Jones Beach. Life magazine wrote a big spread on this unusual weather phenomenon.

The second loss was a C-46 ferry flight from San Antonio to Miami. Approaching Miami, Smitty, the captain, told the tower he had lost elevator control. He tried to land it with the trim tab, but it nosed up and crashed, killing the crew. On inspecting the wreckage they found the cables to the elevators disconnected. Some mechanic had not safety-wired the pins. The plane had just come out of Slick Airline maintenance. There was no record of anybody working on the tail. Wasn't that convenient.

The third loss was the C-46 in the squall line between Cheyenne and Chicago, torn apart in the air, probably by a tornado. The fourth was a C-46 in Louisville, also an elevator control problem. It nosed up on landing and killed all twenty-eight on board.

You have to realize that GG and I were close friends with all these pilots. We knew their wives and children. We were family.

Fate plays a big hand in the flying game. Could things have been different if I had been flying these planes? Probably not. We'll never know. I always felt the most dangerous part of the job was on the freeway getting to the airport.

Corporate Flying 1961 - 1981

I was flying a light Twin Beech for United National Insurance Company in 1961. Charles Russell was the president. This was my first corporate job, and it lasted 2½ years before disaster struck.

When I climbed into this Twin Beech I had a terrible time landing it. I was used to the DC-4s with their heavy controls. On landing the DC-4, the controls were so heavy it took two hands to pull the yoke back to flare. This Twin Beech was so light and goosy, I was just skittish all over the runway at first. But I finally got comfortable with it and went on from there. We did a lot of flying in this light Twin Beech. We averaged about seventy hours a month. The president of the company occupied the copilot's seat. The joke was, I was chief pilot of this company. Well, of course, the punchline to the joke was, I was the only pilot.

The future looked good for the company, so we had a demo ride in an F-27, which was a turboprop. We looked at a Super Ventura. We looked at the Howard 500, which was a faster pressurized airplane. I thought the company was really going places. Later we acquired a Lockheed Lodestar from Signal Oil & Gas, and sold the Twin Beech. The Lodestar was a fun airplane to fly. It was bigger and heavier than the Beech, of course, and it was the same airplane that National Airlines previously used for scheduled service. It was a fine airplane. A crew came with it: Clint Seccombe and Dean Miller. Both were excellent pilots, and, among many other gifts, were superb mechanics. They had flown and maintained this plane at a small facility at Burbank Airport.

Flying the president, I heard about the glamorous future, so I invested my life savings in the company. I invested $20,000. Two months later this investment was worth $40,000. Three months later, it was worth $75,000. The next month it was worth zero. Zip. The company had folded.

I went out to the airport and found the plane chained to the ramp with a sticker on the door. It had been repossessed. The big boys had shut us down. Later I had to go down to the courthouse and testify before the grand jury about the operation, and what I knew about the company. Well, I was the pilot, I could tell them where we went and when, but that was the extent of it.

Suddenly I was broke and out of a job, with a wife and two kids to support. But I was very lucky. I was only out of work for about two weeks.

At Burbank Airport there was an outfit called Trans-California. Larry Mudget, an old pilot friend of mine who I had flown with at Resort Airlines, was president of this company. I went in to see Larry and told him I needed a job. He really didn't need pilots, but he said, “No problem, Frank. We'll put you on the line as a Captain.” I had a Constellation type rating, so he didn't have to train me or check me out.

These were the little Connys. They were the first model, the little 749s. They were really old airplanes. They'd been purchased from Eastern Airlines. We had three of them, and they were really in ratty condition. The carpets were threadbare, the curtains were hanging down, the overhead was sagging, and the engines were covered with oil. But it was a job.

I went right to work for Larry Mudget as Captain, and of course there were hard feelings from the copilots to have this joker come in when they expected to be upgraded. I realized that, and I leaned over backward to be diplomatic and gave them every leg possible to keep up the morale. After a few months we became friends, maybe not buddies but at least friends.

This was a terrible route. It was an all-California route, so you can just imagine. Burbank, Los Angeles, San Diego, Los Angeles, Burbank, Oakland, Burbank, Oakland, Burbank. Back and forth, back and forth. Seventy hours a month. It was so boring, it was hard to keep your mind on the job.

There was one interesting flight. We'd lay over in Oakland, and we had a room in the hotel just off the airport. We arrived at five o'clock and weren't due to take off again until four o'clock the next afternoon. The flight engineer had just had his first baby. We went down to the bar and proceeded to celebrate this new arrival. Well, we got carried away. I guess we closed up the bar about one o'clock, figuring we were going to get a good night's sleep because we didn't have to leave until four that afternoon.

I'd only been in bed an hour when the phone rang. It was the dispatcher. He said, "Frank, wake up your crew, hop in the bird, fly over to Winslow, and pick up a load of Indian firefighters. Take them to Santa Barbara, and you should be back in time for your four o'clock departure from Oakland."

Oh man – I could hardly see straight. But we figured, it's an empty airplane. As soon as we got in the airplane we started to suck on some oxygen. That worked all right, so we fired up and flew the Conny over to Winslow and picked up these Indian firefighters, took them to Santa Barbara, and returned to Oakland.

About a week later we went back to Santa Barbara to pick up the Indian firefighters and take them back to Winslow. I watched their operation. The chief stood by the airplane, and the whole line of Indian firefighters was stretched out. When one Indian firefighter came up, the government would pay him, and the Indian would step forward, hand it to the chief, and get in the airplane. The next Indian would get paid, hand it to the chief, and climb on the airplane. I thought, "Boy, that chief really has a lot of power."

On another flight, we'd gone from San Diego to Los Angeles to Burbank, and, when we got to Burbank, Larry Mudget came out and said that all the passengers had to get off the airplane, that there was an emergency. The passengers deplaned, and they put some FBI agents on board and said, "Head for Reno."

I don't know if you remember or not, but Frank Sinatra's son was kidnapped, and they thought that he had been taken up to Reno. So we flew these FBI guys up to Reno, and they parked us out in the boondocks. We were there for about an hour and a half when they all came back. It was the middle of the night, and we flew them back to Burbank. On the way back to Burbank, this FBI guy came up to the cockpit and said, "Don't say a word to anybody. This is a hush-hush, secret-secret investigation." Of course we said, "Ok."

But the ironic part is, when I got home, GG said, "What in the world's going on? The phone's been ringing off the hook! All the reporters are calling, wondering where you'd been and what the flight was." So much for secrecy.

I don't know whether that kidnapping was a hoax or a publicity event or what. I never did hear. But it certainly was a fiasco. Anyway, Frank Sinatra's publicity department sent me a very nice letter, thanking me for for all the help I gave him in his time of trouble. So that's in my ego room.

I was with this airline one year, and it folded. The second time my airline folded. So here again I was out of a job and ready to start over.

I started calling everybody I knew, knocking on doors, and hoping for the best. A friend of mine, Orlan Sorensen, was the chief pilot and aviation manager for Signal Oil and Gas. He called me and said, "Frank, one of our vice presidents is buying a little Aero Commander to commute

Frank Sinatra

December 19, 1963

Mr. Frank Bray
11222 Canby Avenue
Northridge, California

Dear Mr. Bray:

On behalf of my family and myself, I would personally like to take this opportunity to thank you for being available when we needed an airplane during the terrible time when Frank, Jr. was kidnapped.

It was probably the most important flight I ever made and to all of you people who helped, my deepest appreciation.

May you have a very happy Christmas and New Year.

Sincerely,

Letter of thanks from Frank Sinatra, 1963

from Los Angeles to his home up there in Monterrey. Are you interested?"

I was desperate. I said, "Hell, yes, I'm interested!"

He took me downtown and introduced me to this vice president, and the vice president asked me a lot of questions. I enjoyed his company. On the spot he said, "Ok, you're hired. Go over to the distributor – I've already signed the papers over there – and pick up the airplane." So, wow. I had a job. Of course, it was a light twin, a huge comedown from a Constellation, but it was a flying job.

I went over to the Aero Commander distributor in Van Nuys, and the salesman there was Bob Mays. Bob and I had played tennis together and knew each other well. He looked at me and said, "How the hell did you get this job? I had this airplane lined up for somebody else."

I said, "Just lucky."

The airplane was used mainly for Mr. Keaton's commute. Friday night I flew him up to Monterrey and then ferried back. Then, Sunday night I ferried up to Monterrey and flew him to Los Angeles.

To help pay for this airplane, I got a 135 certificate. This was a certificate that allowed you to charter the airplane. I took a flight check with an FAA inspector and got certified, and they issued me the certificate. I had a small office at the Burbank Airport, and I advertised for charters. I lined up a few, a very few.

A movie star had a home over in Palm Springs. He lived in the Los Angeles area, and he wanted to go over to Palm springs every weekend. So I'd pick him up every Friday night, fly him to Palm Springs, ferry to Los Angeles, pick up Dee Keaton, fly him to Monterrey, and ferry back to Los Angeles. Then Sunday night, the opposite. Sunday night I'd fly from Los Angeles to Monterrey, pick up Dee Keaton, back to Los Angeles, ferry to Palm springs, pick up this movie star, and back to LA. It was quite a deal.

To show you how efficient this little airplane was, one day Dee Keaton had a busy schedule, so I picked him up in Los Angeles at about seven o'clock in the morning and flew him into Palm Springs for a breakfast meeting. He came back out to the airport at about half past ten, and I

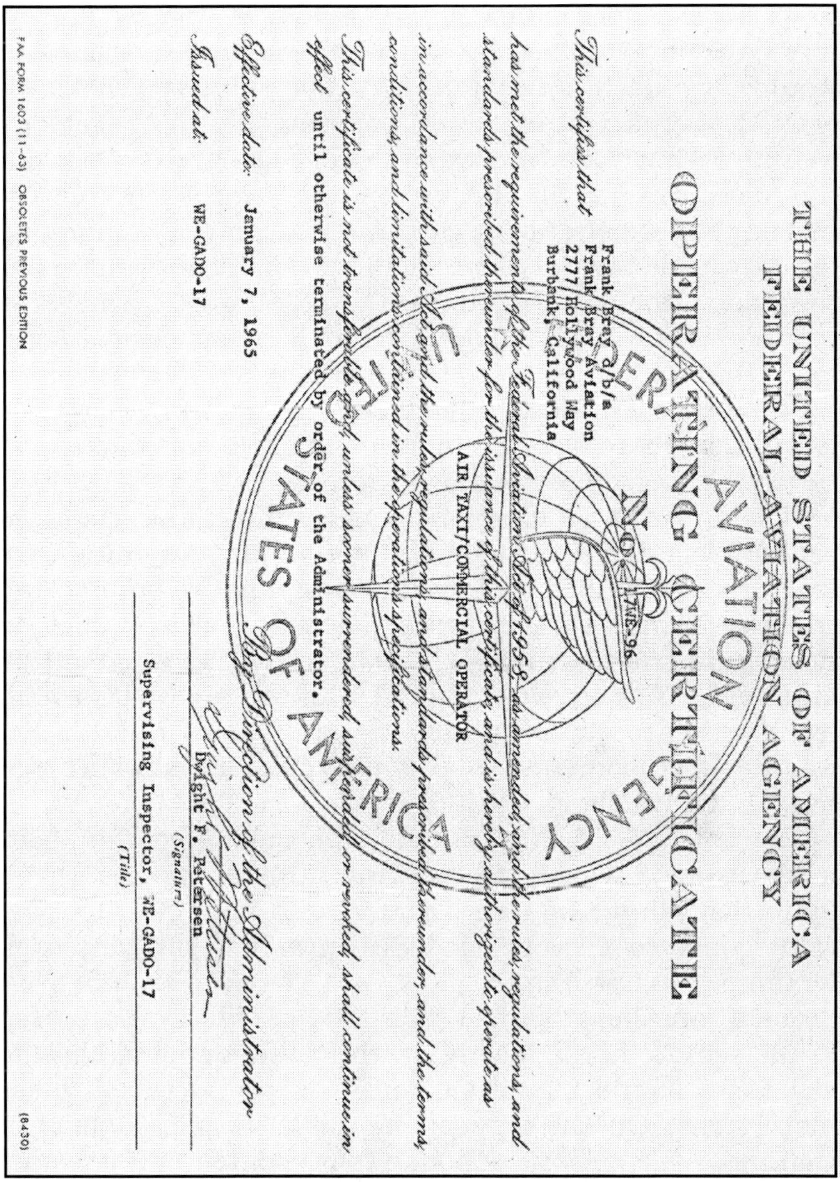
THE UNITED STATES OF AMERICA
FEDERAL AVIATION AGENCY

OPERATING CERTIFICATE

No. 7WE-96

This certifies that Frank Bray d/b/a
Frank Bray Aviation
2777 Hollywood Way
Burbank, California

has met the requirements of the Federal Aviation Act of 1958, as amended, and the rules, regulations, and standards prescribed thereunder for the issuance of this certificate, and is hereby authorized to operate as

AIR TAXI/COMMERCIAL OPERATOR

in accordance with said Act and the rules, regulations, and standards prescribed thereunder, and the terms, conditions, and limitations contained in the operations specifications.

This certificate is not transferable, and unless sooner surrendered, suspended, or revoked, shall continue in effect until otherwise terminated by order of the Administrator.

Effective date: January 7, 1965

Issued at: WE-GADO-17

By Direction of the Administrator

Dwight F. Petersen
(Signature)

Supervising Inspector, WE-GADO-17
(Title)

FAA FORM 1603 (11-63) OBSOLETES PREVIOUS EDITION (8430)

FAA 135 Certificate, 1965

flew him up to San Francisco for a luncheon meeting. Then at two in the afternoon I flew him over to Sacramento to meet with some of the California lawyers there. About four or five o'clock, I flew him back to Los Angeles, and he was back in the office by six. With scheduled airlines, it would have been impossible. So an airplane is a tool.

I flew that little Aero Commander in hellacious weather. That little bird wasn't really designed to fly with the big boys in the heavy weather, but with all my instrument experience, I gave it a go. On one interesting trip, it was a stormy Friday night with lightning and heavy rain, and I took Dee Keaton up to Monterrey. I was going to ferry back to Los Angeles, and while I was filing a flight plan, this soldier came up to me and asked if he could get a ride to Los Angeles. He said that he was on emergency leave, that there were no more flights out that night, and he was desperate to get down there.

I said, "Sure, I'll give you a ride." I put him in the right seat. All I said to him was, "Just don't touch anything." We took off and climbed up into the soup, and we bounced all the way down to Los Angeles. I shot a low approach in heavy rain and taxied in. When we arrived, I looked at him and said, "You know, I got to thinking about it. You're awful brave to climb into a little airplane in this kind of weather with somebody you don't know. I'm not sure you passed the intelligence test."

He said, "Sir." You see, he was calling me sir. "Sir, number one, I was desperate. And number two, I saw you fly in here, and I figured if you flew in here ok, then you were going to get out ok." So anyway I got him from Monterrey to Los Angeles.

On another flight, I flew Dee Keaton up to San Francisco. He had a meeting with Pacific Gas and Light to sell some of the Signal Oil and Gas products – I guess mainly gas. On the way up he said, "Frank, instead of waiting at the airport, why don't you come to the meeting with me?"

I thought, "Oh boy this is going to be an experience. Sure, I'd love to do that."

He said, "I'll just introduce you as my assistant and you won't have to say a word. Just sit there and listen."

I said, "I appreciate it. I'd love to do that."

So we went into this meeting, and it was very interesting. Dee Keaton represented Signal Oil and Gas, and Pacific Gas and Light had about three vice presidents and a couple of accountants with computers there. They were really dotting the i's. All these questions came to Dee Keaton about the volumes, the switching, the barrels and so forth, and he would calculate in his head and spit out a number. The accountants with all their calculators would spin their wheels and hit their buttons and so forth, and a few minutes later they'd say, "Yeah that's right, right on the money." That went on for about half an hour. Dee Keaton was computing in his head faster than these guys could do it with their computers. I was flabbergasted.

Anyway, everybody shook hands and said, "It's a win-win situation." They were happy and Dee Keaton was happy. In the cab back to the airport, Dee Keaton said to me, "Oh man, that went well. I got 40 percent more for our company than I expected. That was a nice day."

It's a small world. After only three months of flying this tiny little Aero Commander, my luck really changed. Orlan Sorensen, who got me this job, was out, and Clint Seccombe, who I'd flown with for the insurance company, was now the chief pilot and general aviation manager of Signal Oil and Gas. He wanted me to fly for him and also fly for Dee Keaton. Clint and I went down to the main office in Los Angeles and up to Mr. Keaton's office to find out if it was all right with him to put me on the company payroll. Of course he agreed to it immediately, because I'd still be flying him, but now he no longer had to pay me. The company would pay me. It was a win-win situation.

Back out at the airport, Clint took me in to the personnel manager. By this time, I'd had my resume updated, and the personnel manager looked at this thing and said, "Oh man, we're going to get you a job with our competitor. We've been trying to get them out of business for years." He saw where I'd been working for these companies and they all folded.

I told him, "Well, my wife has an expression: 'If I go to work for a company, they're in trouble. If I invest in the company, it's fatal.'"

Anyway, he said, "We'll take a chance on you. You're hired."

I was forty-five years old, and this was the first job I'd ever had where there were vacations with pay, hospitalization, a pension, and a savings plan. The savings plan was great. I forget the percentage, but for every dollar that you put in the savings plan, they would add a dollar. It was like a raise in pay. It was great.

The company I worked for was a sort of a conglomerate. The flight department furnished the transportation for Signal Oil and Gas and also for AiResearch Aviation and the Garrett Corporation. They were all one and the same. They were also a distributor at one time – they sold the 125s, they sold Gulfstreams, and there were a lot of demonstration flights. AiResearch had a huge maintenance facility where they did maintenance and installed interiors in new airplanes or refurbished old interiors. They had a huge paint shop where they could paint the exterior. With test flying, demos, and corporate transportation, there were all kinds of flying available.

So started my career with a great company. The first airplane I was trained in was a Gulfstream I. Clint Seccombe was flight manager and chief pilot. He was one of the very few pilot's pilots. He could get more out of a plane than was designed into it. He was also a great instructor, teacher if you will, and a tough taskmaster. Sam Mosier, CEO of Signal Oil and Gas, lived in Santa Barbara. Mr. Green had a vineyard in Santa Rosa, and Dee Keaton had a huge home in Monterrey. So there were lots of empty flight legs. Each of these empty legs the hood would go up, and it was strictly instrument training and running through emergency procedures. Clint kept adding more pressure each flight. He made me a far better pilot. It was a pleasure working for him.

SIGNAL CORPORATE AIR TRANSPORT

Job Descriptions, Qualifications, Recommended Salary Ranges.

COMMAND CAPTAIN

Responsible for:

Flying as Pilot in Command on flights of any nature in light or heavy piston or turbine aircraft, with the sole responsibility for evaluation of all factors affecting safety of flight, and decision to depart, continue, or divert is his alone. (This differs from airline regulations in that an operationally experienced, weather trained Dispatcher assists the airline captain in flight preparation and MUST CONCUR with the captain's decision to initiate any flight.)

Maintaining an exceptionally high level of professional competence. (He has the legal authority in corporate flying to takeoff and land in more difficult conditions than are permitted airline crews, and he must possess the skill to do this safely, and have the experience and wisdom to know when not to).

Ensuring that all practicable non-passenger flying on his trips is used for the additional purpose of maintaining his own or his crew members' instrument flying proficiency.

Taking part in or observing aircraft maintenance as appropriate to augment his continuing effort to increase his knowledge of the aircraft and systems.

Assuring himself that all delegated responsibilities relative to his flights are properly discharged.

Handling financial transactions incidental to the operation as appropriate.

Qualifications:

Airline Transport Pilot Certificate with Multi-Engine and Type Rating in airplanes flown.

Extensive command experience and overall flying background, (7500 flying hours and 15 years and considerable heavy multi-engine time).

Must possess to an above average degree for experienced command pilots: Alertness, intelligence, piloting skill, command ability, judgement, and presence of mind under stress.

Must be of good appearance and bearing, exemplary behaviour, and outstanding in courtesy, tact, and thoughtful consideration for the needs of the people he is serving.

Signal Air's Job Description for Command Captain

I made many interesting flights with this great organization. The Hilton Hotel organization had a very luxurious Gulfstream II, and they had contracted with AiResearch to crew and maintain it. I flew their airplane many times. One of its uses was for a monthly trip from Los Angeles to New York. I took many of these flights. We'd take the Hilton personnel – mainly Barron Hilton, who was the CEO at that time, and his group – to a board meeting. There were limos to meet the airplane when we arrived in New York. Naturally, we stayed at a Hilton hotel. It was very plush. At restaurants we just signed the check. Of course, checking out of the hotel we'd just sign the bill. We were living a great life. It was quite a perk.

Another use for this airplane was going up to a ranch Barron Hilton had in Utah. Barron Hilton himself was a fine pilot, and he was also a very good sailplane pilot. At this ranch, he had a little narrow strip that was probably 4,500 or 5,000 feet long. At the end of the strip, there was a hangar where he had a small piston airplane and a sailplane. He used the little airplane to tow the sailplane up.

The landing strip was on the side of a hill and only fifty feet wide. It was very narrow for a jet to land on. It was at a high altitude, so the air was thinner and therefore your ground speed was higher. It was always a thrill going in there. We'd get way back and fly it just above stall, then come down and plunk it on the runway, hoping we wouldn't veer off, the runway being so narrow. We'd land uphill, which helped us get the airplane stopped, and then we'd take off downhill. If the wind was right, it didn't make any difference.

Dean Miller and I were assigned once to fly Barron Hilton and his party from Los Angeles to Honolulu. The party showed up, and it was Barron Hilton, his wife, and his father, Conrad Hilton, who had started the whole Hilton chain. There were six other guests on board as well. We got a computerized flight plan, and it showed that we were going to have strong winds between Los Angeles and Honolulu, but it showed that we had ample fuel to make it. After we took off, Barron Hilton came up in the cockpit, and we were shooting the breeze. I told him that we were falling behind flight plan, and we might have to turn around. He said, "If there's any doubt, let's turn around now." It just happened that at that point in time I heard one of the United Airlines departing Honolulu, and he was on the same radio frequency. So I called him and asked him if he could give us the wind. He said, "Yeah, we just leveled off at thirty-seven grand, and we've got 110 knots on the tail." That meant we'd have 110 on the nose.

Immediately, Barron Hilton said, "Turn around."

I said, "Yes, sir."

There was no way we could make it. We turned around, and instead of going back to Los Angeles we flew to San Francisco, because San Francisco is about 170 miles closer to Honolulu than Los Angeles. We got another computerized flight plan, and this flight plan said we had ample fuel to make it on this route. Number one, the route was shorter. Number two, it had a better angle on the winds, so it didn't decrease our ground speed that much. I said to Mr. Hilton, "I'll do anything you want. We can lay over tonight and go over to Honolulu tomorrow, or if you want to go right now, I'll fuel it up and file a flight plan and we're on our way."

He'd gone up to the weather bureau with me, and he'd looked everything over, being knowledgeable on this subject. He said, "We've got everybody on board; let's go right now."

I said, "No problem."

I went back and fueled the airplane, got a little extra catering, and took off. Fortunately, everything went according to plan. We were right on the computerized flight plan and landed at Honolulu with plenty of reserve. But that was a mighty long day. Los Angeles, a couple of hours out, turn around, an hour and a half back to San Francisco, a couple of hours on the ground, and then a five and a half hour flight to Honolulu. We were dragging when we got to the hotel that night.

Elvis Presley was another perk with the Hilton airplane. He was one of the biggest moneymakers for the Hilton Hotel in Las Vegas, so a part of the deal was that each year Hilton would furnish Presley an airplane for his tour. I was assigned to one tour. We picked up Elvis and his party, and the first concert was up in Seattle. We flew Elvis and his party up to Seattle. At each city where we took him, they made sure that the crew received passes to the show. I went to the first show and sat in the second row. The amplifiers were so loud that my chest was vibrating. I could hardly stand the noise. Elvis was up there on the stage gyrating and singing. You couldn't really tell if he was lip-synching or actually singing; everything was so loud. But all the women around me, regardless of age, were hollering, screaming, and jumping. It was quite a show, but once was enough. I didn't go to any more of his shows.

I flew him to seven different cities, and each time he'd show up with a gorgeous young lady. On each flight, he and this gorgeous young lady would disappear back in our lounge blue room to give themselves some privacy. We'd arrive at our destination, and they would still be back there. It might be twenty minutes before they would come out. When they did come out, Elvis would say, "Goodbye," and go to the hotel. Each leg was a different beautiful young lady. Well, of course, us old duffers, we were happily married, but if we weren't, we just might have taken his rejects. We wondered how many times he joined the Mile High Club. No wonder he died young. But that's the story on Elvis Presley.

Our company got a call from Elizabeth Taylor's group stating that Elizabeth Taylor and Richard Burton were in Honolulu, and they would like a demonstration flight in our Gulfstream II. We were selling Gulfstreams, and they were potential customers. I flew the airplane with a salesperson from Los Angeles to Honolulu. We spent the night, and the next morning Elizabeth Taylor and Richard Burton showed up.

Somehow, Richard Burton was extremely scared of flying. He hated flying. The only way he could get in an airplane was to be absolutely inebriated. His group practically poured him into his seat on the airplane, put the seatbelt on, and he immediately went to sleep, very happy.

This is my only bid for fame with Elizabeth Taylor. We had a blue room in the rear of the airplane, and she used the facility. A short time later, I had an urge and went back, and by golly, the seat was still warm. That's as close as I could get to Elizabeth Taylor.

Anyway, it was a routine flight from Honolulu to Los Angeles. We landed at Los Angeles and spent the night. The next day Elizabeth Taylor and Richard Burton boarded for a flight to Acapulco. When Elizabeth Taylor showed up she was in blue jeans, ratty tennis shoes, and a T-shirt. However, she was still gorgeous. We proceeded to fly down to Acapulco.

Their agent came up to the cockpit as we were flying over Mexico and said, "Ms. Taylor is not ready to deplane, can you slow this airplane up or circle?" Well, sure we could, so we pulled the power back and made one huge circle. Then I had a fuel problem, so went in and landed. Elizabeth Taylor had gone back to the blue room to change her outfit. We were on the ramp at least twenty minutes before she came out of her blue room – you can call it a dressing room now.

What a transformation! She was absolutely, marvelously, beautifully gorgeous. We opened the door, and there waiting to greet her were immigration, customs, a limo, and the clapping Mexican people. She stood at the top of the doorway and smiled and waved. I'll tell you, it was a beautiful arrival. There was no such thing as paperwork or formalities. The customs and immigration people graciously escorted her to her limo, and away she went. It turned out that they weren't interested at all in buying an airplane. All they wanted was some free transportation. But I don't think the company cared, and it was an interesting flight.

Our outfit did the maintenance for Walt Disney's Gulfstream I. Disney was a good customer of ours. One summer, one of their pilots went on vacation, and they needed a loaner pilot. They asked AiResearch if we had anybody who would be willing to take a trip to New York with them. I volunteered for it. I was qualified in the Gulfstream I, and I went as the copilot. I went over to Burbank, and, would you believe, Walt Disney himself was on the airplane. The Disney organization was running some of its employees back and forth from the Los Angeles area to New York as a morale booster and public relations deal. It was really fantastic. Walt Disney acted as flight attendant, serving all his employees. There was no liquor on the airplane, but he was serving them soft drinks and coffee. They'd catered the flight as well, and he served them lunch. Walt Disney came up to the cockpit and asked us what we wanted for lunch and what we wanted to drink. So I was served lunch by Walt Disney himself. It was mind-boggling.

Another interesting celebrity I flew was Frank Sinatra. He had his own jet, and our outfit, AiResearch, did maintenance for his airplane. As often happens, the airplane didn't come out of maintenance on time. When an airplane didn't come out on time, we would furnish the customer one of our airplanes and a crew member. So I was assigned to go over to Palm Springs and pick up Frank Sinatra and take him up to Las Vegas. I flew him three or four times, but he was strictly a businessman, an entertainer. We as pilots were bus drivers. There was no hello, goodbye, good landing, nothing. He just climbed on the airplane and did his work with never a word. There was no problem with that. That was his personality.

Then I had a flight for Kirk Kerkorian, the billionaire who owns MGM Grand in Las Vegas. His wife had been over in the Hawaiian Islands, and she had been scuba diving. She was down fairly deep, and her lead-belt came off. She popped to the surface, and it damaged both her eardrums. They were good customers of ours, and their airplane was not available, so they wondered if we could go over and pick her up and bring her back to Palm Springs. I flew the airplane over there. It was one of our new JetStars with Garrett engines. It had these little fan-jet engines, and it was pretty efficient. I flew the JetStar over to Honolulu, and we spent the night.

I talked to the doctor who was taking care of Mrs. Kerkorian, and I explained that, due to fuel, I had to get some altitude. However, I could keep the cabin pressure below 2,000 feet, and would that be satisfactory? He thought it over and said, “Yeah. We're sending a couple of nurses along with this lady. If she has problems as the cabin comes up to 2,000, let down again and come back. If not, continue.” With jets, the higher you go the more efficient the airplane is. If you fly too low, then you burn too much fuel and you can't make it. I figured with this problem I could fly the airplane at 29,000 feet, and the cabin would be 2,000 feet. A computerized flight plan said that at that altitude I could make it from Honolulu to San Francisco, then refuel and fly to Palm Springs.

Halfway over there, we were doing pretty good. We had the equipment that told our ground speed and distance, so I refiled direct to Santa Barbara. It was more on the direct route to Palm Springs. About an hour outside of Santa Barbara, things were looking so darn good, I figured we could go all the way to Palm Springs and land with forty-five minutes of fuel, which was my bare minimum. So I refiled for Palm Springs. We flew this JetStar from Honolulu to Palm Springs at 29,000 feet, nonstop, which was quite a feat for a little corporate airplane.

Phil Stacey was the chief pilot for Kirk Kerkorian, and he got word from the boss to give this crew a pass up at their hotel in Las Vegas and be their guests for a week up there. A while later, GG and I went up there and checked in, and, oh, what a beautiful suite. We had a spa in the room. It was unbelievable. It was all on the house and compliments of Kirk Kerkorian. That was a real perk.

I have to tell you this story about Kirk Kerkorian. I wasn't flying it, but I met his chief pilot, Phil Stacey, over in Luton, by London. We were talking, and he received a phone call from Kirk Kerkorian, who was in downtown London. He said, “Phil, I've got a buddy that I want you to run over to Burbank and drop off. Then I want you to come back and pick me up.”

One of the presidents of the broadcasting company wanted a ride back, but he couldn't wait another day until

Kirk Kerkorian went over. So Kerkorian told his pilot to run him over there. The kicker to this story is that Kirk Kerkorian's private airplane was a four-engine 707 transport – a huge airplane. Can you imagine the amount of kerosene that was burned for this big 707 transport to fly from London to Burbank with one passenger and then ferry back to London? That is wealth.

While I'm dropping names, I might as well keep going. For three days I flew Governor Pat Brown around the state of California. He was on a stumping tour, running for reelection. Back in those days, the company would furnish an airplane for both the Republican and the Democratic politicians in case the company ever needed a favor. Later on, the government came in and said, "You corporations can't do that. Anybody who uses your airplane has to pay." So the gratis rides ceased.

There was another little trip that was sort of a mystery. I flew Steve Martin and Bernadette Peters from Los Angeles down to a little town in Texas. There was no conversation. I didn't get to talk to either one, and I never did find out who gave them authorization to use the airplane, but obviously they knew somebody pretty high up. We dropped them off and then just ferried home. That was the end of that.

One of my most interesting flights during this time was for the Howard Hughes organization. I wrote a letter after I came home from that trip so that I could remember it in detail.

Saturday. It all began with a telephone call from our dispatcher. Ramona said, "I thought you would be smart enough not to answer the phone on a weekend. I guess you and Roy Nielsen are nailed for a flight that just came up." And that is about the way it works on a weekend. The pilots the office can reach are the ones who go.

It seems the Howard Hughes organization had called Mr. Hilton and requested the use of his Gulfstream II. Since AiResearch crewed the bird, we were called. The

Pat Brown, former governor of California

only word we had was that we should pack for three days and that we would leave either Sunday morning at nine a.m. or Monday at nine. Destination unknown. Naturally, after the sudden Hughes move out of Nassau, the imagination ran wild. Was this another move? I knew many Hughes pilots, and it seemed the old man did a lot of his work in the wee hours of the morning. Thus it wouldn't have surprised me to get a call in the middle of the night.

Sunday 0900. We got the word. Take off at noon. Destination unknown. To be gone three days. So we packed and went to the airport. We stocked the plane with life rafts, survival kits, maps, charts for Central and South America, cases of drinking water to try to ward off the *tourista*, booze and beer just in case, and passports. We wanted to have a flight plan on file so we could quickly get airborne, so we filed for Houston, which seemed like a logical possibility.

Sunday 1130. Phone call at the airport. Take off now at 1330. Eight passengers. The destination was Guadalajara, Mexico (but we were to keep it quiet). Could we have hot meals put on board?

So we changed the flight plan, ordered food, went to the terminal and tried to get the required Mexican Tourist cards, but no luck.

Sunday 1400. Phone call. Take off now set for 1500. Two more passengers, and could we get some special cognac?

So we ordered more food and went to many liquor stores trying to locate the brand of cognac. No luck.

Sunday 1530. Many cars showed up at the plane. Some were big, long, and black with telephones in the back seat. I am happy to report that the Hughes organization appeared about as efficient as any other big company. There was much dashing in and out of the plane, last minute phone calls, instructions, ideas, suggestions, coordinates. It seems the left hand really didn't know what the right hand had done or was doing. Most passengers had little or no advance notice of the flight.

Sunday 1600. The plane door finally closed. We taxied out and called for clearance. The controller asked if we wanted to go to Houston or Guadalajara. It seems the computer didn't get the word to cancel the Houston flight. We replied that we really wanted to go to Houston but guessed we would have to accept the Mexico one. Moments later we roared off for Guadalajara, the second largest city in Mexico and some 1,300 miles southeast of Los Angeles. It got dark rapidly, but a full moon made for a beautiful flight. Even from 37,000 feet we could see Guadalajara from 150 miles out.

On the flight down, we got to know a little about our passengers. *Very little.* Attorneys, directors, PR men, real estate men – all Hughes employees on the way to confer with THE man. Our arrival in Guadalajara was about 8:35 p.m. local time, sans tourist cards. It took us some two hours to get this little problem solved. With two Hughes men typing as well as the Mexican immigration officials huntng and pecking, we finally got the necessary forms filled out. The passengers told me we would leave the next day about noon for Managua, Nicaragua. We never did learn what the folks wanted to see or do in Guadalajara.

Monday 1200. We taxied out on schedule with a Hughes Air West station agent helping to pave the way. The only hitch was we were told to return to the ramp by the tower. We had all the copies of the flight plan on board and had to return some.

We had a beautiful flight down to Managua. We flew over Mexico City but could hardly see it with all the smog. We also flew by Guatemala City, but it was covered with clouds. However, we had a fine view of San Salvador as we went by. The distance from Guadalajara to Managua was 1,300 miles or 2½ hours in flight time.

We called Managua tower for landing instructions and were amazed to hear the voice of Bob Worely, who is the chief pilot for Hughes Las Vegas. He just happened to be in the tower, but had not been expecting us. Once again, the old right hand not knowing what the left was doing. I was told to park by the Hughes JetStar.

When we arrived, there was a huge iguana on the taxi strip. As we approached, he went waddling over the field at a rather fast clip. It seemed almost appropriate for our arrival in Nicaragua.

The passengers were met and whisked off without the bother of Customs or Immigration. It must be great to be buddies with General Somoza, the dictator of the country. This Hilton Gulf Stream II had a large "H" on the tail, so naturally the word spread that it belonged to Hughes.

Monday 1700. We checked into the newest and best hotel in Managua, the Inter-Continental. You may have seen pictures of it in the newspapers. It is shaped like a pyramid and relatively small. Hughes had the top three floors. The hotel was full, so they gave us rooms on seven and eight that belonged to Hughes' men who were out of town at the moment. The rooms still had their clothes and personal belongings in them. At the end of our hall was an armed guard twenty-four hours a day. There was a closed-circuit TV camera that could scan the hall, a squawk box, and a peep hole. It took two keys to open the end door. After one man went in, we heard what sounded like a huge slide bolt ram home.

If you pushed the number 9 in any of the two elevators, nothing happened. The elevators were evidently rigged not to go to 9. The whole atmosphere here at the hotel was amusing or strange, depending on how one saw it. Everyone knew Hughes was there in the hotel and had the top three floors, so when we pushed the elevator button for 7 or 8, the tourists did a double take and looked us over with interest. We were questioned by newsmen and stared at by people sitting in the lobby and the bar. Everyone wonders who is who and why.

Tuesday. No word on when we are to leave or where we are to go. There has been some talk of Merida in the Yucatan Peninsula and some talk of Acapulco.

Wednesday. No word yet. Told to stand by. Went sightseeing.

Thursday. Hughes crews have been known to sit for a month just waiting for some word of a flight. It seemed strange, but many of our passengers met us in the lobby and would ask if we had heard when we were leaving.

Back home when flying is slow, we have been known to generate a flight by calling company X and telling them that company Y has a flight going to Houston and there are seats available. Then we call Y and tell them X has a flight going to Houston and there are seats available. First thing you know, we have generated a flight where none existed.

So for the last few days, we told everyone we were leaving Friday morning.

Thursday 1700. We got word we were scheduled to leave at nine Friday morning for Acapulco, Mexico. Same passengers on board. We would stay there four hours and then on to Los Angeles.

Thursday 2100. Roy became deathly ill. It was food poisoning, most likely. When he wasn't on the pot with a wastebasket in front of him, he lay in bed moaning and groaning. I was in the next room and went over three times to see if I could get him a doctor. I woke up at five a.m. and didn't hear any groaning, so I went over to his room to see if he was still with us. He was... just barely.

Friday 0900. Roy was just able to get out to the plane. Frenchie, the third crew member, and I did all the work, as Roy was just hanging on.

Friday 1000. The flight from Managua to Acapulco was 960 miles in two hours. We passed a volcano with smoke coming from it. We heard all the passengers were happy; it seems they all accomplished what they came to Managua to do.

Friday 1500. While we were waiting for the passengers at the airport in Acapulco, we received a telephone call from the Hughes company in Los Angeles. Locating a strange crew in a foreign airport is some feat. The message was for Mr. Davis, Hughes' number one attorney. He was supposed to call the Managua traffic desk before take off, as the message said "Urgent Report Do Not Leave Without Making Call."

Friday 1800. The passengers were now two hours late. While waiting, Bernard Diedreich, the TIME LIFE Bureau chief of Mexico City came out to the plane. He wanted to know if the old man was on board. He said he had a tip and flew down from Mexico City just to meet this plane. I said I wished he would call his office and find out when we were going to leave to return to Managua. This Bureau Chief reported that Hugh Hefner's Playboy black DC-9 was due to arrive in Acapulco at six p.m. He wondered if there was any connection between Hughes and Hefner. Now that would be a twist. The playboy DC-9 landed at six thirty. We were parked about half a mile down the ramp, and a few moments later we started the engines and taxied up to the terminal to pick up our few remaining passengers. By just a coincidence, I think, we parked right behind the DC-9. The passengers walked under the DC-9 wing. Without shutting down the engines, we popped open the door, loaded the passengers (the first one on said, "Keep eyes straight front"), closed the door, and immediately took off. One really couldn't tell if someone had gotten off the DC-9 and onto our plane or not. What a laugh.

The leg to Los Angeles was 1,700 miles and took three hours and twenty minutes. We arrived at eight p.m. local time, and the passengers were soon on the phone with big ear cups – a scrambler phone box. I assume they were calling Managua.

We left the airport thinking, "Now there is a dream world to end them all." It was mighty interesting, but I wouldn't want that sort of life for a steady diet.

One of the great successes of AiResearch at Garrett was its small fan-jet engine. Many years ago there was no such thing. AiResearch had been building APUs for the airlines for years. Some engineer got the bright idea to take this APU jet engine and put a fan in front of it, and it would be ideal for light corporate airplanes. So they did. It took years to perfect it and get it certified, but once they got it certified, all the airframe manufacturers had to have it. Lear, Falcon, DeHavilland, Lockheed – they all wanted

THE SECRETARY OF HEALTH, EDUCATION, AND WELFARE
WASHINGTON

December 9, 1969

Dear Frank:

I can't remember a flight which I have enjoyed more than our trip from Los Angeles to Washington, D.C. several weeks ago. Your and Clint Seccombe's professional expertise in the cockpit coupled with Dean Miller's generous hospitality in the cabin made our flight most comfortable and convenient. Needless to say, I could easily become accustomed to flying with you and Airesearch.

Many thanks for taking such good care of us. It was a pleasure flying with you again.

Sincerely,

Robert H. Finch
Secretary

Mr. Frank D. Bray
Pilot
Flight Operations Department
Airesearch Aviation Company
6201 West Imperial Highway
Los Angeles, California 90045

A letter of thanks from the Secretary of Health, Education, and Welfare, 1969

A corporate airplane is a business tool. Here's a couple of letters to prove the point.

Signal Oil and Gas Company

General offices: 1010 Wilshire Boulevard, Los Angeles, California 90017
Telephone: 482-0722 • Cable address: SIGOILGAS

F. D. LORTSCHER
CHAIRMAN OF THE BOARD

July 7, 1972

Mr. Frank Bray
AiResearch Aviation Company
6201 West Imperial Highway
Los Angeles, California 90045

Dear Frank:

Our sincere thanks. The job you did flying our people to and from their Houston pre-transfer trips was, as they say, above and beyond the call of duty.

We've received nothing but enthusiastic praise about the flights from our people upon their return. "The food was really good" (usually with a touch of disbelief in their voices) . . . . "The time went by so quickly." . . . "Those pilots are great guys. They're so friendly." I'm sure keeping the bar stocked alone must have been a full time job for one of you. Seriously, making a long, normally wearisome five-hour flight pass like an enjoyable afternoon get-together with friends takes a special effort. And I want you to know we appreciate it.

It seems to me that when you get any endeavor off on the right foot, you've got the battle over half won. And we have you people to thank for doing just that. You might be interested to know that out of the 131 employees we flew down to Houston, only two came back and said they'd decided not to transfer. Most who intended to buy, found and bought homes. Most who intended to rent, located apartments. Now that's what I call a pretty darn good record.

Again, our heartfelt thanks for a job very well done.

Very truly yours,

F. D. Lortscher

one of The Signal Companies

A letter from one of our Vice Presidents, thanking us for the service we provided our own company in helping transfer one of our organizations from Los Angeles to Houston. We had a flight a day for about three weeks. We enjoyed it, and obviously the passengers did, too.

OFFICE MEMO

SFAR-5037-0829

TO: Mr. Lou Berger | DEPT. AAC | DATE: August 29, 1975

FROM: F. A. Ryan | DEPT. 35-3 | EXT. 2135 | COPIES TO: Crawford, J. V., Los Angeles; Derbes, D. W.; Richardson, H. L. AAC

SUBJECT:

Dear Lou,

The purpose of this quick memo is to inform you that we have positive proof that your group and the activities associated with the use of the aircraft have materially contributed to the receipt of two major awards at Garrett.

You might recall that on July 28, 1974, we asked for the aircraft to fly to Toronto to pick up some important gentlemen at the Toronto Transit Commission, fly them to Los Angeles on the 29th, to Pueblo on the 30th, back to Toronto on the 31st, and return to Los Angeles on the same day. This was, obviously, a tight schedule and pretty demanding on your pilots, and the whole thing was handled in a very friendly, efficient manner in spite of the long hours.

Subsequent to that, your group flew Hawker-Siddeley key personnel from Los Angeles to Pueblo on November 5, and up to Thunder Bay, Ontario, on November 6. I recall distinctly that this was also quite a long day as we didn't even leave Thunder Bay heading for Los Angeles until approximately 10:00 o'clock that night.

During the course of the negotiations on both contracts, the Hawker-Siddeley personnel and the Toronto Transit Commission personnel referred many times to the proficient manner demonstrated by the Company and the use of its aircraft.

One contract was received from Hawker-Siddeley in July for 134 propulsion systems for the Toronto Subway. A contract was received last Monday for 200 systems for the Toronto Streetcar System. The sum of the two contracts is in excess of $40 million. We are enclosing with this memo an analysis that shows the potential business through follow-on from these contracts to be of substantial magnitude.

Just want to say one more time, Lou, that the Los Angeles Division and certainly the Ground Transportation Group fully recognizes and very much appreciates the assistance you gave us in obtaining this business.

Frank A. Ryan

FAR:kj

CREW: BRAY - BISSELL

Enclosure

A memo of thanks for a flight I made into Toronto to pick up some customers

this engine because, with this new technology, the same fuel capacity increased its range by 45 percent. None of the big engine manufacturers had this small engine. Pratt & Whitney, General Electric, Rolls Royce – no one had a small fan-jet engine, so we had a monopoly. It was great.

We had a real good deal. We would buy the first production airplane with our engine off the line. For instance, we bought the first Learjet with our engine and brought it to Los Angeles. We got six crews typed rated in the airplane, and then we flew it eighteen hours a day, seven days a week, until we got over 2,000 hours on the airplane. The theory was that we wanted any problems with this engine to happen to us before it happened to a customer. So we filed flight plans from Los Angeles to Seattle and back, Los Angeles to Kansas City and back, Los Angeles to Houston and back. We'd only land in Los Angeles, because that was where our maintenance was. The whole time, we were keeping accurate records of everything. We'd fly a round trip and have a crew change; round trip, crew change; round trip, crew change; and keep going until time for maintenance. We did that with the Learjet, and we did that with the Falcon. It was a fun deal to just bore holes in the sky with an empty airplane.

This engine was manufactured in Phoenix. We were selling this engine to the airframe manufacturers, and to sell more engines, our boss decided to convert airplanes with the old engine to this engine. Mr. Wetzel decided the first airplane to convert would be a Lockheed JetStar, because he could sell four engines instead of two. At our hangar in Los Angeles, we converted fifty-two JetStars with the old Pratt & Whitney engines (the straight turbine engines) and put on our four Garrett engines. They now had 45 percent more range. It was tremendous. However, it was horrifying to see these airplanes in the hangar torn apart with hundreds of miles of wires strewn over everything. You wondered, how in the world can they ever get all this back together again?

There was a lot of test flying to be done. Bill Baxter was in charge of that, and I had a lot of trips with him on those test flights. The first time we got a converted JetStar, we spent maybe five hours just sitting on the ramp with the engines running, going through every switch on the airplane. Once we were satisfied with that, then we took it out and told the tower we just wanted to take a high-speed run down the runway, abort, and come back. When they had clear traffic, they'd let us do that. We'd get it up to 120 mph and then full thrust reverse; the airplane would shake, rattle, and roll. Then we'd taxi it back and go all through the airplane to see if anything had shaken loose.

We knew there was going to be a lot of testing on this conversion, and we weren't test pilots – we were line pilots. Glenn Gray had done the original testing on this airplane for Lockheed, so the boss hired Glenn to come up to Los Angeles and start in on the testing.

Lou Berger, our aviation manager, went with him as copilot on the first flight. Glenn was in the left seat, and Lou was in the right seat. They were doing a few maneuvers when the airplane flipped over on its back. Glenn calmly recovered, and he said, "Oh, that's interesting. Let's see if we can make it do that again."

Lou looked at him and said, "Take me back. You get your own copilot!" That's the difference between a test pilot and a line pilot. The test pilots are tigers.

The first flight after putting four new engines on it, you never knew what to expect. So the ground rule was it had to be good weather to take off. You couldn't take off on the instruments, because if something happened, you couldn't get back fast enough. We test flew all of these fifty-two conversions, and each airplane took at least five or six flights to test out and eliminate the bugs.

The big bugaboo was trying to set the stall warning system. They would set it on the ground, and then we'd stall it. If it wasn't correct, they couldn't adjust it until the plane got back on the ground. So we were up and down, up and down. Finally, somebody devised an electronic box where they could check this in the air.

These test flights weren't too comfortable. You'd take it up to altitude, pull the power back, and pull the nose up until the airplane stalled. On a stall, the airplane shook violently. It shook so badly that the dashboard and the instruments were a blur. If you happened to be back in the cabin and looked out the side windows, you saw two engines on a pylon on the right and two on the left going up and down maybe a couple of feet. You'd think they were going to snap off. It was horrifying.

Along with this, the FAA decreed that you had to have a stick pusher to warn the pilots of a stall. It's ridiculous: the airplane was shaking so darned bad you knew it's going to stall. You didn't need a stick pusher.

That brings on this next story. The FAA was going to certify our airplane, so the inspector was in the left seat and Roy Nielsen was in the right seat. I happened to be in the jump seat. This inspector was stalling the airplane, and he said, "I can't feel the stick pusher."

Well, he couldn't feel it because the airplane was shaking so badly. After he tried it two or three times, Roy Nielsen said, "Hey, try once more."

So the inspector slowed it up. It was approaching stall, and the airplane was shaking like mad. Roy put his knee against the yoke and pressed forward, and the inspector said, "Yeah, I feel it now. Ok. Let's go back." So that's the way we got the airplane to pass.

Once in a while I was assigned to the Los Angeles-Phoenix shuttle. Monday through Friday, Los Angeles ran a shuttle over to Phoenix, and Phoenix had an airplane that ran the shuttle from Phoenix to Los Angeles. We were shuttling engineers, accountants, and customers back and forth. It was a daily trip. The Phoenix airplane and the Los Angeles airplane would both take off at seven in the morning, and we'd pass each other every day over Blythe. I'd leave Los Angeles at seven, and it would only take an hour to fly over to Phoenix. Then we'd lay over all day. The company didn't care about money, so we'd get a hotel room, play tennis, go swimming, take a nap, and then come back out to the airport at four in the afternoon and take the folks back to Los Angeles. What a great life.

The worst part was the direction that we flew. We were going eastbound into the sun, so we got the sun in our eyes on the way over there in the morning. In the evening we had the sun in our eyes again coming back to Los

With Roy Nielsen

Angeles, westbound. The Phoenix crew, on the other hand, got the sun on their back in the morning, and they got the sun on their back in the evening. With the sun and the smog in Los Angeles, coming back in you could never see the airport. It was always an instrument approach, but instrument approaches are part of the fun.

At one time, we had an unusual situation with the bosses. Harry Wetzel was the president of the Garrett Corporation, and he was an ex-Air Force pilot. Bill Pattison was the vice president of the Garrett Corporation, and he was an ex-Navy pilot. Not only that, Forrest Shumway, who was CEO of the whole organization, was also a pilot.

We got these new jets. Harry Wetzel and Bill Pattison had never flown a jet, so they wanted to fly it. On many occasions, they'd come out and say, "Do you mind if I fly this leg?" Well, of course, we let them; we couldn't possibly say no. So, Mr. Wetzel, for instance, would be in the left seat, and I'd be in the right seat. The copilot would be in the jump seat, so I'd handle all the checklists, radio work, and navigating. Mr. Wetzel would fly the airplane. If the weather was good. If the weather was bad for an approach, he'd get out of the seat and say, "I think it's time for my martini. I think I'll go back in the cabin." He was very diplomatic.

Bill Pattison was in the Navy, and I was in the Navy. He claimed that when I was in Norman, Oklahoma, I was his instructor and taught him how to fly. I got my log books out and went through them all, and I couldn't find his name. I tried to tell him that I had not been his instructor. But he had it in his mind that I taught him how to fly. Every time he'd introduce me to one of his friends, he'd say, "This is Frank Bray. He taught me how to fly. He's one of the best pilots I've ever been with!" I figured, well, I've tried to explain it; I'll just accept that I was his instructor and go from there.

Bill Pattison didn't care what the weather was; he wanted to fly the airplane. I can remember one time, we were going up to Seattle, and Bill was in the left seat. (I was on a first-name basis with the vice president – not the presidents or CEOs, just the vice president. I was in the right seat, and the copilot was in the jump seat. They had a low ceiling in Seattle, and we had been cleared for a circling approach. However, as we were coming up to the airport, they changed it to a straight-in approach. Wow. Now we really had to dump everything and pull the power back. There I was in the right seat trying to handle the radio and tuning in frequencies while telling Bill what to do. It was damned uncomfortable.

This went on for some time, and then the board members told Mr. Wetzel and Bill Pattison, "If you guys are going to fly, we're going on the airline. We're not comfortable with this. You hired professional pilots, and

Bill Pattison, ex-Navy and Vice President of the Garrett Corporation

you guys are taking the seat." Fortunately the FAA heard about this, and they backed it up. They told the president and the vice president, "If you're going to fly, you've got to be type rated in this airplane. You've got to go to ground school and take your flight checks." That put an end to that, but it was an interesting period of time.

As I mentioned, the chairman of the board, Forrest Shumway, was also a pilot. I'd flown him on literally hundreds of flights. I took him around the world four times, and not once did he ever come up to the cockpit to see what was going on or to offer any advice. He never left the cabin. He never conferred with me before or after the flight. He figured that was my job, and he'd just let me do it. I just thought, being a pilot, he might be interested in some of the aspects of the flight, but he never came up to the cockpit.

At Christmastime, it almost seemed like we flew a shuttle out of Los Angeles into Aspen, Colorado. Our top executives had condos up there. Before Christmas, we'd fly them from Los Angeles up to Aspen, and then ferry home. Then, just before Christmas, we'd fly to Aspen to pick them up and take them back to Los Angeles, so they could celebrate the holidays. After Christmas, we'd fly them back up to Aspen, and just before New Year's we'd go back to pick them up and take them back to Los Angeles. After New Year's Day, we'd fly them back up to Aspen and then ferry home. A week or so later, we'd ferry back up, pick them up, and fly them home.

The only problem is that the Aspen airport is down in a valley. With winter conditions – snow and ice on the runway plus snow showers – it was a hairy operation. The airport is also on a slope, so you fly down into this canyon. When you land, you're landing uphill into the canyon. The city's at the end of the runway. For takeoff, it's the other way around. You get up on the high end of the runway and takeoff downhill, down the canyon. The minimums are very high, naturally, because of the mountains. But we survived and had no major problems there.

Once a year there were interesting flights for an organization called the Conquistadors. Once a year these people meet at this deluxe ranch in the middle of nowhere in Wyoming. This was a group of airline people, airline manufacturers, aerospace – anything to do with aviation. These were the highest echelons meeting in this out-of-the-way place.

It was a very high airport, and there were no landing aids there. You had to go in by visual flight rules. It had a very narrow runway, so it was a challenge to fly in there. Once a year, all these corporate jets were flying instrument flight rules into the area, and then they would cancel their flight plan. I can just imagine the air traffic control thinking, "Here's the top money people of the United States, and they're all flying into an unknown place. It must be the end of the world."

Anyway, we flew our chairmen of the board and our presidents up there. I flew our president up once, and there was an extremely strong crosswind. Mr. Wetzel was in the jumpseat.

He said, "Frank, do you think we ought to try this?"

I said, "Sir, no problem."

Hughes, a few days earlier, had brought a Convair into this narrow strip, and when the pilot put his props in flat pitch to slow the airplane, one of them went in and one didn't. This sloughed the airplane off the runway and down a ditch, and sheared the gear. The Hughes' airplane was beside the runway, and it was totaled. We could see that from a distance.

I told Mr. Wetzel I could handle it. I flew back out and lined up. With a strong crosswind, I was crabbing as you approach the runway. Just before the wheels touched, I kicked the rudder to straighten it out. The wheels touched and immediately went to full aileron. I jammed the nose down on the runway, jammed the downwind brake, and kept it on the center line. That was a thrill, but being a non-sked pilot, I'd handled worse. I think Mr. Wetzel gave me a couple of brownie points.

Then we ferried back home. We didn't leave the airplane there because there was no ramp. There was no tower. There was no terminal. There was nothing. It was just a strip out there in the wilds of Wyoming. Later, when we got the word, we brought the airplane back to pick up our people. I got the word to go back up there, and, fortunately, there was no crosswind this time. It was just a piece of cake.

We picked up our people and had a full load. The runway isn't all that long, but it had quite a slope to it, and there was a speck of a wind. I elected to go downwind with a couple of knots of tailwind. It was a downslope. I taxied all the way to the very end of the runway, using every foot, and I turned it around. I stood on the brakes, and brought the power up to full power. I let the engines spool up until they were up to maximum rpm, then I released the brakes and started rolling. I was hoping for the best, and at the end of the runway, I pulled back on the yoke and away we went. We started climbing.

One of our passengers was an astronaut. I forget what his name was, but after we got up to altitude, he came up to the cockpit and made that oooh sound. He said, "Man, that was interesting." He realized what we were doing and how we got the job done. He sat there in the jumpseat for a while, and we shot the breeze.

I think I flew in and out of that airport for five or six years. Just once a year we'd take them up and drop them, ferry back, and then ferry back up to pick them up. It was an interesting operation.

Signal Oil and Gas had a plush, corporate DC-3 that we used quite a bit, and with all my past DC-3 time, it was a good fit. One of the things they used it for was to take potential customers and VIPs down to Cabo San Lucas for fishing. Cabo San Lucas is right at the tip of Baja California, and, at that time, there were no roads leading into Cabo. There was no big airport down there. All they had were little grass fields by a couple of hotels, so the only way to get into Cabo was to fly in or come in by boat.

We'd go down there on a fishing trip and land on this little grass strip beside the hotel and then walk across and enter the hotel. The place was so isolated down there. There was no theft whatsoever. You could leave your door unlocked with your wallet on the top of your desk and go fishing all day, and nothing would be touched because everybody knew everybody down there.

An interesting situation came up while we were there. We had an airplane, but we didn't have a yacht in Cabo. Douglas Oil had a yacht, but they didn't have an airplane. So we would take our people down, and they would use the Douglas yacht. Then we'd take the Douglas people down and they would use their own yacht.

On one trip, I took the Douglas people down, and the president called me up before we left and said, "We're going to be gone a week – why don't you and your copilot bring your wives along?" Oh boy, that was a great deal. So the copilot and I took our wives along, and we had a blast.

We went down to Cabo and spent four or five days there. Then we flew the whole group over to Guadalajara, had a great time there, and then brought them home. One of the vice presidents came up to the cockpit to give us a bonus for providing such great service. I diplomatically told him, "Joe, we can't accept money. You've given us more than enough already. We're on salary, and we're very happy with the situation." I don't know whether I handled it correctly or not, but I just couldn't see accepting money after all they'd done for us.

One time we had a new secretary who was acting as dispatcher, and I was scheduled for a flight from Los Angeles to Washington. I looked at my trip sheet, and I saw she had made me a reservation in Philadelphia. I said, "Mary, we've got this trip to Washington. How come I have a hotel reservation in Philadelphia?"

"Well," she said, "they're both on the East Coast aren't they?" From then on we made our own hotel reservations.

On another occasion, my trip sheet showed our destination was Washington National Airport. We were flying Mr. Wetzel, and we landed at Washington National. As we were taxiing in, he came up to the cockpit and said, "There must have been a screw-up. I wanted to go to Dulles Airport. But that's okay. I'll just hop a cab over there." I said, "No, sir, we'll have you there in about ten minutes."

It was late at night. There was no traffic on the airport, and we were the only ones there. I immediately told the tower our dilemma and requested tower-to-tower clearance from Washington National to Dulles. The tower said, "No problem; just keep taxiing." We got to the end of the runway, and they cleared us for takeoff. We immediately went to departure control, and they said, "That's the quickest turnaround we've ever seen. How did you guys do that?" We probably weren't on that ground more than three minutes. We got the boss over to Dulles. But this was another worthy dispatcher who thought, Washington is Washington, and didn't realize there were two different airports there.

One day I had a very short flight. It was from Los Angeles just up to Palmdale. Lockheed was running an evacuation test up there, and they were using emergency slides that our company had built. Some of our vice presidents and engineers wanted to go up and witness this demonstration. It was a military-controlled airport, and I called for landing instructions. The tower asked if we had the necessary clearance to land there. I explained we had military and insurance papers for other military airports, but not that particular one. He said, "Stand by; continue approach."

He asked me another question, and I answered it. Here again, he said, "Stand by, but continue your approach."

By this time we were down to about 500 feet. The runway was right in front of us, and the tower came on and said, "You are denied landing. I suggest you pull up and go over to Fox Field."

Being an old non-sked pilot, I figured, ah, the hell with it. I'm just going to land and get my people where they want to go. I'll sort it out later. So I continued the approach. I was down to about 200 feet now, and the tower said, "If those wheels touch, it'll be a $2,000 fine." I immediately advanced the power levers, pulled up, and proceeded to Fox Field. What was really funny was that some other pilot, listening on the same frequency, in the dead silence said, "That'll get your attention."

From then on, if something happened, that was the answer: "That'll get your attention." We landed over at Fox Field, got a couple of cabs, and got our people over to Palmdale. As a matter of fact, I went over with them to watch the demonstration.

Here's an interesting story. I was running a demo flight in our Lockheed JetStar for a potential customer. I flew over to the East Coast, picked up this group of people, and then flew them into London. Their chief pilot was aboard. Routine flight to London. We flew them in and out of Europe and ended up in Luton, England.

The next day we were bound for Frankfurt, and, unfortunately, one of our engines had a problem. So we shut it down, came back to Luton. When we pulled the oil filter there was a lot of metal in it, so obviously the internal part of the engine was coming apart. We had to have an engine change. This chief pilot pleaded with me to three-engine ferry to Los Angeles, get an engine change, and fly the airplane back so we could keep flying his people. To three-engine ferry across the Atlantic wasn't even an option.

He was very unhappy, but I said, "Why don't you charter another airplane and continue your tour with your people?" So he did. This was a Wednesday.

I called the office to notify them that we needed an engine change and to tell them to send mechanics and an engine over to London. Then I went down to the local Garrett office in London, walked in, and said, "I need $10,000 for expenses." They looked at me – they'd never seen me before in their lives – with an expression that said, "Who is this joker? He must be a nut."

I said, "I understand you don't recognize me, but just call Harry Wetzel. You have his phone number. He is the president at Garrett. I'll just wait."

So they picked up the phone, called Los Angeles, got the word, and said, "No problem. We'll get you your ten grand, and we're instructed to give you any assistance we can." Now I had expense money.

Friday, two of our AiResearch mechanics flew in. It was Al Martinez and his partner. These were crackerjack mechanics, and they'd brought their own tools.

Saturday morning, the engine arrived at Heathrow Airport, and it was down at the customs building in bond. I hired a cab and went down to the customs building. Nothing moves on Saturday. Anyway, I paid the duty and got the engine released. Then I called a trucking company to take this engine from the warehouse up to Luton, about fifty miles away. The trucking company responded, "We don't operate on Saturday."

I said, "I need a truck, regardless."

They responded that if they sent a truck out it would be double time. I said, "Not a problem. Send it out."

The truck came out, loaded up the engine, and took it up to Luton. Earlier on Friday, I'd gone to the base operator there and told them that we were changing the engine, but we'd be out of there by Sunday night. They looked at me like I was crazy.

"You won't be out of here before next Wednesday. You've got to change an engine."

I said, "I'd like to pay my bill now, because you folks are closed on Sunday and I won't be here."

They said, "Ok. If you're gone, we'll just bill you."

I said, "That's fine."

I arranged for them to furnish one of their mechanics who would like to learn about changing one of our engines. He could keep the shop open on the weekend and get us odds and ends, like cleaning fluids, rags, and whatever. They assigned a young mechanic of theirs to learn the procedure.

Saturday afternoon, we got the engine up to Luton, and our two mechanics came out and went to work. These two mechanics had been changing these Garrett engines for three years. They knew the engines; they knew the airplane. They didn't need the manual. It was like changing a tire. Their wrenches were just a blur. They yanked that engine off, yanked the accessories off, cleaned the accessories, put the accessories on the new engine, and installed the new engine. They didn't stop for breaks. They didn't stop for meals. They didn't stop for anything. Start to finish, they just worked.

Later on, I pulled the young British mechanic aside and asked, "What do you think of this operation?"

With his slow British drawl he said, "I didn't anticipate the fast pace of this drill." He was absolutely flabbergasted.

By Sunday afternoon, that engine was changed. We ran it up; it ran good. I filed a local flight plan and went up to test fly it. Everything was fine. I came back and arranged to have the old engine shipped back. By Sunday night we were gone, on the way back to Los Angeles. It was quite a show.

Garrett mechanics replacing a JetStar engine at Luton

Another time, we were up in Edinburgh, Scotland on a Sunday morning. We went out to the airport to pick up our airplane and fly it over to Prestwyck for a Monday morning departure. Our people were over in Prestwyck, and we were just going to ferry from Edinburgh over to Prestwyck. We got out to the airport, and there wasn't a soul there. The airport was closed on Sunday. How do we file a flight plan? How do we get out of there? Finally, I located one of the caretakers, and he said, "The airport's closed. You can't take off. There's no tower. There's no clearance."

I requested the telephone number for the airport manager, and he gave it to me. I called the airport manager and told him my problem. He said, "I'm sorry, the airport's closed. You can't leave until tomorrow morning."

I said, "I'll tell you what. I'll just take off, visual flight rules, and I'll call the center when I get in the air."

"Oh," he said, "I wouldn't advise you to do that. No, you can't do that."

Finally he said, "I'll tell you what. The Prime Minister's airplane is at the airport, and they are departing at three this afternoon. We will bring out an air traffic controller and a tower operator, and after they depart, you can depart."

So we had five hours to kill and decided to stroll around the airport. As we were going around, we saw the Prime Minister's airplane, and we walked over to it. They had a single bobby there, and he was their security. We struck up a conversation with him. We were just flabbergasted at the lack of security. Here was the Prime Minister's airplane, and just a single bobby guarding it. If it was an American President, you couldn't get near the airport to say nothing of getting near the airplane.

We waited. Finally, at three o'clock the crew and the authorities came out, and we were able to file a flight plan for Prestwyck. The sequel to the story is that when we arrived at Prestwyck, it was fogging in. We were cleared for an approach there, and after coming up on the outer marker and starting our letdown, the tower said, "Good luck there," with a British accent.

It piqued my curiosity, and I asked, "What do you mean, 'Good luck?' "

You have to appreciate the British accent: he said, "Well, you know, the last chap didn't make it." We came down anyway and could see the runway. We made a normal landing, but that was it – "Well you know the last chap didn't make it."

One day I had a flight from London to Los Angeles, and if we flew a great circle route, we could get by with just one fuel stop. If you have a globe and take a piece of string, stretching it from London to Los Angeles, that shows you the shortest distance. The great circle route took us up over the tip of Greenland. Halfway to Los Angeles, there was an airport in the middle of nowhere called Frobisher. Frobisher is on Baffin Island. It was just a little south of the Arctic Circle. To give you an idea of how far north it was, it was on the same latitude as Fairbanks, Alaska.

Greenland from the air

It was a routine flight from London to Frobisher. We landed there and taxied in. The fuel truck driver came out and said to us, "Boy, you guys are sure lucky."

Of course we asked, "Why are we lucky?"

"Well," he said, "we've been out of fuel for three weeks, and we just got it in yesterday." Oh, man, if we'd landed a week earlier, I could just have imagined our chairman of the board, the president, and their guests stuck in this out-of-the-way place for a week. I would have been fired for sure. I don't know why we didn't catch it on the International notems. We eliminated this "I gotcha!" just by a pure stroke of luck. A lot of times it's better to be lucky than skillful.

This is one of my most embarrassing stories. We were in Houston, because we had a facility there. We had our old JetStar with the Pratt & Whitney engines on it. The board of directors came out to the airport and boarded. We were to fly them to Los Angeles. They got out to the airport an hour early, so we weren't ready for them. It was the hurry-hurry deal, which causes accidents, and it did.

We boarded the people, but we didn't get a chance to run the pre-start checklist. As we taxied out, one of the passengers was in the cockpit, asking about a small airport. We were taxiing and trying to talk to him, and then the tower came in. Instead of a long taxi for the usual runway, they turned us a shorter distance to another runway. Then the tower asked if we could expedite. Well, hurry, hurry, hurry. So we didn't get a chance to run the before-takeoff checklist.

We thought everything was under control, and they cleared us for takeoff. Roy Nielsen and I were both type rated in this airplane, but we weren't very experienced in it. Roy was in the left seat, and I was in the right seat. He advanced the throttles, and we rolled down the runway. I called out V1, which is your go-no-go speed, and we went a little faster. Then I called VR, which is your rotate speed. Roy pulled back on the yoke and... nothing. It wouldn't rotate. He immediately pulled the throttles back and went into four-engine thrust reverse. We were so darn heavy, and those brakes were so weak, that we weren't slowing down. I said, "More brake!" He was pressing the brake pedals trying to get more brake, and I had my feet on my brakes, trying to push the brake pedals right through the front bulkhead. He had his hand on the thrust reverse levers pulling back. I had my hand over his, and we were both trying to rip those thrust reversers out of the pedestal. It was horrifying; it was like slow motion. The sucker just would not slow down.

It did finally slow down, but the end of the runway came up. We were still going thirty miles an hour, and we sailed off the end of the runway and through the bushes. It had been raining, and twenty-five yards off the end of the runway we became mired down in the mud with the engines going full power. So, we shut it down, and there we were sunk in the mud at the end of the runway. Roy got out of his seat, opened the door, and just started walking. He left me in the airplane to face the whole board of directors.

Off the runway in Houston

I went back in the cabin and said, "Sirs, we're not sure what happened, but we're going to sort it out. I see that our company's station wagon is approaching. We're going to put you all on a commercial airline and send you home. When we find out what has happened, we will give you a report." And that was that.

What had happened was that we had turned the trim tab to zero when we landed the previous night. It was out of range, and, being in a hurry, we had not run a preflight to make sure that the trim system was working accurately. We had not reset it. In newer airplanes, that trap is built out of the airplanes. If you advance your throttles and the trim tab is not set correctly, you get a warning horn that tells you that your trim tab is not set correctly. We didn't have that warning system, and, being hurried, we blew it. Fortunately, there was no damage to the airplane, but it was pilot error. It was inexperience.

The next day, Roy Nielsen had to go in and see the president of the company to explain what happened. The president, Harry Wetzel, was a pilot, and Roy told him, "We screwed up. It was our fault. It shouldn't have happened. It won't happen again."

The president told him, "Roy, if you had told me any cock-and-bull story, you were fired. The fact that you're honest – ok, we'll chalk it up to experience." So we lucked out on that one.

But that little episode might have saved my life. Later on, I had a flight up to Santa Rosa. I took people up, and there was also a full load coming back. It was a Friday night, and we had ten passengers and a lot of baggage. Not only that, they also came on with ten cases of wine. Everything in that airplane was forward CG, Center of Gravity. The more you load, the more you have to set the trim tab farther back to be able to rotate the airplane. We also had a 250 pound man in the jumpseat, so that made the plane even more nose-heavy.

Here again was a hurry, hurry situation. "We've got an appointment down there in Los Angeles. Can't we expedite this flight? Come on, let's go." We loaded everybody up and fired up. They had a relatively short runway here. It was 5000 feet, which was ample for a normal takeoff. We were roaring down the runway, and the copilot called V1. Then he called VR. I pulled the yoke back... nothing. Oh boy, that Houston flight flashed through my mind. The trim tab button was on the yoke, the wheel, and I laid my thumb on that. That old trim tab started to whir, and I just kept my thumb on it, getting it back in the proper range. Fortunately, as I got to the end of the runway and pulled back on the yoke, it took hold. We were in the air, and away we went.

The trim tab was against the stop. We were so darned nose heavy it was unbelievable. When the passenger in the jump seat wasn't looking, I tapped the copilot on the knee and pointed to the trim tab. He saw it was against the stop and knew we were lucky. If it hadn't been for that Houston episode, I don't know whether I would have thought fast enough or not. This was an item that no one had trained us to do. The learning curve is hell.

This is a cute story. At least I think it's cute. We were sitting in our four-engine jet on the taxiway at La Guardia Airport. We were about number six for takeoff, so there was a lot of time for conversation. We had a full load of

National Business Aircraft Association

Pilot Safety Award

to

Frank D. Bray

In recognition of having been first pilot on aircraft operated in the conduct of business for a total of

3,028,420

or more consecutive plane miles without accident involving damage to property or injury to persons, this safety certificate of merit is awarded.

By order of the Board of Directors

ATTEST: DATED: June 30, 1977

Randall H. Carpenter, CHAIRMAN, SAFETY AND AWARDS COMMITTEE — PRESIDENT — William F. Gilbert, CHAIRMAN OF THE BOARD

NBAA Pilot Safety Award, 1977

This was before we ran off the runway...

passengers, and on the jumpseat between the copilot and myself sat a beautiful young lady. She was trying to make conversation, and she asked me where I was trained.

I said, “I was trained in World War I.”

“Oh, she said, “that’s interesting.” She turned to the young, good-looking copilot, Phil Laisney, and they had a bit of a discussion.

Right in front of us was a DC-10. During a lull in the conversation, I pointed out this DC-10 and said, “Do you see the center engine at the rear of his airplane? That nacell is exactly the same size as a DC-3 fusilage.”

And she said, “What’s a DC-3?”

I knew right then that time had passed me by, that another generation was coming along, and it was time for me to hang it up

I guess the highlight of my flying career was taking our corporate four-engine, ten-passenger jet around the world four times. Our flight department had twelve pilots, but I was assigned to each of the trips.

Back then, I was a detail, take-charge type of guy. My background of non-sked flying was invaluable. A non-sked pilot has to do all his own flight planning, paperwork, forms, reservations, and permits, and deal with all the various authorities. The big skill is solving problems as they come up. Getting the bird from point A to point B is the easy part.

At the time it didn’t seem like all that big of a deal, but, looking back on the flights, I’m amazed the corporation trusted me with the responsibility of the CEO, President, and their wives and guests. Mrs. Shumway, the CEO’s wife, complimented me once. She said,”Frank, you are good at dealing with these rude officials.”

The secret was to always remember that we were playing in their ballpark and to go with the flow. Never, ever lose your cool, no matter the amount of stress, and, most importantly, keep smiling. Usually a satisfactory solution could be negotiated. If not, you could go to plan

B with no burned bridges. The CEO and President never said a word. It was what they expected. Anything less would not have been satisfactory.

In Part II of this book I have included detailed accounts of my flights around the world and some other notable flights I made for the Garrett Corporation.

All corporations set their own compulsory retirement age for their pilots. Garrett had set theirs at fifty-eight. Our Aviation Manager, Lou Berger, reached fifty-eight first. He played golf with the corporate officers, and he got them to raise the age to sixty. When he approached sixty, he sold them on the fact that we all took a first class physical every six months, so sixty-two was a reasonable retirement age. But when he was approaching sixty-two he was told, "Sorry, Lou. But you will stay on as a consultant with the same pay. You only have to be available to play golf with us."

I wasn't offered the same deal, so I retired at age sixty-two. Being in good health and still wanting to fly, I went into contract flying.

THE GARRETT CORPORATION

GARRETT

AIRESEARCH AVIATION COMPANY
6201 WEST IMPERIAL HIGHWAY · LOS ANGELES, CALIFORNIA 90045

March 21, 1980

VICE PRESIDENT
AND
DIVISION MANAGER

Dear Frank:

My heartiest congratulations to you on your 15th anniversary with AiResearch!

Frank, we are all well aware of the tremendous job you do for us as Captain on the JetStar, not to mention your many other contributions. You have remarkable capabilities, and we couldn't ask for a better man. As Lou says, you are "a willing, wonderful employee."

We deeply appreciate everything you've done for us and wish you continued success and happiness, Frank.

Sincerely,

H. L. Richardson

Mr. Frank D. Bray
11222 Canby Avenue
Northridge, California 91324

HLR:fc

A letter of congratulations for my fifteenth anniversary with AiResearch

AIRESEARCH AVIATION COMPANY
A DIVISION OF THE GARRETT CORPORATION

GARRETT

6201 WEST IMPERIAL HIGHWAY · LOS ANGELES, CALIFORNIA 90045

VICE PRESIDENT
AND
DIVISION MANAGER

March 17, 1982

Dear Frank:

March 22nd will be your 17th anniversary with us. Congratulations once again!

This letter is being written with a somewhat sad feeling since it will be the last anniversary letter from me to you. You have been an ideal employee in every way. Your flying skills are very superior, and your professional approach to your position is unquestionable. Believe me, Lou is very unhappy about your leaving, as are the rest of us.

But on a more cheerful note -- we all wish you the happiest, most peaceful retirement ever. You deserve the best, Frank. We will miss you.

Thank you and God Bless You.

Kindest personal regards,

Bill

H.L. Richardson

Mr. Frank D. Bray
11222 Canby Avenue
Northridge, California 91324

HLR:fc

A letter of congratulations for my seventeenth – and final – anniversary with AiResearch

Contract Flying 1982 -1987

I flew for the next five years after my retirement, from age sixty-two to sixty-seven. I felt very fortunate. Commercial airline pilots have compulsory retirement at age sixty. I was able to enjoy my great career for another seven years.

The first call I got was from a pilot by the name of Neil Looy. His boss, Glen Larson, was a producer for Twentieth Century Fox, and he had just purchased a Lockheed JetStar. Neil was not type rated in it, so he wanted me to ride with him for a period of time until he was up to speed and got his type rating, and go from there. Glen Larson produced *Quincy*, *Fall Guy*, and *Magnum P.I.* among other TV shows, and he was filthy rich. He had, if you can believe it, his own personal limo. It was a Rolls Royce limo. He had homes in the Los Angeles area, Palm Springs, and Honolulu. Not only that, but he purchased a huge yacht, so he was a very interesting individual.

Neil was a crack pilot, very experienced. He was a retired Air Force fighter pilot and a squadron commander. So it didn't take him long to get up to speed and take his flight check and get rated in the Lockheed Jetstar. Neil had me train a copilot for him. I gave the copilot ground school, some flight training, and sent him on the way with Neil.

Standing with Neil Looy in front of Glen Larson's jet

A month or so later, Neil called me up. He said, "Hey, Frank, how'd you like to come work for me full time as a copilot?"

I laughed, and I said, "What happened to that copilot I trained for you?"

Neil said, "We had a personality conflict, and I got along so well with you that I want you to work for me."

At this stage in the game, I didn't mind riding copilot, so I said, "Sure, under two conditions. I'd like to handle the landing and takeoff once in awhile, and I will not come out to the airport every day just to hang around. Only when you need me."

Neil said, "That's fine."

So we had a great relationship for the next four years. In those four years, I think we made twenty-two flights from California to Honolulu, taking the boss, Glen Larson, back and forth. He had a beautiful home in Hawaii just off of Diamondhead, right on the beach. It was a gorgeous facility. There was a huge guesthouse where I would stay. It had tennis courts, swimming pools – the whole bit!

One evening at the cocktail hour I was invited to Glen Larson's house. I stood on the deck there with him. The sun was going down, and it was a beautiful sunset. You could see the surf.

Just to make conversation, I said, "That is certainly a million dollar view."

Glen Larson turned to me and with a straight face said, "It's slightly more than that!" You can't even have a million dollar view anymore!

I had many long talks with Neil's father. His father and I were peers. His dad stated he was glad I was riding with that tiger son of his, that I would be a safety pilot so to speak and possibly have a calming influence on him.

We'd go into an airport to refuel the airplane. Of course I was the old duffer, baldheaded and chubby, and all the ground crew would assume I was the captain of the flight! They would come up to me and ask what service I needed, and I'd say, "You'd better ask the captain over there, that young good-looking guy!" They'd look at me and wonder what in the world I was doing riding copilot. But I didn't have an ego problem. As a matter of fact, it was very relaxing to be enjoying the flight and not having the responsibility for the catering and the flight planning, the weather, the fueling, the maintenance. I could ride along, and just enjoy the scenery.

Glen Larson, being a producer and in charge of everything, wasn't very considerate of the crew. For instance, one Christmas morning at nine o'clock – we hadn't even opened up the Christmas presents yet – Neil Looy called me. He said, "Hey, pack a quick bag, get to the airport, the boss wants to leave for Honolulu in two hours." So I packed a bag and shot on out on Christmas morning, and we flew Glen Larson to Honolulu.

Another time we were over in Honolulu at Christmas time. We were going to be there for a week, over New Year's Eve. So GG flew over commercial and stayed with me. We all went out New Year's Eve. Of course we partied, did a bit of drinking, and ended up bringing in the new year. We went to bed around one a.m., with no flight scheduled the next day.

About two o'clock in the morning, the boss called Neil and said, “I've got a script that has to go over to another island because my partner is going back to Hollywood and it's the only way to get it back over there in time. So I want you guys to fly immediately over to this island.”

So Neil and I, feeling no pain, went to the airport, took the covers off and filed a quick flight plan and flew it over to the other island. It was an empty airplane so that was no big problem. It just shows that we were taxi drivers, and that was what we were paid to do.

In the four years that I flew with Neil, we only had one difference of opinion. We were over in Honolulu and had been there for four days. We were scheduled to depart the following day for Los Angeles. I went out to the airport to preflight the airplane, stock it, and make sure everything was ready for the following morning. I went through the airplane, picked up a sofa, and there was no life raft! When we flew domestically we took the life raft out of the airplane so we didn't have to carry all that weight. There was a bin under the sofa built specially for that so when we fly over the ocean, it's installed. Neil had a mechanic by the name of Dave Chamberlain, and in the hurry up he forgot it, and in my hurry up inspection I'd forgotten to check it. So we'd flown over there with no life raft. I scurried around the airport and tried to borrow one, tried to rent one, tried to buy one. There wasn't a life raft to be had.

I called Neil back at the house and told him we couldn't leave tomorrow morning because we didn't have a life raft. I guess when Neil told the boss, the boss reamed him out, so Neil reamed me out. He said, “Hey, you should've kept quiet, and no one would've known this.” And I said, “Neil, you're thinking like a nonsked pilot now. If it was just the two of us, I'd go with you in a minute, not a problem. But you have the boss, you have the boss's wife, you have the boss's children aboard. If we should have to ditch and no life raft, it would be murder!” It was interesting – he was talking like a nonsked pilot and I was a nonsked pilot talking like a conservative pilot. My point was that we were not being paid to take chances, but to use good judgment. Well, that blew over and from then on we immediately put the life raft on the checklist.

Any time Glen Larson was on the airplane, Neil was in the left seat as it should be. However, I did get to fly as the captain for a few flights. Glen Larson bought a huge, beautiful yacht, and it had been sailed over to Fort Lauderdale because Glen wanted to tour through the Bahamas. Neil Looy elected to be a crewmember on this yacht. Since he'd be on the yacht, I'd fly his airplane for him. The yacht went to the various islands in the Bahamas, and I flew the airplane following the yacht. Glen Larson wanted to go sightseeing. So we went sightseeing. There we were roaring around about five hundred feet over all these islands, and it was a gorgeous flight.

Another time I got to fly captain was interesting. Neil was out of town or on another project, and I was assigned to take his place. Glen Larson had written a script for a movie, and he wrote his airplane into the movie. There were some flying scenes in it. In order for me to be in the movie, I had to go down to Hollywood and join the Actor's Union. I went down, and it was just a matter of paying a fee. They gave me a certificate showing that I was a member of the Screen Actor's Guild. The hero was a pilot. So I was in this flying scene, and I was supposed to represent the hero of this movie. They dressed me in the exact same outfit that the hero was wearing. The ironic part was that I was inside the airplane and they were filming from outside the airplane. They could never see who was in the left seat anyhow! I wondered what the difference it made.

But it was interesting to see how these films were made. In the main scene, the hero flying in this airplane roared down the runway, and the bad guys were at the end of the runway shooting at him. He had to pull up sharply to dodge the fire and bullets. I arranged what we were trying to do with the tower. The cameraman was down at the end of the runway, and they were all set to film it. I was at the other end, and when the director said everything was ready to go the tower gave us clearance. I poured the coal to it. As I got down to the cameras I pulled back sharply on the yoke and flew up and around and that was it. For a few years, I received a check in the mail, residuals, for my part in the movie. And this residual check was six dollars a month. Big deal, but very fascinating.

As I said before, it was a fun four years flying with Neil Looy. He was a great person and a fine pilot. I was really lucky.

At various times for a year, I flew Larry Flynt, the porno king. He was the publisher of Hustler magazine. His chief pilot was offered a job with Northrop flying Gulf Streams. Naturally he jumped at that, but he remained chief pilot for Larry Flynt. He hired me to fly as captain when he wasn't available.

When I was notified of a trip, I would go to Century City, up to the twentieth floor of the Hustler building, and tell the girl at the front desk that I had to go back to the accounting department. So this sweet young thing would come and escort me back there. As we walked down these hallways, these many porno proofs covered the walls from floor to ceiling. They were only tacked up there to decide what would be in the next magazine. I had trouble not looking at them. I just looked at the girl. She was just a girl who worked there and saw it everyday and didn't think anything of it.

These flights worked on a cash basis. When I got back to the accounting department, they would hand me $10,000 expense money for the trip. Well, $10,000 doesn't sound like much in this day and age, but you have to realize this was twenty years ago. I would sign for the $10,000, they'd put it in the envelope, and I'd be on my way. The parking garage was in the basement of this building. I was always wary of being robbed. If a robber did stick me up, I hoped they'd shoot me, because no one would believe that I lost their ten grand. This money was for everything, for hotels, catering, fuel, and salary. I'd pay myself. I'd pay the copilot. Everything was on a cash basis. So rather than taking this money home, I'd take this money to the airport, go to Larry Flynt's airplane, and stash it in a hiding place. Of course in an airplane – behind drawers, under cabinets, behind the wall furniture – there are plenty of places to hide things. So I used the airplane as the bank.

We made a number of trips down to the Cayman Islands. I suspect Larry Flynt was laundering money there. Years back he had been shot, and they did not get the man who had shot him. The shot paralyzed him. He carried three armed bodyguards with him all the time, and he carried two nurses. So these bodyguards were armed, and I called customs down there in the Cayman Islands and explained the situation. I asked if it would be okay for these armed guards to come in there with their weapons. They were very congenial and said that when we landed, the guards would have to put their guns in bond and they would be returned when we left. It was such a small island, and they knew everyone on the island and there was no crime there. I explained this to Larry Flynt and he said, "okay."

It was interesting when we landed in the Cayman Islands. Customs came out and met the airplane. They wheeled up a little dolly. As the guards came off the airplane, the customs said, "Okay, fellas, put your toys on this dolly." So the guys took their 45s out of their shoulder holsters and put them on the tray. Customs said, "Come on guys, ammunition, too." So they dug in their pockets and took out their spare clips and put those on the tray.

But to show you how paranoid Larry Flynt was, even though this was a small island, one of the guards would be on the roof of the hotel during the night, one of the guards would be walking around the perimeter of the hotel, and the other one would be sleeping. So they would switch off.

On a couple of trips, GG flew down commercial because we were going to be there for a week, so we were having a vacation at *Hustler*'s expense. On one trip Larry

Larry Flynt's jet: HM stands for "Hustler Magazine"

Flynt knew that GG was down there and offered her a ride back with us. But she elected not to. We said that she was going to stop over and see friends in Houston. So that took care of that.

Then I took Larry Flynt on numerous flights to Las Vegas. He loved to gamble. Here again it was interesting because he was still scared that someone was out to get him. So he would always sit at a gambling table with his back to a wall, and one of the guards would be on the balcony with his eyes roving over the whole casino. I would go talk to the guard. The guard was professional. He never looked me in the eye, and he never took his eyes off the casino. He was constantly scanning to see if anybody was approaching Larry Flynt.

One night coming into Los Angeles about two o'clock in the morning there was no traffic, so approach control said, "Say, we're just curious. What does Hotel Mike stand for?" And I said, "Hustler Magazine." There was silence, and finally he said, "Well, that figures." Of course 69 is a porno number. So here we were going all over the country asking for various things using our tail number, which is a porno number.

One of the funniest things happened when we stopped for fuel at Colorado Springs. It was about ten o'clock at night and extremely warm and humid. In this little terminal there were a bunch of pilots waiting for their people to come out. One of the guards stayed in the airplane, and two of the guards came with me into the terminal. They had taken their jackets off. So here were these two big, six foot three, two hundred pound guys with shoulder holsters and 45s. They were just standing there having a Coke and shooting the breeze.

I was presented a fuel bill, and I said, "I assume you accept cash." The bill was for $2,000 for this jet fuel. The young lady at the desk was startled. No one ever pays cash for fuel. It is always paid for with a credit card. I pulled out this wad of bills and started peeling off the hundreds until I got up to the amount of the bill. Here I was, a little, fat, baldheaded pilot peeling out all these hundred dollar bills, and there were two huge guys standing there with 45s, and these other pilots never said a word. But you could see their eyes were wide open, thinking, "What is this? The mafia? Gangsters? What in the world is going on here?" It was a fun deal.

One interesting side note: Larry Flynt's jet originally belonged to Elvis Presley. After Larry Flynt stopped using it, the jet sat abandoned at Garrett AiResearch. It has since been returned to Graceland.

I had one flight with Bob Hope. He had a Lockheed JetStar. It was a quick flight from Burbank to Palm Springs, and their copilot was unavailable. So I hopped out to the airport, and we flew Bob Hope over to Palm Springs. He had a speaking engagement over there.

On the way over I went back to the cabin and asked him if I could get him a coffee or something to drink. That was the extent of it. We waited around for about four or five hours, and then at one in the morning we flew him back to Burbank. About a week later I received a personal

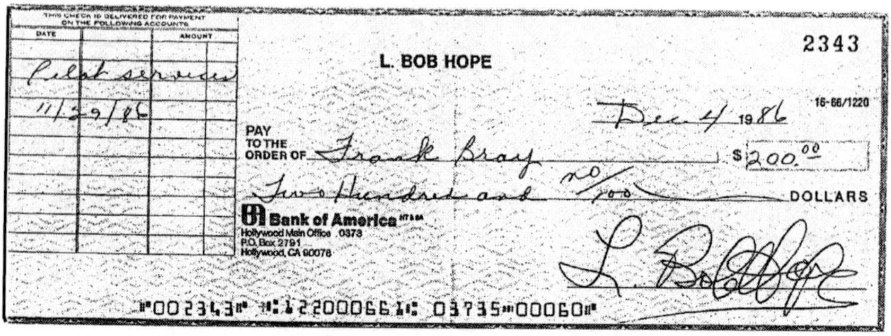
THIS CHECK IS DELIVERED FOR PAYMENT ON THE FOLLOWING ACCOUNTS
DATE AMOUNT
Pilot services
11/29/86
2343
L. BOB HOPE
16-66/1220
Dec 4 1986
PAY TO THE ORDER OF Frank Bray $200.00
Two Hundred and no/100 DOLLARS
Bank of America
Hollywood Main Office .0373
P.O. Box 2791
Hollywood, CA 90078
L. Bob Hope

I have Bob Hope's autograph – on a paycheck!

check for two hundred dollars from Bob Hope for services. That was my one and only trip with Bob Hope.

I flew Kenny Rogers off and on for two years. Kenny Rogers had two airplanes, a DC-9 and a Lockheed JetStar, but he only had two pilots. So anytime both the planes flew at the same time, they had to hire two contract pilots. I was type rated on the Lockheed Jetstar, as copilot. I did get to fly Kenny Rogers as captain for a week on one of his concert tours. His chief pilot was unavailable, so they hired me as captain.

Kenny was the greatest guy in the world. He would come up to the cockpit and shoot the breeze. He was very hospitable and wanted to know if he could get us a cup of coffee, a Coke, or anything. Then he always made sure that we as a crew had passes to all his shows. He made sure that we had backstage passes so that if we wanted to go backstage and talk to the other performers, we could. Anytime he met us backstage he always made a point of saying, "Are you guys getting taken care of? Is there anything more we can do for you?" He was just a wonderful person.

The one thing that was interesting was the fact that Kenny Rogers' chief pilot was a karate expert, so he was in charge of Kenny Roger's security as well as being his chief pilot. In the hotel, for security reasons, the chief pilot karate expert would be in a room next to Kenny, and on the other side of his room would be the copilot. On this

"Kenny was the greatest guy in the world"

tour, I was always in the room next door that was normally occupied by the chief pilot, supposedly for security. Of course what Kenny Rogers did not realize is that he had no security. I was the pilot, not the guard.

I spent two weeks with that operation down in the midst of Georgia. Kenny Rogers had a huge, beautiful farm with a small airport and a tower, but it was out in the middle of nowhere. I have to say that this farm was unbelievable. It was a horse farm. The barns had stained glass windows, oak stalls, and tiled roofs. It was more beautiful than a lot of homes. It also had a swimming pool and was air-conditioned indoors for the horses. It had a ramp in the center aisle so they could lead the horses down into this pool and walk them around inside the pool for exercise! Of course they had a display ring. It was in a huge barn where they could demonstrate the thoroughbreds. I think they had an Arabian horse there also.

They used that little airport in Georgia as a hub. Kenny Rogers would come out to the airport at about seven o'clock at night, and we'd fly him up to New York. He'd give his performance, and at one in the morning, we'd fly him back to Georgia. Then the next day, we'd go up to Philadelphia and back. Maybe the next day up to Washington and back, and the next day we'd go up to Chicago and back. So we used his home and airport as a hub.

When we flew back to this airport Kenny would use the telephone and order up a bunch of pizzas because he only lived five minutes from the airport. The runway lights would be on, but not another soul would be at that airport. As we landed, the pizza truck would drive up, and Kenny would get out of the airplane, pick up these boxes of pizzas, get into his station wagon that was parked right there on the ramp and go home. This happened night after night.

One time when Bill Mato was the pilot and I was the copilot, Kenny Rogers was producing a cowboy movie up in Sheridan, Wyoming. We flew him up there and stayed with him for a week while the production crew was shooting this film. What was fascinating was that it was a very small town, and the film crew had permission to have twenty wild horses race down the main street. They brought in all these horses in trucks, and positioned them at the end of town. They blocked off all the intersections, and then when the cameraman said, "Roll 'em," they released the horses. These horses galloped down the main street of this little town. Well, evidently the film didn't turn out exactly the way they wanted it, so they corralled all these horses and took them back to the end of the town again. It took about two hours to get everything set up for the next shot of this same scene. They released the horses, and the horses galloped down the main drag. It was interesting watching them make this movie. Of course, Bill and I had passes, so we ate with all the actors, the stage hands, and producers. It was a fascinating two weeks.

We got caught short on that trip. Kenny Rogers was also a famous and very knowledgeable photographer. They weren't shooting this film on the weekend, so he wanted to go down to Rock Springs and spend Saturday and Sunday taking pictures. I think he wanted pictures in the Green River area. So we flew him down to Rock Springs, and he rented a car. He and his assistant took off and said that they wouldn't be back until Saturday night. Bill and I put the bird to bed, put the covers on it, went in, and got a motel room. By this time it was dinner time, so we had a few scotches and ordered up a couple of steaks and a carafe of wine. We weren't going to leave until ten the next night after all.

Well, we'd just finished our steaks and, feeling no pain, were about to order an after-dinner drink, when Kenny Rogers came in and said, "Oh, I've changed my mind. I'd like to go back to Sheridan right now."

Bill and I looked at each other and said, "Sure, we can handle that." Fortunately there was no weather involved. We went out, took the covers off the airplane, and did our preflights. We sucked on a little oxygen, but made a routine flight back to Sheridan. That's the way pilots get caught short. The boss changes his mind at the last minute.

Finally the phone stopped ringing. So ended my contract flying. There seemed to be no demand for an old, bald, deaf, blind pilot.

This story is bound to be inaccurate, because I wrote it as I remembered it. It is now 2006, and at the age of eighty-six, I think back and realize how lucky I've been to have all these beautiful toys to play with and get paid besides! It has been a great ride with a lot of wonderful memories.

FRANK BRAY AVIATION

Pilot Record

Name Frank Bray — Address 11222 Canby, Northridge, CA 91326
Birthdate 3-25-20 — Occupation Pilot

[redacted]

Cert.# ATP 368008	Type/Cert.	Type Rate in Following A/C:
Marital Status Married	Commercial	DC-3 DC-4 C-46 Constellation
# Dependents 1	ATR X	Lodestar G-I G-II DH 125
Yr. Orig. License 1944	Flight Instr.	Falcon 20 Lear Jetstar

FAA Medical Certificate: Date 3-1-85 Class II Waiver None (If none, so state)

Describe Flight Training U.S. Navy, American Airlines, National Airlines, Lake Central Airlines, Resort Airlines, World Airways

PILOT EXPERIENCE

A/C Make and Model	PIC	Co-Pilot	Total	Last 12 mo.	L/90 days
1. Jetstar	3410	132	3542	200	60
2. Falcon 10					
3. Lear 24,25,35	194	50	244		
4. Gulfstream G-159	1214	200	1414		
5. Gulfstream G-1159	522	193	715		
6. Falcon 20	615	80	695		
7. Citation					
8. DH-125	1546	74	1620		
9. Merlin II,III,IV	206	60	266		
10. Misc under 12,500	1924	600	2524		
11. Misc 2 eng Ov/12,500	8040	500	8540		
12. Misc 4 eng Ov/12,500	7700	700	8400		
13. Other King Air	76	6	82		
TOTAL	25447	2595	28042	Inst. 2308	Nite. 7575

As Pilot-in-Command or as Co-pilot, have you: (If yes, explain fully on reverse side)
1. Had or been involved in any aircraft accidents? No X Yes ___
2. Had any violations of Federal Air Regulations? No X Yes ___

Has you automobile drivers license ever been suspended or revoked? No X Yes ___

Have you ever been arrested for operating an automobile under the influence of alcohol or drugs? No X Yes ___

Have you had any automobile accidents within the last five (5) years? No X Yes ___

I warrant that the answers given are true and complete to the best of my knowledge and belief and that no material information has been withheld.

Date: May 1, 1985 Signed Frank D. Bray

This pilot record is filed in connection with the Insurance Application of:

Copy of Pilot's License & Medical Attached X (Check)

My pilot record from May, 1985 showing 28,042 hours of flight time. That is more than three years in the air.

PART II:

INDIVIDUAL FLIGHTS
1975 - 1981

The JetStar 731– I flew this airplane around the world.

In the cockpit of the JetStar 731

1975 Flight to Tehran

March, 1975

When our boss said he wanted to go to Tehran in Iran in our JetStar, we thought he must be kidding. After looking into the problems involved, we hoped he was kidding. This plane still had the old Pratt & Whitney engines, so it only had about an 1,800 mile range. Considering what places were available for overflying or stopping for fuel, it didn't appear we could get there from here.

It is not possible to overfly Yugoslavia, Bulgaria, Turkey, Syria, Saudi Arabia, Iraq, or Iron Curtain countries without prior permission. You can fly into Greece or into Turkey, but you cannot cross the Greece-Turkey border, as they are mad at each other. The same applies to the Israel-Egypt border.

To begin, we had a routine flight from Boston to Gander in Newfoundland. It was a beautiful day in Gander. You could see clear into yesterday.

From Gander it is 1,600 miles to Keflavik in Iceland. We go over lots of water, but we also go over the tip of Greenland. On this trip Greenland was covered with clouds, but on a clear day it is a magnificent sight with the ice, snow, mountains, and fjords.

It was a typical day in Iceland: cold, rain, a low ceiling, and wind. From Iceland we flew on to London. By this time, it was dark, as London is five hours ahead of the East Coast. Flying over Scotland at night was fantastic. It was clear with no smog. The lights of the cities and towns appeared orange, which seemed strange. We landed in London at ten p.m. in the middle of a rain squall. The wind was blowing twenty-five to thirty-five with gusts. The poor old bird bounced like a cork in river rapids.

We spent a day in London to rest up. I learned of more problems when I filed the flight plan. Apparently fuel service was on strike in Athens, but the strike should be over when we arrived. Since one cannot land in Italy just for fuel, it put us in a bind. Luckily, the strike was over when we landed at Athens.

Then, we flew on to Beirut in Lebanon, refueled, and then on to Tehran. We had permission to overfly Turkey, so we flew north and then east to Tehran. Approaching the Turkey border we couldn't get anyone to answer our calls, so it was with an uneasy feeling that we proceeded over the country. It was dark, we were tired, and we had been warned to make contact before crossing, all of which contributed to this uneasiness. However, we made contact later and routed on to Tehran.

Since there are mountains just north of town, it was a relief to see the light of Tehran about a hundred miles out. We were glad to be there.

Tehran reminds me of Denver. It is high, about 4,000 feet, with a mountain range just north with lots of snow. The highest peak is 18,000 feet.

The ride to town was the most dangerous part of the trip. All the cabs seemed to think it was a Le Mans Race. Red lights were just something to slow down for and zip through. Left turns were just a game of chicken. The car nose kept edging into oncoming traffic until someone stopped and made way. All of this was accompanied by much blowing of horns. It was enough to drive a person to drink!

Mack Truck has an assembly plant in Tehran, and Garrett has a sales office there. So it was business and pleasure. Our office there arranged for us to fly within Iran. Monday we took a full load of folks down to Isfahan, about 200 miles south of Tehran. It was the former capital of Muslim Persia and had huge flowered domes on the mosques and giant minarets. We spent two nights there, and it was most interesting.

Then, since we had picked up more guests, we made two flights down to Shiraz, another 200 miles south. We went out and saw the ruins of Persepolis and learned the history of Cyrus and Darius. That night, we went to a remarkable "Sound & Light" show that described the history of Persepolis. It was great, but a cold rain started and we couldn't wait for it to finish.

The next day we took a full load back to Tehran. We dropped all the baggage and one of our Vice Presidents and then flew north over the mountain range to Ramsar on the coast of the Caspian Sea. The Caspian is eighty-seven feet below sea level, and the airport in Ramsar is fifty feet below. We spent the afternoon there and went back to Tehran.

We came home by the same route: Tehran, Beirut, Athens, London. Out of Athens, the #3 oil pressure started to flicker and the #1 engine's TVI (Turbine Vibrator Indicator) was jumping up a storm. I thought for sure we would have to land at Geneva or Paris, but it held on and we landed in London ok. I checked the oil in #3 and found it almost dry.

The next morning we found a hydraulic leak in the down-line of the landing gear, so there was a two-hour delay while a new part was made up.

The plan was to fly from London to Iceland to Gander and then spend the night in Bangor, Maine. I found the winds were too strong to make Iceland to Gander, so I replanned for Iceland to Sondrestrom in Greenland, then Gander to Bangor. From London we flew north and landed in Iceland with the usual rain, wind, cold, and low ceilings.

On filing a flight plan for Sondrestrom, I learned the field was closed due to an ice storm. A DC-8 from Copenhagen to Sondrestrom was returning to Iceland.

When he landed, we talked to the Captain, and he convinced us not to try it. It didn't take much convincing. That was his regular run, and his judgment was good enough for us. So there was nothing to do but spend the night there, with the prospect of more nights due to the weather.

Early the next morning, I made an $85 call to Universal WX in Houston, and the weather appeared good from Iceland to Frobisher, on Baffin Island, and from there down to Gander. We departed Iceland, climbed up through the dark rain, and broke out on top in beautiful sunshine. Things always seem better in sunlight – even if the #1 TVI was still dancing.

On crossing Greenland, we requested the Sondrestrom and Frobisher weather. We were very much surprised to learn that Frobisher had bare minimums in snow, but Sondrestrom was good. What a dilemma! If Frobisher went down, we did not have enough fuel to go any other place, so we decided the decision point was halfway between Sondrestrom and Frobisher. At that point, Frobisher went below minimums, so we turned back to Greenland.

What a sight! All the snow and ice. The airport was up a fjord and, as they say, "it was like landing in a ditch." There were walls of hills on both sides, so you landed up the fjord into the end and took off from the opposite direction down the fjord.

Now we couldn't make Bangor non-stop, so we had to go down to Goose Bay and then on. It turned out to be a long day: Iceland to Sondrestrom to Goose Bay to Bangor to Des Moines and finally to Los Angeles. Needless to say, we were a mite tired.

The next day, we learned that we had been lucky. A stud had pulled loose on the #3 oil pump, and that was the reason we were losing oil. Then maintenance found the front bearing on the #1 starter-generator gone, and that's why it was vibrating and causing the TVI to dance. It is amazing it lasted from Athens to Los Angeles, some twenty-one hours.

All-in-all this was an interesting trip, but it was great to get home!

1976 Flight to Europe

The First Flight to Europe with the New Garrett Engines

August, 1976

AiResearch has a modification program to convert the Lockheed JetStar with the original Pratt & Whitney engines to the Garrett 731 engines. This is a fan-type engine with low fuel specifics. Thus, with the same fuel capacity, it gives the JetStar some 45 percent increase in range. There are other benefits such as lower noise, more performance, and a quieter cabin, but the added range is the big factor for the pilots.

First, we flew non-stop from Los Angeles to Bangor, Maine. We covered a distance of 2,150 nautical miles (2,480 statute miles) in five hours and thirty-five minutes. We burned 15,200 pounds of fuel, or an average of 2,720 pounds per hour. This flight would have been impossible in the older JetStar. We would have run out of fuel just about over Detroit.

From Bangor, it was a short hop to Gander in Newfoundland. This was only 641 nautical miles, one hour and thirty-five minutes air time.

The next day was the Gander to London leg. We used a computerized flight plan for best wind track, altitude, and burn-off. This conversion is so new, the computer still thinks a JetStar will not make it. It would not accept our flight plan, so the programmer merely fooled the computer by calling us a Learjet 36 (which also has the Garrett 731 engines). Of course, the fuel burn-off would be much different, but we were primarily interested in the course and wind component for each portion of flight.

The flight plan showed 2,107 nautical miles (2,400 statute miles) in four hours and forty minutes, cruising at mach 0.76 at 37,000 feet all the way with a +15 wind component. This was a random track and due to heavy crossing westbound traffic, we were given three choices by air traffic control. One. Take a far southern track and get the altitude we want. Two. Take the track we want at 39,000 feet. Or three. Take the track we want at 29,000 feet.

The first choice was poor due to added distance and less wind. Number two was impossible; we were too heavy to get up there. So we flew from Gander to London at 29,000 feet. This was a great credit to these fine engines. We flew the whole way at 433K true air speed, and time en route was four hours and forty-seven minutes. We burned a total of 14,900 pounds of fuel, or an average of 3,150 pounds per hour. This is phenomenal when one considers the older JetStar could not have made Shannon (some 350 nautical miles less) at this altitude.

JetStars have been to Europe countless times, but with the new 731 Garrett engines life is going to be far easier and more relaxing for the pilots. We need all the flexibility and range we can get to do the best and safest job for our people.

Another example of the versatility of this 731 JetStar was shown on the London to Munich leg. We departed London with 9,900 pounds of fuel and a gross weight of 36,000 pounds. After take-off, the Center asked us if we could accept 41,000 feet. We could, and did. We leveled off at 41,000 in twenty-one minutes and burned only 1,300 pounds total in climb. Another feat impossible with the older JetStar.

London to Munich is 560 nautical miles (645 statute). Flying time was one hour and twenty-five minutes and the total burn was 4,300 pounds or 3,050 average per hour.

Now, after that glowing report, here is the real life.

The Los Angeles-Bangor leg was as advertised. A beautiful day! Hardly a cloud in the sky the whole way. It is most unusual to fly coast-to-coast and not pass or fly over a storm someplace en route. We had on board a new Bendix RDR-1200 digital radar, but didn't get a chance to play with it as there were no thunderstorms to look at.

On takeoff from Bangor, #3 and #4 generators dropped off the line. It is not unusual to lose one of the four generators, but to lose two is almost unheard of. However, after much button pushing, we discovered #2 was knocking #3 and #4 off, so we shut #2 and then had 1,3, and 4 on the bus. This unit is a combined starter/ generator, so it was our first clue it would create a problem – and it did.

We spent a short night in Gander, Newfoundland. We got six hours of sleep (the alarm was set for 6:30 local time), but our body clock or Los Angeles time was only at two in the morning. It made us tired just thinking about it.

The airplane had to be moved at Gander for fueling, and #2 started fine. After filing the flight plan, loading, catering, and boarding passengers . . . you guessed it. We started 1, 3, and 4, but #2 refused to turn over. The starter just plain gave up. This was not a complete surprise as we had anticipated this possibility and had a spare starter on board. Allied Aviation provided two mechanics, and, with the help of our three VIP passengers (Mr. Azar, Group Vice President; Mr. Richardson, Vice President; and Mr. Carr, head Sales Manager), we had the starter changed and were on the way within the hour. Thinking back, that was some high-salaried talent as mechanic's helpers.

On our climb out of Gander, the #1 fuel computer decided to act up. There was a bit of engine surge. We went to manual mode and after a while went back to automatic. From then on the engine decided we were going anyway, so it purred like a kitten the rest of the flight.

The weather was clear over Ireland and England, and it was a sorry sight. Both countries are usually beautiful with all different shades of green, but due to the lack of rain all the fields were a scorched brown.

We landed at Luton Airport some fifty miles north of London. Here customs and limos met the plane and in a very short time the passengers were on their way to town. After they left, we sat down in the plane and had a spot of scotch with Her Majesty's finest customs agents. This was an enjoyable and very relaxing way to clear up the necessary paperwork.

The purpose of this flight to Europe was to fly potential customers for our new engine to demonstrate how fuel-efficient it is. For the next two weeks I flew demonstration flights out of London, Munich, Ibiza, Paris, Frankfurt, and Vienna.

At last came go-home day. It was a bear. We flew from Vienna to Shannon to St. Johns in Newfoundland to Green Bay, cleared US customs, and then to Los Angeles. Fifteen hours and twenty minutes flight time; on duty time was some twenty hours.

The sales manager, Landis Carr, was pleased with the interest and the prospects for orders. Looks like the new engine is a winner.

JET TRANSPORT FLIGHT ITINERARY
FORM 19-35 (R 12-72)

TENTATIVE SCHEDULE

DATE: August 11, 1976

PREPARED FOR: | AIRCRAFT MODEL AND NO.: 731 Jetstar N731A | TAS (KNOTS): 430 - 450 | FLIGHT NO.: --- | PREPARED BY: Frank Bray

AIRPORT	GMT DATE	GMT TIME	* TIME FACTOR	LOCAL TIME	LOCAL DATE	DISTANCE TO FLY	** BLOCK TIME	GROUND TIME	REMARKS
DEPART LOS ANGELES	Aug 20	1600Z	+7	0900	Aug 20	2413	5+40		Request computerized flight plan - LAX - BGR
ARRIVE BANGOR (KBGR)	Aug 20	2140Z	+4	1740	Aug 20			+35	
DEPART BANGOR	Aug 20	2215Z	+4	1815	Aug 20	641	1+40		
ARRIVE GANDER (¢YQX)	Aug 20	2355Z	+3:30	2025	Aug 20			12+35	Advise Allied of ETA
DEPART GANDER	Aug 21	1230Z	+3:30	0900	Aug 21	2057	5+00		Need computerized flight plan CYQX/EGGW at Allied by 0800Z.
ARRIVE LONDON (EGGW)	Aug 21	1730Z	-1	1830	Aug 21			5 NITES	Luton A/P. No handling. We will advise McAlpine
DEPART LONDON	Aug 26	1300Z	-1	1400	Aug 26	550	1+30		
ARRIVE MUNICH (EDDM)	Aug 26	1430Z	-1	1530	Aug 26			1 NITE	No handling necessary.
DEPART MUNICH	Aug 27		-1		Aug 27	788	2+10		
ARRIVE IBIZA (SPAIN)	Aug 27		-1		Aug 27				No handling necessary.
DEPART IBIZA (LEIB)	Aug ?		-1		Aug ?	830	2+20		
ARRIVE LONDON (EGGW)	Aug ?		-1		Aug ?				McAlpine Aviation
DEPART LONDON	Aug 28	0830Z	-1	0930	Aug 28	550	1+30		
ARRIVE MUNICH (EDDM)	Aug 28	1000Z	-1	1100	Aug 28				Request handling this flight.
DEPART MUNICH	Aug 31	0900Z	-1	1000	Aug 31	200	+55		
ARRIVE VIENNA (LOWW)	Aug 31	0955Z	-1	1055	Aug 31			3 NITES	Request handling Vienna.
DEPART VIENNA	SEPT 3	0900Z	-1	1000	SEPT 3	1040	2+55		Req. computerized flt. plan Shannon/St.Johns leg/be in Vienna 0500Z
ARRIVE SHANNON ((EINN)	SEPT 3	1155Z	-1	1255	SEPT 3			1+05	Request handling Shannon
DEPART SHANNON	SEPT 3	1300Z	-1	1400	SEPT 3	1727	4+50		with copy of computerized flight plan
ARRIVE ST JOHNS (CYSJ)	SEPT 3	1750Z	+3:30	1420	SEPT 3			+45	No handling required
DEPART ST. JOHNS	SEPT 4	1230Z	+3:30	0900	SEPT 4	1050	3+20		
ARRIVE BUFFALO	SEPT 4	1550Z	+4	1150	SEPT 4			1+00	CLEAR U.S. CUSTOMS
DEPART BUFFALO	SEPT 4	1650	+4	1250	SEPT 4	1950	5+50		
ARRIVE LOS ANGELES	SEPT 4	2240	+7	1540	SEPT 4				
DEPART									
ARRIVE									

Flight Itinerary for the first 731 JetStar flight to Europe, 1976

1977 Around the World Flight

The First of Four Flights Around the World

February, 1977

It all started about three weeks ago when Mr. Harry Wetzel, the president of the Garrett corporation, called Lou Berger, my immediate boss. Lou is manager of the Aviation department. Mr. Wetzel told Lou to plan on leaving on the fourth of February for an around the world flight, and Lou in turn assigned me the project of making the necessary arrangements for handling, landing permits, overfly permits, fuel requests, fuel allocations, shots, visas – all the details necessary to make this flight run smoothly. I've been working on it for the last two weeks, and I think we have everything lined up.

This trip involves some twenty-four different countries. We are now on our seventh revised flight itinerary, as every couple of days Mr. Wetzel will call Lou and tell him, “Say, we have a change in plans, and instead of going there we'd like to go here, and could you make the necessary arrangements?” Naturally, Lou tells me to “have at it,” and I do.

So at the moment I think the schedule is pretty well finalized. We're going from Los Angeles to Honolulu, New Zealand, Australia, Indonesia, Singapore, Malaysia, overflying Thailand and Burma, to India, then Pakistan, overflying Afghanistan, landing at Iran for fuel, overflying

Turkey, Bulgaria, Yugoslavia, and Austria, and landing in Germany.

Mr. Wetzel would like this flight to go westbound instead of eastbound. This in itself is interesting. The advantage of going westbound is that you have a long day. You can get up at a reasonable hour, leave at a reasonable hour, and, in effect, chase the sun. You can have a long flight and still land at your destination, which is usually a place you've never seen before. It's a strange environment, and landing in daylight is a tremendous help. You check into the hotel before the dinner hour, usually at cocktail hour, shower, have a good dinner, and a full evening. You've had a tremendously long day, and therefore you can sleep.

If you're going eastbound, the days are short. You usually land at your destination in the darkness. By the time you check into the hotel all the restaurants are usually closed. You try to go to sleep, but you've had a short day. Your body is not tired, so you can't sleep. You toss and turn, the alarm goes off at five thirty in the morning, and it's time for another short day. So the advantages of going westbound are clear.

The disadvantage of going westbound is that you're fighting the prevailing westerly head winds. Therefore you are restricted on range – you can't go as far with full tanks as you can when going eastbound. If you were out to set a speed record or go around the world on the least amount of fuel, you'd go eastbound. But I'm kind of glad we're going westbound, even though it does create some range problems.

Our first day's flight on Friday the fourth will be from Los Angeles to Honolulu. This will be the longest leg on the entire flight. It is the critical leg because there is no place to land between California and Honolulu for fuel. So our first choice naturally is to try to go from Los Angeles to Honolulu. However, if on the morning of the fourth the winds are such that we can't make it with a good reserve, we'll go instead from Los Angeles to San Francisco, fill up with fuel, and then from San Francisco to Honolulu. Strangely enough, the distance from San Francisco to

Honolulu is 150 nautical miles shorter than Los Angeles. Most people think of San Francisco as being north of Los Angeles, but in actual fact it's more west than north and therefore closer to Honolulu. Odds are we'll have to fly from Los Angeles to San Francisco and depart from there.

We're planning on spending the night in Honolulu and departing at eight in the morning for Auckland, New Zealand, which is a fair distance across the Pacific. Here, again, we are debating how we can do it. The wind that morning will determine which route we go. The ideal route would be from Honolulu to Pago Pago, 2,275 nautical miles. This is the extreme edge of our range for the JetStar. Pago Pago to Auckland is 1,566 nautical miles, which is very acceptable. If the winds are light we could go Honolulu to Pago Pago to Auckland with only one fuel stop.

However the chances are against it, so the other ideal route would be Honolulu to Canton Island in the Phoenix group, from there to Nandy in the Fiji group, and from there to Auckland. It would be two fuel stops and three very acceptable legs. The only problem with this route is that Canton Island is military, prior permission only, and from all reports it appears an impossibility to get permission to land there for fuel.

I did some checking with our Washington office, and they called the Pentagon. The Pentagon gave them the name of the man in charge. It so happens in the Garret Organization that we have an ex-general working with us, a General Bradley, so I got in touch with General Bradley and told him the name of the man in charge of landing permits for Canton Island. He then called the man, and it turned out they knew each other. So we got the permission to land and the fuel allocation. We were told to keep it on the QT. They didn't like to give civilians permission to land. They didn't want to set a precedent. However, we do have permission so we're planning on getting two computerized flight plans, one from Honolulu to Pago Pago, and one from Honlulu to Canton, when we get up in Honolulu on the morning of the fifth. If the one from Honolulu to Pago Pago shows it will be too critical, then we'll go Honolulu, Canton, Fiji, Auckland.

It is now Sunday the seventh. At the moment I am sitting back in the cabin of our airplane. We are cruising at 35,000 feet and making a ground speed of 500 mph. I'm looking out the left window down at the beautiful dark blue water. The sky is covered with fleecy white clouds – it's just an absolutely beautiful day.

To go back two days, the trip started out on a sour note. The day before we were to leave, the jet stream moved down from the north, giving us a wind component that made it impossible to reach Honolulu even from San Francisco. The computerized flight plan said it would take about six hours and thirty minutes. We only have about six hours and forty-five minutes of fuel in this airplane, so it wouldn't be a safe operation. There didn't seem to be any hope in the immediate future of the winds dying down so that we could make it. We can live with a head wind component of fifty knots against us, but the day we were to leave the wind was a -62. The passengers elected to leave from San Francisco commercially to Auckland, New Zealand. They got on Pan American and flew from San Francisco non-stop, fourteen hours, to Auckland. We were to stay there and, when the winds died down, catch them as soon as we could and proceed on schedule. I set the alarm for five o'clock the following morning and called our computer service down in Houston. He gave us a wind component of -20. I couldn't believe it.

I said, "What happened to all those strong winds that were supposed to be here for five or six days?"

He said, "The patterns changed. There's still eighty to ninety knot winds, but they swung around." Now it was coming from the northwest, so it's a much better wind component.

Before this had happened we debated going from San Francisco to Seattle to Cold Bay up in the Aleutian chain, and from Cold Bay down to Honolulu. When we got the report we went to the airport, loaded up with fuel, and took off for Honolulu. The computerized flight plan was fantastic. It was so close. It said it would take us five hours and twenty-three minutes en route. It took us five hours and twenty-five minutes. The winds on each leg were within two or three knots. It was just a fantastic flight plan, and it's very ironic that if this could only have happened the day before, the trip would have gone as smooth as silk. Anyway, here we are, flying across the Pacific with three crew members and an empty airplane. It's as if we have our own private jet to tour the world with.

The flight to Honolulu as I said was very routine, and it was really a beautiful sight to see the islands coming up over the horizon. We first picked up the island on our radar, which has a 200 mile range, and then we slowly began to make out the tops of the mountains. Then, as we let down into Honolulu, we could see the beautiful water with the blues, the greens, the white surf, the sand and the palm trees. Just absolutely beautiful. The sun was going down. There were quite a few clouds and a haze and this big ball of fire slowly sinking into the sea. We spent the night in Honolulu.

This morning we received our two flight plans, and, inasmuch as we don't have any passengers with us, we decided we'd just make the two stops. We'll land at Canton, go down to Fiji, and then down to Auckland.

I looked in my log book, and it seems the last time I flew into Canton was in 1945. I was in the Navy then. So it is going to be interesting to visit there once again.

It is now Tuesday, February the ninth. At least I think it's Tuesday, February the ninth. The days seem to run into each other, and it becomes very confusing. In any event, I'm now sitting in our hotel in Auckland, New Zealand.

The only problem we had out of Honolulu is that the fuel truck rolled up right on time. However, it broke down, and we couldn't get fuel from the truck to the airplane.

This created a twenty minute delay, which wasn't drastic, and from there it was a routine flight down to Canton.

As we approached Canton, I said "beautiful" too often, but it's the only word I know to describe the sight. It's a small atoll almost in a complete ring. The highest point on the island is maybe six or ten feet. Inside this ring of sand is a very shallow lagoon, with all these colors, the turquoise, the greens, and the blues. On the largest stretch of land is the runway. The runway starts at the water line and ends at the waterline; it takes up practically the whole island.

We landed there and found thirty-six people on the island, thirty-four men and two single girls. We sort of smiled at that. One of the guys told us the two single girls have their steadies and that sort of protects them, but it seems like an interesting situation inasmuch as these are all civilians, and they go out there on a years contract tour of duty. They work for Global Associates. At the moment Canton Island is in a caretaker status, but it was in the missile program. They tracked the missiles that were sent out from Vandenberg. But, inasmuch as the missile program has wound down now, they are on caretaker's status.

One interesting thing they told us was that there were two whale sharks living out there in the lagoon. These animals were very docile. People could swim in the lagoon and ride the whales' backs. They suggested that after we take off we should circle the lagoon at a low altitude and look for them. However we didn't do that. We fueled up and departed for Nandy in the Fiji group.

Between Honolulu and Canton Island we witnessed a weird sight. I've crossed the equator a few times in the past, but this is the first time I've been able to see us crossing the equator. We have on board the Litton inertial nav system, which gives a constant readout of our position. It updates itself every six seconds. We were watching as we approached the 0° latitude from the north. It kept working down, then suddenly crossed over, and now we're over in the south latitude. It was interesting to see the instant that we crossed the equator.

Between Canton Island and Nandy in the Fiji islands we had another interesting experience. We crossed the International Date Line. Here it was broad daylight, and suddenly we crossed from Sunday to Monday. We left Honolulu on Sunday morning, flew all day, and when we landed in Auckland it was Monday evening. I'd just finished filling out my expense account, and it seems strange to have a day in the week missing. There was no hotel for one night because there was no night there.

At any rate, we had a routine fuel stop at Nandy. It's a beautiful island that reminded us of Panama or Costa Rica. Very high humidity. The temperature was about 85°, and the humidity appeared to be about 100%. We climbed out of the airplane, and it was just like stepping into a sauna bath. We took our cameras out, but I don't believe we could have taken any pictures because the lenses immediately fogged up. They'd been cool and comfortable in the airplane, and going out into that high humidity they immediately fogged over. It was a beautiful place.

However, we were just as glad to get out of there. It was a routine flight down to Auckland. We landed there, and customs seemed quite perturbed by our arrival. We have all kinds of booze on the airplane, and they wanted to know how we were going to lock it up. I suggested we just lock up the airplane, use the whole plane as a container, and they could put that in bond. We could give them the key, and when we depart, instead of taking the liquor out of bond, we just open it up, and away we go. After much head shaking they allowed that maybe that was the most practical solution. They washed their hands of us and sent us on our way.

We have a tech rep in Auckland, a fellow by the name of Bill Juno, and he happened to be out there. He took us all down to the hotel and got us settled. Eventually, that is. We arrived at the hotel about seven o' clock, and, inasmuch as we were a little bit late, they'd sold our room. It was the height of tourist season here in Auckland. So they scouted around and found us a little lodge on the outskirts of town. Well, it isn't much but it's comfortable and beats sleeping in the airplane.

We went touring today in Auckland, and on one of the sundials I saw some of the distances that we covered. Honolulu to Auckland is 4,400 miles, and from San Francisco it's 6,500 miles. So in the last two days we've covered over 6,000 miles. We have a day off today and leave tomorrow morning at eleven o'clock. We're going down to Pemberton North on the North Island in New Zealand and pick up our passengers, and from there we'll go down to Christchurch.

On the tour, we passed over one of the bridges that crosses the channel here. When they built the bridge they built four lanes, but like everything else by the time they completed it, it was a bottleneck. When they decided they didn't have enough lanes, they put it out for bid to enlarge the bridge. The Japanese tendered an offer. They put extensions out, used the same foundation and put two lanes on each side. So it's now known as the "Nippon Clip-On," which brought a groan from everyone.

It is now Wednesday, February the ninth, and I'd like to give just a few impressions of New Zealand. One thing that is most unusual is the attire of many men here. They wear shorts, business shoes, socks up to their knees, a business shirt and tie, and many times a business jacket. So in effect it looks like the top half of their body is attired for business, and the bottom half of their body is attired for either pleasure or sports. It doesn't seem to fit. However, it does appear to be very comfortable, and in this warm climate I'm sure it's very cool.

Of course another thing that is unusual is that it's daylight savings down here. It doesn't get dark until half past nine at night, and it gets light about half past six in the morning. It's warm, very comfortable, in the eighties. It seems strange to have the people tell us they get freezing weather and some snow in July and August. Most unusual.

Today an unusual thing happened. We were at the airport getting ready to depart, and the agent for New

Zealand Airlines took me over to customs to check us out. He very suddenly said in a whisper, "You don't have any drugs or you don't use drugs do you?"

I said, "No, of course not."

He said, "Well, okay, fine. If you had, I would have taken you a different way, because a customs agent with a drug sniffing dog is coming toward us." And the dog did pass within a few feet of us. He added, "If you had any drugs on you that dog would have turned."

We flew from Auckland to Pemberton North, which is about 200 miles south of Auckland. We flew down there to pick up our passengers that left us in San Francisco. We landed at Pemberton North, and it was fantastic. The people there were either very curious or they hadn't seen a jet or both. People flocked to the airport. All the people working in the airport came over. We must have had 150 to 200 people climb on the airplane and examine it and look at it. Someone called up the local newspaper, and a photographer and reporter came out and took pictures, and I gave some information to their newspaper. When we took off I looked out the window, and there must have been fifty to a hundred people lined up at the edge of the ramp watching the departure. It just seems very strange to me in this day and age that a jet could create that much interest.

From Pemberton North we flew south to Christchurch. At the moment I'm sitting in a hotel room in Christchurch and about to hit the sack. I have to get up at five thirty for an eight a.m. departure for Sydney, Australia.

It is now Saturday the twelfth, and I'm sitting in a hotel in Brisbane, Australia. It was a routine flight from Christchurch to Syndey. On the climb out we flew by Mount Cook, which is 12,400 feet high. It was really amazing to see the amount of snow on the mountain, inasmuch as it is summertime down here. From Christchurch to Sydney is about 1,300 nautical miles, so it took us a little less than three hours. However, as we were still flying westbound, we picked up about two hours. We were off the ground at eight fifteen and landed in Sydney a little after nine o'clock.

In Sydney, we went up to the top of a small building. It was a forty-eight story building, and they had what they called a sky walk that went around the top of the building. But the amazing thing was the express elevator. I timed it. We went up the forty-eight floors in thirty seconds. It climbed so rapidly we were really concerned about whether the thing was going to stop or go out through the top of the building.

At Brisbane the next day we went to the airport to clean the plane, order fuel and catering, and file a flight plan. While I was in the terminal a TV camera crew showed up at the plane. They wanted pictures and the copilot let them take all they wanted. I would not have let them inside. It was to be shown at six that night. We watched it, and I was horrified at how the reporter bad-mouthed the corporation. The theme was, this is how the executives spend and waste the stockholders' money.

The next day the CEO, Forrest Shumway, asked me, "Frank, did you see the TV news last night?" I thought I was about to be fired. Then he said, "That was the funniest thing I have seen." What a relief. I can't believe that the third largest city in Australia would find a corporate jet newsworthy.

Back in Christchurch I saw something very fascinating at a post office. The post office had a very small courtyard, and in the center of this courtyard was a turntable that was maybe twenty-five or thirty feet in diameter. Trucks would come into this dead-end courtyard at fifteen or twenty miles per hour, go onto this turntable at a little bit of an angle, and slam on the brakes. The turntable would start spinning, and when the truck had reversed 180° they'd back into their docks and that would be that. The courtyard was so small it would have been a hardship to turn the trucks around. So here they had the turntable in the center, and it was all self-sufficient.

We were scheduled to go up to Cairns on the north-east coast of Australia. The folks wanted to go up there to visit the Great Barrier Reef. However, they've had eighty-nine inches of rain in the last four weeks. A lot of the streets are underwater. According to the newspaper, there are two cyclones off the coast bringing in stormy weather, high winds, and lots of rain. So we canceled that outing and spent an extra day here in Brisbane. We leave tomorrow morning for fuel in Alice Springs, which is in the center of Australia, and from there over to Bali.

While we were here we went out to a park where they raised koala bears. We call them koala bears, but we were told they were not bears – just call them koalas. They're the cute, little, fuzzy, teddy bear-like animals, and they are just as cute as a button. They were playing and climbing and eating. I took quite a few pictures of them, and they were just absolutely fantastic. They also have kangaroos there, and you'd walk in among them and pet them and examine them, and they'd examine you. All in all it was very fascinating.

It is now Monday the fourteenth. Yesterday we left Brisbane in the sparkling clear morning and flew to Alice Springs, a distance of some 1,200 miles. It took us two hours and thirty-nine minutes. Alice Springs is about the center of Australia. I think Australia is about the same width as the United States, so landing in Alice Spring would be something like landing in North Platte, Nebraska. The country between Brisbane and Alice Springs is interesting. It was all arid and desert-type land. However the colors would put our Painted Desert to shame. They had bright reds, vivid oranges and the color was just sparkling. It was really fantastic.

We landed in Alice Springs and it was just like landing in a town in Arizona. They had the sage and the sand, and they're about 2,000 feet high. Fortunately they have 8,000 feet of runway, because the temperature was about 95°. These jet engines don't like altitude or heat, and when you combine the two of them, they really don't like it. We loaded the airplane full of fuel because we wanted to make a side trip on the way up to Bali. When we poured the coal to it, started to roll, and we rolled and rolled and rolled. There is always a doubt in your mind as to whether the thing is going to start flying or not. It finally did, and we climbed up to 28,000 feet and proceeded down to Ayer's Rock.

The brochure says Ayers Rock is about 180 miles southwest of Alice Springs, and it's the world's largest monolith. I'm going to have to look that word up. It says Ayers Rock is a great sandstone rock about 1,200 feet high and about three miles around in circumference. It looks like a monstrous whale just sitting out in the middle of the desert all by itself, sticking up out of the ground. The brochure says, "At sunset the colors often change dramatically from burnt red to brilliant orange and then to crimson and finally to delicate purples and blues. At sunrise the first rays of the sun may make the rocks glow with fire. With moisture in the air it takes on a mantle of more subtle hues." It's hard to believe all these pictures in this brochure are of the same rock, because they have red pictures and blue pictures and gray pictures. When we saw it from the air it just looked like a rock. It would have been a rock in Arizona, but I will say it's a monstrous piece of sandstone. From there we climbed back up to 35,000 feet and headed for Bali.

From Alice Sprigs to Bali is 1,700 miles, and it took us about three hours and forty minutes. Between Alice Springs and Bali we crossed the point exactly opposite Los Angeles, so we're past the halfway point around the world.

Landing in Bali was like going into another world. Up until this point we'd been in English speaking countries. New Zealand and Australia were relatively dry, but very comfortable. Bali was very hot, very humid, and we immediately encountered the language problem. The Indonesian national airline agents handled us. They had trouble understanding us, and we had trouble understanding them. But we finally got our passengers on their way into the hotel, got our airplane cleaned, closed up, and headed for the hotel ourselves.

We got up this morning and toured Bali. I guess this is my second most favorite spot to visit. My first favorite was Venice, with its waterways, canals, boats, and so forth. This is a close second. It's a different world, something I've never seen before. Every available bit of land is terraced to grow rice. You'd think the ground of the hillsides is level, but if you look at it it's all terraced. They have the oxen out plowing in the water, and the Indonesian people are planting rice or picking rice, and the streets are just teeming with people and motorcycles. There are kids along both sides of the roads. There is a stream that's very muddy and dirty, but the kids are in there swimming, and people are washing clothes in it.

Now it's Wednesday, February the sixteenth, and as they say in the movies, "If it's the sixteenth it must be Singapore." We are sitting in Singapore. To go back to yesterday, I have just a few more thoughts on Bali.

The women with their sarongs were very attractive. They carried heavy loads on their heads just like the gals in Haiti. Some of the loads where so heavy it was hard to imagine how they got them up on their heads without considerable help. Also about half of the people in crews working on the roads were women. Here again it was all hand labor. They carry stones and rocks and sand and mortar. The girls had large, flat, platter-like dishes on their heads with these rocks and stones, and that's the way they carried it over the spot they were repairing. They were just most interesting to watch.

All of the crew has been complaining about the missionaries. We had always heard about the topless in Bali. We did see about five topless. Unfortunately, all five were well over sixty and not too attractive.

We visited one temple, walked around the corner, and there was a gal taking a shower. It happened to be a temple of the water gods. She wasn't a god or a goddess, but it was rather unexpected. The many temples in Bali are so attractive with their peaks and their stones and ornaments made out of concrete. It's just an amazing place.

It was hard to get used to the money there, though. There are about 425 rupees to the dollar. So the landing fee, for instance, is 152 American dollars, which came out to 64,600 rupees. Dinner was about 4,000 rupees, breakfast 1,500. Roy carried the money to buy fuel. Fuel was cash only there, so I had to get half a million rupees to pay for the fuel. Fantastic.

We departed Bali in extremely heavy rain. As they say in Texas it was a real frog strangler. We got soaked pre-flighting the airplane and getting fuel and getting our passengers on board. We flew to Bandung, which is about sixty miles southwest of Jakarta.

We were concerned about whether we'd be able to land there because of the location of the airport. It's down in a little saucer like valley, and it's a VFR (visual flight rules) operation only. When we broke out below the clouds we could look over and see the valley, so we proceeded on and landed.

Bandung is a combination military and civilian airport, and we did need special permission to land there. When we landed, the Indonesian Air Force came out and drove up to see this strange bird that had descended upon them. We sat there for four hours waiting for our passengers. We managed to make arrangements while we were there to go from Bandung to Jakarta, clear out of Indonesia there, and then up to Singapore. It would save us about two hours of flying and about 1,000 miles. Unfortunately, it was a disaster. The man who got us clearance into Jakarta assured us there would be customs in the North airport. We landed there and taxied in, and no one was expecting us. No one was willing to help us. First they wanted their landing fee and their parking fee, and it turned out there was no customs and immigration there. So things were going from bad to worse.

They said we'd have to go to the other airport. We didn't have a landing permit for the other airport. And time was running out. The airport at Singapore has a night curfew, and if you don't get in there by eleven o'clock, you can't land there. The big airport at Singapore takes special permission. The way things were working we figured we might have to spend the night in Jakarta. But fortunately one gentleman took pity on us, and he went to work and called the other airport. He made arrangements for customs and immigration to take a taxi and come over to this airport and stamp our passports, clear us out of the country, and get us going. They came over in a cab, and they inspected the plane and stamped our passports.

With a sigh of relief we fired up just as the sun was going down and proceeded to Singapore. It's only a distance of about 600 miles. It only took us about an hour and a half. Fortunately the weather was fine at Singapore, so we found the airport and landed. We sent the passengers to the hotel, and we thought, "Boy, after this long day our troubles are over."

But we had one more incident. They have a fixed base operation in Singapore with a name of Helio Orient. One of their men came into the cockpit and was going to direct us to a parking spot. We saw the taxiway across the field, and it looked like it was dirt. We didn't want to taxi on it. He said, "No, no, there's a steel mat on it. The grass is coming up through the steel mat, and it's perfectly solid." So, as much as it was his operation, like fools we listened to him and started to taxi.

He said, "No, turn left, turn left." We started to turn left and ran off the steel mat, and the airplane started to sink in the mud. We thought, man, this is really a disaster. We shut down, got our flashlights out, and inspected the situation. We were sinking in, but it wasn't up to the axles, and the mat was about eight to ten feet in front of us. We got in and fired up all four engines and, with lots of power, drove it right through the mud and back up on to the mat, and there we were. The moral of the story is, don't listen to anybody.

After our fiasco at the Singapore airport we had a very pleasant surprise when we checked into the hotel. We were in the Mandarin Hotel. It was late and they had overbooked the rooms. We had reserved three singles. They had two singles, and inasmuch as they didn't have a third, they had a presidential suite open. So they put me in the presidential suite at the same price as a single room.

When I walked through the door, it was really quite a sight. It was a monstrous living room. The living room was about the size of our living room and family room combined at home. It had a built-in bar, well-stocked with all the different wines, liquors, brandies, and ice. It had stereo music in all the rooms. Along one wall was a long closet to take care of fifteen to twenty suitcases. Back in the master bedroom was a double king size bed. Indirect lighting, stereo music, and in the vanity section a wall-to-wall mirror. Just absolute luxury.

A curious thing happened. Here I was on the eleventh floor in all this luxury, and, as I was sitting here reading a book, out of the corner of my eye I saw a mouse run out and into the bathroom. I went in there to see where he had gone, and he had just plain disappeared. So here's a Singapore mouse living in the presidential suite on the eleventh floor, and that must be a little bit of something for the mouse.

Another thing amid all this luxury. I look out the window and can see hovels, shacks, lean-tos, obviously quite a bit of poverty. It just doesn't seem right that so few have so much.

Last night we went out on the town. This one section was a monstrous parking lot by day, but by five or six all the cars are gone. It's a nightly occurrence that people bring in cooking stands, tables, and chairs. We walked through, and there were all kinds of things cooking on barbecue grills. They had gas stoves, frying grease. Many of the things smelled delicious. Some of the frying grease didn't smell too good, but it was quite a sight to see all the different squids and fishes, the meat barbecuing, and people eating with chopsticks. We were tempted to eat there, but thought better of it. We thought, with as much flying as we had to do the next day, we couldn't take any chance with food poisoning.

Yesterday we had a routine flight from Singapore to Penang in Malaysia. It's only a distance of 350 miles. It took us about an hour. We landed at a pretty airport. It reminded me of an island in the Caribbean. However, this island is covered in a dense jungle. The airport's on the south side of the island; the hotels are on the north side. The north side has really wide, beautiful white beaches, like Daytona Beach. They're setting this up as a tourist center. They're building a new runway at the airport, a new terminal to take jumbo jets, and new hotels adjacent to these wide, beautiful beaches.

Today we took a little tour. The highlight of the tour was the Temple of the Reclining Buddha. They have a female Buddha made out of plaster or concrete, and it must be at least 150 foot long. Just unbelievably long. Underneath the Buddha there's a room with thousands of little cubicles. In each cubicle is an urn containing ashes of somebody who has been cremated. There's a little plastic door in front of each cubicle and it has the dates of the life of the person and also a photo of the person. 98 percent of these urns were porcelain. However, some of them were tin cans. As a matter of fact, a couple of them still had labels on them. Like a Campbell's soup can. One of them was a kerosene can. I though that was very interesting.

On the way back to the hotel we went by the waterfall gardens. This was a holiday, and there were literally thousands of people in this beautiful park. Lots of flowers, trees, and a stream. The monkeys were the most fascinating part. Hundreds and hundreds of wild monkeys came out of the jungles. They came to the edge of the park, and people fed them bread and peanuts. The monkeys would be looking at the people and the people at the monkeys. It was all most fascinating.

We left Penang a week before yesterday. In some respects it seems like it was a month ago. When we arrived at the airport at Penang, pre-flighting the airplane we noticed all the Malaysian airplanes were taking off downwind, and we wondered about it. Because we were heavily loaded, maybe a bit overloaded, and the runway wasn't that long, we wanted to take off into the wind. They cleared us to do so. When we were taxiing out, we ran over our pre-flight check list. Then we rolled down the runway, and we had just reached about ninety knots when all of a sudden there was a loud crack, and we dipped down. It was evidently a sharp depression in the runway, and the jolt was quite startling. All of us jumped and wondered whether there'd been any damage to the airplane. We even wondered if the landing gear would come up. Later on inspection, there didn't appear to be any damage. At any rate we found out why the Malaysian airlines were taking off downwind. The opposite end of the runway was so rough they didn't want to use it. I really felt like somebody could have mentioned the fact to us and saved us a bit of agony.

We departed Malaysia and overflew Thailand, Burma, Bangladesh (which used to be East Pakistan), and then entered India over Calcutta. It seems strange talking to air traffic control centers in Bangkok, Rangoon, Calcutta, and Delhi when we're used to air traffic control centers in Los Angeles, Cleveland, Chicago, and Dallas. We made landfall in India at the mouth of the Ganges river, and it reminded me very much of the Mississippi River Delta. This river through the centuries has brought down lots of silt and has produced a monstrous delta area.

About fifty miles inland, we overflew Calcutta. It was a clear day and we could see the river. From there we went up into Dehli. Originally, we had requested to overfly Nepal so we could circle the Himayalas, particularly Mt. Everest. However, that overfly permit did not come through. Maybe it was just as well that we didn't get the overfly. Due to the warm weather and heavy load we had consumed much more fuel than we originally anticipated. It took us over five hours to fly to Delhi, and when we landed we had about forty-five minutes of fuel in reserve. Normally, we'd have about an hour and forty-five minutes.

We attributed it to the warm weather, the heavy load, and the fact that we couldn't really fill up the tanks at Penang.

When we landed at Delhi, they parked us in the boondocks on an unused runway and brought buses to take the passengers in. On both sides of us were Russian airplanes. There was a monstrous Russian turboprop parked just to the left of us, and they were loading two or three tons of mail sacks. I asked our agent, "What in the world could be in all those mail sacks?"

"Oh," he said, "those are diplomatic messages." There must be a communication gap somewhere, because I couldn't believe there were that many mail sacks of diplomatic messages.

The original plan was to fly down today, Monday, to Agra, pick up our people, go back to Delhi for customs, and then on to Lahore in Pakistan. But customs canceled that idea for us as we had lots of baggage, liquor, gifts, cameras, and so forth on board. They wouldn't let us fly to Agra with all of that, thinking that we'd maybe go down there and sell it. They wanted us to unload the entire airplane, put everything in bond, go down to Agra, pick up our people, come back, and get our things out of bond before leaving the country. But looking at the airport and the situation, we could easily imagine that everything might not get back on the airplane.

We even tried to talk customs into sending an Asian along. He could ride along with us and watch everything on the airplane, ride back with us, and we would pay him for his time. One of the young agents was all in accord with that. I think he wanted the ride and the time off. But the head customs man vetoed the plan, so that was that. I discussed the situation with our boss, and he said, "No way." They would drive back to Delhi from Agra, and we would depart from here. We put seals on all the doors, all the windows, on the belly hatches, and we left the airplane parked there.

Yesterday we rented a car in Delhi and drove down to Agra, which is about 125 miles southeast. Agra is where the Taj Mahal is located. We wanted to see that. The ride down there took about three and a half hours. It was one of their main roads, but by our standards, it was a third-rate road. It was just teeming with humanity: motorcycles, bicycles, oxen, camels, taxis, tractors, buses. Naturally, we couldn't make any time.

When we were on the outskirts of Delhi, we saw some sort of religious ceremony coming up the road. There was a horse-drawn cart with lanterns, colors, and lights, and maybe two or three hundred people chanting and throwing fire crackers. We stopped to take some pictures. I was very concerned about whether we were doing anything that would arouse the anger of these people. But the cab driver assured us that tourists here were a privileged group. The government wanted tourists, and whatever pictures we wanted to take were okay with them.

It was amazing to see huge oxen in teams pulling monstrous wooden carts with extremely heavy loads of lumber or hay or things covered with hay. These carts had huge wooden wheels. They might have been six feet in diameter and made out of solid wood. It's similar to what you might see in pictures of Malaysia.

I had never associated camels with India, but we saw hundreds of camels and it was amazing. People riding camels, camels pulling carts, people herding camels; I just had not expected to see them. There was commotion along the road ahead, so we stopped. A pack of six or eight dogs were working over the carcass of some large animal. Surrounding this scene were maybe twenty or twenty-five huge vultures waiting for the dogs to finish so they could move in. We were told that the vultures were scared of the dogs, so they didn't try to drive the dogs off.

It was Sunday, but there were lots of people working on the roads, and here again the tools were very primitive, picks and shovels. The women in this country also carried loads on their heads – heavy loads. The women carried loads of sand, gravel, and rock in flat pans on their heads. There were also hundreds of women carrying water on their heads in bright, polished brass jars. They would go down to the stream, fill these jars with water, and carry them back to their huts or homes.

We stopped for cold beer about halfway to Agra, and there were some gypsies at the entrance of this little restaurant. They had dancing bears. One man had a cobra that must have been twelve to fifteen feet long. They had snake charmers and snakes coming out of the baskets. We went out and took pictures and everyone started jabbering about money for having their picture taken. So we had to take care of that.

While we sat there having a beer, we saw maybe twenty-five or thirty wild parrots up in the tree. The colors were vivid and very beautiful.

Further on we stopped at a temple, and there was a young lad there with a burlap sack. In the sack he had a cobra. In his arms he had a mongoose. He wanted to put on a fight for us. I don't know why we declined. It would have been interesting to have seen it. We planned to stop there on the way back. But by the time we got there, we were tired and it was getting dark, so we didn't get to see a mongoose-cobra fight at all.

The scenes along the highway were out of the last century: little mud huts, dirt floors, thousands of people, little cooking fires, roadside stands. Most of the people looked like they hadn't had a bath possibly in all of their lives. The living was extremely primitive, just hard to believe. But people appeared to be happy and laughing.

The transportation was most unusual. They had three-wheeled bikes with the pedaler or driver up front and a seat across the back two wheels. We saw as many as four or five people sitting on the seat in the back of one bike, with this poor driver trying to pull the load. But the amazing part was that you would see these things way out in the country. They'd be pedaling along, and you'd just wonder where they came from and where they were going to. There might not appear to be anything within five or six miles of the place. These tractors pulling carts loaded with maybe fifty people were also on the highways. The people were hanging all over the tractor. We passed a bus where the people were jammed in like sardines. You wondered how, if it did come to a stop, a person in the back would ever get out. We saw people hanging out the windows and hanging on the back of the bus.

We saw the Taj Mahal, and it's really everything it's cracked up to be. It's beautiful, like going into another world. The ride down to Agra was desolate, dirty, and dusty, showing all sorts of poverty. But when we went through the gate to the Taj Mahal, everything was sparkling clean, green, gleaming. It's obviously one of the seven wonders of the world.

The workmanship on the Taj Mahal was just fantastic. We were told that there were 20,000 men working on it for twenty-two years, and they carried the marble from a spot 180 miles away. They built a camp every ten miles. The people would carry the slate ten miles, spend the night, carry another ten miles and spend the night – a constant production line. I'm going to have to buy a book about the Taj Mahal. Now that I've seen it it's really aroused my interest.

We also saw a wedding yesterday in the streets of Agra. It turned into a Chinese fire drill. The groom sat on a horse dressed entirely in gold – gold jacket, pants, shoes, and hat – and the bride was nowhere in sight. I don't know what her situation was. But surrounding the horse were maybe seventy-five people chanting and laughing and knocking sticks together. They were holding up money. I don't know what that was all about, probably a good luck charm of some sort. A ragged five piece band led the procession. From the sounds of the music I wasn't sure if they were all playing the same piece. They all seemed to be doing their own thing on their musical instruments. Everyone seemed to be very happy except for the groom. He sat on his horse, looking very dejected, as though he wished the whole thing could get over with.

Yesterday was ulcer time.

It was just a short flight from Delhi to Lahore in Pakistan. We had requested the direct route from Delhi to Lahore, which is a distance of about 350 miles. However, the military in India would not allow that route due to military restrictions. The only route they would approve was straight west into Pakistan and then back north to Lahore. It doubled the distance to about 700 miles. The clearance was only good for an hour, and our passengers were an hour late. The authorities threatened to cancel our flight plan, to in effect make us start over. We were really, really nervous.

We loaded the passengers and fired up the engines quick and requested clearance. We were ten minutes over time, but they gave us clearance. As we poured the coal to it and breathed a sigh of relief, a light flashed on our panel indicating that our #3 computer had dropped offline. So we reverted back to manual. It wasn't too important; it just meant that we couldn't get full power out of that engine. However, we had three other engines, and we just kept right on going, really breathing a sigh of relief to be on our way.

The charts say specifically that before entering Pakistan we must establish contact with their air traffic control. We called, and we called, and we called, and by this time it was pitch dark. There was no moon whatsoever. We had entered Pakistan without clearance. We were entering Pakistan also on a route that had not been approved. We were in Pakistan thirty minutes before we made contact. All these countries are so security conscious, so we didn't know if we'd be intercepted, or what our reception would be.

We finally turned north and managed to contact a little tower at some small airport. We gave him our position and had him relay our information to Lahore traffic control center. A few minutes later he came back and said the center had cleared us down to 29,000 feet. He instructed us to contact the Lahore control on such and such a frequency. It finally seemed that things were going much more like they were supposed to. We let down and finally saw the lights of Lahore coming into view. As we were landing, we noticed that they had runway lights indicating the runway, but beside each electric light was a flare or smoke pot. It was almost as if they didn't trust their generating system, and if their lights failed they would still have these flare pots to mark the runway.

One of the reasons we were extremely nervous going into Lahore is that Lahore is in the northeast corner of Pakistan, and it's not too far from the China border.

When we taxied up to the terminal a whole mob of people met us, some in uniform, some in rags. However, they were all friendly. The only problem was that everyone was trying to help and contradicting each other and consequently getting nothing done. But we finally cleared customs and got checked into the hotel. Once again we had hotel problems. We had arrived late, and they weren't sure whether we were coming or not, so they sold our rooms. But they did scrounge us up a few, and we had to double up for once.

Today we have a long flight. We're leaving at eleven o'clock. The flight will take us out of Pakistan, over Afghanistan, and into Iran. We will land at Tehran for fuel. All these countries require overfly permits with route and time stated in the request. From Tehran we'll fly over Turkey, Bulgaria, Yugoslovia, and Austria, and then head into Germany. The big bottleneck here is Bulgaria, a very strict iron curtain country. We do have an overfly permit, but they've been known to turn back an airplane that's approaching the border even though they have a permit. Once we get by Bulgaria we feel like we should be home free.

I never realized that so many countries in the world drove on the wrong side of the street, on the left side. Every country we've been in so far has driven on the left side: New Zealand, Australia, Indonesia, Singapore, Malaysia, and now Pakistan. We've been driving on this side of the street for so long now it's going to seem strange to be back on the right side.

The day before yesterday wasn't one of our better days. We got up in Lahore and, after a short breakfast, had a wild ride to the airport. Our cab driver was absolutely berserk. He'd skin cars and pedestrians who were walking across the street – it appeared as if he was seeing just how close he could come to them. We tried to get him to slow down, but he just grinned at us and kept on driving wildly. The copilot almost put his feet through the floorboards two or three times. It was with a sigh of relief that we reached the airport.

On the way, at every street corner there must have been five or six policemen. It seemed strange. When we got to the airport there were all kinds of military. We found out that one of the Arab princes was leaving. His Falcon Jet was sitting out on the ramp. They had a red carpet that must have been two hundred feet wide and at least sixty or seventy yards long. It was a monstrous carpet. Of course there were all kinds of military spectators. The prince arrived in a big, long limousine that drove right out onto the carpet with its escort. He got out of the limousine, into his airplane, closed the door, and away he went.

We got off on schedule, climbed up to altitude, overflew Afghanistan with no problem, and entered Iran. The territory was absolutely desolate, barren desert. It was hard to believe it could support anything. Someone remarked that he couldn't see how Alexander the Great got his troops across such forbidding land.

Approaching Tehran, we tried to raise a ground handler who had been set up for us by British Airways. We couldn't raise him, so we tried to raise Pan Am. We couldn't raise them, so we landed without any contact with anybody. I was a bit tired already. The distance from Lahore to Tehran is 1,500 miles, and it took us three hours and fifty minutes flight time. We started out without too much headwind but ended up with 100 knots.

There we were on the ground in Tehran, parked out in the middle of the boondocks. No one was there to meet us, no customs, no immigration, no fuel, no nobody. I finally flagged down a passing vehicle, and, with sign language, got them to take me up to British Airways. They weren't too happy because they weren't expecting us, but when they found out that I already had the flight plan ready to file and was willing to pay the landing and parking fees, they took us through customs and immigration and got the flight plan filed and away we went.

The distance from Tehran to Stuttgart, Germany was a long haul, 2,400 miles, and had the winds been as forecast we could have just barely made it. As it turned out the winds were much stronger than forecast, and it didn't take us long to decide that we were not going to make it.

After departing Tehran, the first country we flew over was Turkey. We were amazed at all the snow on the ground. We'd been south of the equator, and everything had been hot. Now we were flying over snow. Next we came to Bulgaria. Bulgaria is communist, really the bottleneck of the whole route. The distance in Bulgaria is only 200 miles, but it's the most important link in the whole flight. They evidently had our permit and cleared us through.

We sailed across Bulgaria into Yugoslavia. By this time we realized we had to land somewhere for fuel, and we were in a quandary as to where to land. We looked in the book and decided some place in Austria would be the logical location. We called ahead to Graz and asked if they had jet fuel, and they did. We asked if they had Shell because by this time we were out of money, and they said that they did. We got a revised clearance and let down and landed in Graz.

We had a shock after we landed as there was only one fuel truck, and it was British Petroleum. We didn't have a BP credit card, and he wouldn't take a Shell or Exxon credit card. It was cash. We had about $900 left, having gone through $8,000 so far for various expenses. So we said, “Ok, we'll pay cash.” He started pumping. I pulled out a traveler's checkbook and started writing out a traveler's check. The poor fuel man almost had a heart attack. He grabbed the checkbook and slammed it on the ground and jumped up and down and got red in the face and said that we'd promised him cash, and now we weren't going to give him cash. We'd always thought that traveler's checks were good as cash, but in this case they apparently weren't. I had to hit the chairman of the board up for $500 cash, and the president of the Garrett

Corporation donated $200. In the end I had $200 left. That got us on the way. The CEO laughed and said it was the first time he had to pass the hat to pay for fuel.

From Graz to Stuttgart is a distance of about 400 miles. It took us a little over an hour, and we landed in the dark about an hour and a half late. As we taxied up and opened the door, two big limousines drove up with Garrett representatives who had been waiting there for our people. They loaded all the baggage into cars and were going to whisk them to the hotel when I said, "Hey, I think we really ought to check in with customs and immigrations before we leave the airport." They allowed as that'd be ok, so they went down to the terminal to check with customs and immigration.

All in all it was a long day. We flew ten hours. The flight from Tehran to Graz was five hours. And then Graz to Stuttgart was a little over an hour. Ten hours of flying, and duty hours were about fifteen. We picked up four hours, so it was still early in the day, but the body clock said it was around midnight. Needless to say we were a bit tired. We got to the hotel and had a couple of beers and something to eat and then hit the sack.

I called GG from Stuttgart. The phone system is fabulous. You just dial a five digit code, the area code for California, and the home phone number, and the phone starts ringing, bang, right from the hotel room. The charge is billed to your room automatically. Of course the next day I had a bit of a shock. It didn't seem to me that we'd talked all that long, but the bill was $48.

We got up yesterday morning in Stuttgart and planned to spend the day doing a little sightseeing. But the boss called us and said, "Hey, change in plans. We want to go over this afternoon to Strasbourg in France and spend the night there." The only problem was that the copilot and I had already sent out our laundry. We called the desk, and they managed to trace it and stop it before it was sent out, and they sent it back up to the room.

It's only eighty miles over to Strasbourg. The weather was beautiful, and the scenery was beautiful. We landed, and... another day, another country. We went downtown and saw the Cathedral, and the famous clock was very beautiful.

From Strasbourg to Zurich is only about 100 miles, but you cover three countries. From France, you overfly Germany and then land in Switzerland. It was a routine flight. We took our boss there to catch a 747 from Zurich to New York. He had a meeting the following day, so he couldn't wait for us. We were met there by Jet Aviage, who rushed him over to the terminal to catch his flight. After looking around for a bit, we flew back to Strasbourg and arrived there about eleven o'clock.

We were supposed to depart at three, but our people didn't show up until six. We were getting tired by this time, and their arrival at the airport was perfect timing – in the wrong direction. They arrived right in the middle of a thunderstorm. By the time we got all the people and all the baggage on board, everybody was soaked.

From Strasbourg up to London was only about an hour and ten minute flight, but here again we had poor timing. We arrived over Luton airport, which is fifty miles north of London, about the same time as the thunderstorm. There were showers in the whole area, and it was pitch dark, of course. Lightining and heavy rain. We were cleared for an ILS approach. The president of Garrett was sitting in the jump seat as we shot the approach. He's a pilot also. Unfortunately, the computer for the integrated flight system on the left side wasn't working too well, so it was sort of a sloppy approach. We saw the approach lights off to our right as we broke out under the overcast and with the shallowest turn we landed, full reverse, and taxied in, tired but very glad to be there.

At the moment we're in London. It's rainy, dreary, and cold. We went out to the airport today to do the chores, clean the airplane, and get ready for the final leg of the flight.

At the airport we ran into a man by the name of Phil Stacey, who is a pilot for Kirk Kerkorian. Kerkorian is a multimillionaire from Las Vegas and owns one of the few private 707s in the world. They'd arrived non-stop from Newark into London last night with a distinguished passenger on board. They brought Frank Sinatra over for his concert tour, with about twelve other people. The twelve people had over a hundred pieces of baggage. It filled the back cargo pit. We went through his airplane, and it was just like a flying apartment. It had a master bedroom, a shower, of course a bar, a kitchen, a film room, murals, and a thick rug. It was just like a house aloft, just beautiful.

The last day is always the worst. It's such a long day. The distance from London to Los Angeles is about 6,000 miles and involves flying four legs with ground stops, approximately thirteen hours of flying.

We got up at about five in the morning, which is the same as nine the night before, Los Angeles time. We departed at nine a.m. for Shannon, which is a little less than 400 miles, just about an hour's flight. We like to land at Shannon and fill up with fuel for the flight across the Atlantic to make sure we have plenty of kerosene to get us to the shore. There's usually very strong prevailing winds from the west across the Atlantic, and, as a rule this time of year, we have just about an hour's reserve when we hit Newfoundland. However, yesterday when we flew over, we had +1 component, so we had lots of fuel when we saw the coastline.

Gander and St. Johns were very soupy. They had freezing drizzle, fog, and very low ceilings. We elected to continue onto Stephensville in Nova Scotia, which was another 180 miles west. The weather was good there, though very cold. We landed in Stephensville and cleared customs, got kerosene, and took off for Green Bay, Wisconsin.

We'd been into Green Bay a couple times before to clear customs, and they were excellent. The customs officer came on the airplane and took care of any excess duty and cleared us right there without unloading a single bag. We were looking forward to another easy inspection. However, when we were about 200 miles east, the center told us that they had word that we were not to land at Green Bay, that we were to land at either Milwaukee or Minneapolis. We questioned the reason why, and the reason was that there was no immigration available at Green Bay at that time.

Since we'd come around the world, the airplane was loaded with trinkets, gifts, boxes, and bags. It was packed like a sardine can. We could picture a bunch of customs guys meeting the airplane and having to unload everything. But we were rather low on fuel, so we didn't have much choice.

We landed at Milwaukee, and it was a real foul up. Immigration had sent word that we should land at Milwaukee, so they cleared us. But customs didn't show up, and they didn't show up, and they didn't show up. After an hour immigration was pretty embarrassed by the whole thing. They called customs three times. I guess they were busy some place else. Finally they said, "Oh, the heck with it. Tell them they're cleared, and go on home." So customs never did poke in our airplane or charge us any excess duty for all the things we had on board. We fired up and departed Milwaukee for Los Angeles.

As I say, it was an extremely long day. 6,000 miles in thirteen hours. We landed at Los Angeles at six p.m., which by our body clock was two in the morning, London time. Needless to say, we were thrashed.

To summarize just a bit this whole around-the-world flight, we flew about sixty-four hours. It was an average ground speed of about 430 mph. We flew 27,600 miles and burned about 29,000 gallons of kerosene. That comes to about $18,000 for kerosene alone. As you can see, it's just a little bit more than a gallon per mile, which isn't very efficient. But considering the airplane had four engines, I suppose it was not too bad.

All in all it was a very interesting and wonderful trip. But having been away for three weeks, it felt wonderful to be back home.

1977 Paris Air Show

June, 1977

We started planning this flight on the first of May for a third of June departure. GG left for Europe on May tenth and was to meet me in Paris on June fourth. Our airplane went into maintenance on May twentieth, and they found a cracked frame that grounded the plane. It was a six week job to change this frame, and we knew immediately that that airplane could not make the schedule.

We had another airplane that had just been converted to Garrett engines, but it had never flown. They put three shifts a day on it working like mad to get it ready for the scheduled departure. Well, they managed to get it ready, and we test-flew it. As a matter of fact, I took it on a sales demo tour two days before June third, worked the bugs out of it – at least a majority of the bugs – and we were on schedule for Paris.

Our schedule began with Los Angeles to Newburg, NY. We were to pick up two people in New York, then fly on to Gander in Newfoundland, fill up with fuel, and jump off non-stop for Paris. In Los Angeles I filed a flight plan for Los Angeles to Newburg. At the last minute the chairman of the board showed up and requested we drop two members in Washington. Naturally I said, "Yes, sir," and changed the flight plan. This added two hours to an already long day. We had a three man crew, so it wasn't all that bad. The weather was good all the way, and that made life a lot easier.

It was about eleven p.m. local time when we departed Gander for Paris. We noticed two interesting things on this leg. First, we were flying so far north that we could see a streak of light from the sun all the way over, just below the horizon. It was like first light before sunrise all the way across. The second interesting thing was that we could see a contrail from another airplane in the moonlight about a mile off to our right, and we paralleled this contrail from Gander all the way to Shannon, a distance of about 1900 miles. As the bloomin' Navy says, it was off to our starboard. We have an inertial computer on board. These inertial computers are extremely accurate. They're never off more than two miles in 2000 miles. Obviously, the other airplane had an inertial nav hooked to its autopilot as well. I thought it was phenomenal that there were two airplanes at the same altitude in the sky and the tracks more or less parallel a mile apart for that great a distance.

From Gander to Paris is about 2,500 statute miles, and it took us five hours and twenty-two minutes. The time change from Los Angeles to Paris is nine hours, so we landed there at about nine in the morning, having been on duty for eighteen hours. This is a long time, but we don't do it every day.

At the moment I'm sitting in a hotel in Bergen, on the west coast of Norway. The date is June the fourteenth. The last ten days have passed so rapidly, but I'll see if I can go back and recount a few of the things that happened.

The last time that I reported was June fourth, and that was the day we arrived in Paris, and I met GG. Not having seen her for some three weeks, it took us a while to catch up on the news and the odds and ends.

We were lucky there in Paris. The Garrett Corporation had assigned our crew a car with a full-time driver, for whenever we wanted to use him to go to the air show or sightsee. So we had this car and driver at our disposal 100 percent of the time. He was the same driver we'd had two years ago, and he's really a character. He's a Turk and speaks fluent French. His English is quite good, too. When he was assigned the job of driver, they wanted to assign him to a VIP, but he said, no, he wanted to drive the crew or he wouldn't drive anybody. So they assigned him the crew again.

We had a good rapport with him. The man is seventy-three years old and drives like a wild man. We had trouble keeping him slowed down. He claimed that he had never touched a fender. We took bets on how many days it would be before he did crease a fender. It was four days. We got him to slow down finally.

Anyway, this seventy-three year old driver is a tennis instructor. He teaches tennis, and when professionals come to town and need a partner to practice with, he practices with them. He tried to get me to play with him, but GG was there, and it was raining most every day. I didn't have my equipment anyhow, which is probably just as well.

The hotel, by our standards, was about fourth rate, a little Parisian hotel, narrow, with dark hallways, and very small rooms. Our room had two single beds in it which were practically wall to wall. Only one of us could get dressed at a time. The other had to stay in bed. It had a satisfactory bathroom. The hotel did have a little bar, so we managed to get by, no problem there.

One amusing thing did happen at that hotel. We came in late one night and stepped into the elevator. There was a little Frenchman standing in front of the buttons. There always has been a language problem, so I held up two fingers, pointed to the controls, and requested he push number two. In perfect English he came back and said, "I know what two means." Well, we laughed about that ever since.

I don't know where the week got to. We went out to the air show three times, I guess. The Garrett Corporation has a chalet right on the edge of the runway with a bar and a dining room where they entertain customers and VIPs.

You can sit out on the patio and watch the air demonstrations, the fly-bys.

In the other parts of the airport they have the static displays, with various types of airplanes. All of the equipment displays are in the large buildings. I got to go through the Concorde, which was fascinating.

In Paris we went to the Montmartre twice. We went to the Lido one night, and would you believe we went to a Chinese restaurant, too. I know it sounds awful strange to go to Paris and go out for Chinese food, but it was a little spot that GG had found, and it was delicious.

GG was scheduled to leave for home on the Friday the tenth. That day came all too soon. I took her to the Charles de Gaulle Airport, and she departed from there.

That same morning we had a flight from Paris to take some people to Copenhagen. When we arrived at the airport it was raining cats and dogs, just teeming. It was a real frog strangler, as we say in Texas. We preflighted the airplane in all this rain and got soaking wet, of course. We put power on the plane, and evidently two of our engine fuel computers had shorted out, which meant that we wouldn't get full power out of two of the engines. However, we were relatively light, so it was no major problem.

Paris to Copenhagen is about 600 miles, an hour and twenty minutes – nothing drastic. We arrived there, and, while we were refueling the airplane (we have centerpoint fueling), the fuel went through the vent and started pouring out on the ramp. Everybody was running around, concerned. We shut it off, and they called the fire department. The fire trucks came and unwound the hoses and washed all this kerosene down the drain. Everybody was looking at us. I didn't feel like we were overly welcome.

As we taxied out we were instructed to follow another airplane. When we arrived at takeoff position the control asked us if we had permission to cross a runway that we crossed. We told him that we understood that we had. He said, "Well, ok, no problem, but I don't think you did." We took off.

This was an empty leg going back to Paris. We only had a two man crew at this point. Inasmuch as it was an empty leg, Art was flying the airplane from the left seat. He's a very conscientious, good pilot. However, this was his first jet, and it's an awful lot to learn at once. First jet, first APU, first centerpoint fueling, first HF radio, first inertial nav, first European flying. It's an awful lot to learn at one time. Anyway, we just leveled off at 35,000 feet and I was doing paperwork and handling the radio when I heard him exclaim, "Hey, I can't control this thing!"

We were in a bit of a dive, and it looked like we were right on the red line. I thought it was a mach problem. When you approach the max mach, the plane tends to tuck under and go into a dive. I pulled the power back, and it turned out that wasn't the problem. Pulling the power back exaggerated the problem. It turned out that somchow or other the trim had been disconnected, so I went to emergency trim and got it back under control.

As we were climbing back up to altitude the ground controller came in and said, "Did you guys leave your altitude?" Our transponder gives a readout of our altitude, and it must have startled him to see us dive 2,000 feet. I told him the autopilot had malfunctioned, and we were climbing back to altitude. He said, "Well, ok, no problem." We proceeded on back to Paris. This just wasn't one of our better days.

That was on Friday the tenth, Paris to Copenhagen to Paris. On Saturday the eleventh, we took our regular eight passengers from Paris to Oslo, Norway, a distance of about 850 miles. We had eight people, but I believe we had enough baggage for fifteen. I've never seen so much baggage in my life. But we have two families on board, and of course the women pack for Paris, they pack for Oslo, they're going to Leningrad, they're going to Budapest – party dresses, walking outfits, the whole shebang.

Then on the twelfth we had to go back to Paris to pick up another group of people, then back to Oslo. We got in rather late.

We were up at five o'clock to depart Oslo on Monday for Bergen. Unfortunately, the weather was a bit stormy. We couldn't see any of the ground. Normally they tell us it's a very beautiful flight from Oslo to Bergen, with all the mountains and snow and the fjords and so forth.

I read in a pamphlet that Bergen was founded in the year 1070. That really makes us think that our country is very young. Bergen is the second largest city in Norway. It's a very beautiful spot. It reminds you of Cape Cod or other parts of the New England coast. It's a seaport.

Along the wharf they have all these counters and stands set up where they're selling all different kinds of fish. The housewives, and the tourists as well, swarm down and watch the selling and the haggling. These fishermen are unbelievable the way they can clean the fish right on the spot. The knives must be razor sharp. Within three strokes the fish is clean and in the package and delivered to the housewife.

On the same wharf the florists have their displays of plants, flowers, and shrubs, all with vivid colors. Then up the side of the hill they have a cog railroad car. Funicular as they call it. You take this to the top of the hill and you can look down over the whole city, the harbor and ships, and see clear into yesterday because the air is so clear. It's like looking down on a play village, with all the tiny cars and ships. I guess it's the old clichè; it just reminds you of a postcard, it's so beautiful.

We're so far north that we're in the land of the midnight sun. It stays light until about ten thirty at night, and then the sun comes up about three in the morning. A few days ago in Oslo, I had set the alarm for five o'clock and left the drapes open, knowing I had to get up early. I woke up, and it was broad daylight outside. I jumped out of bed thinking that the alarm had failed to go off. I looked at the clock, and it was three thirty in the morning, broad daylight. Most hotels here have real heavy drapes so that you can close them and get some darkness. The latitude here is about the same as Juneau, Alaska.

Another interesting thing here is that the telephones don't have a bell. They make a little chirping sound, like a bird, instead of ringing. Roy woke up out of a sound sleep the other night, and he thought he'd left his window open. He heard this chirping and he thought a bird was in his room. Groggily, he got out of bed and looked around for this bird, and it turned out it was the telephone.

Another unusual thing here, they have big thick down comforters instead of blankets on the beds. I don't like them at all because if you put one on, shortly you're too hot. So you throw it off and then you're too cold, and you bring it back on and you're too hot again. I finally just got rid of the comforter and used the bedspread, and that seemed to work out pretty well.

They run hot water through the towel rods in the bathroom here, which is a good idea. These rods are so hot they're hot to touch. You hang your bath towel on the rods, and they dry out rapidly and are nice and warm to use.

Today is June seventeenth, and we're in Helsinki, Finland. Two days ago we flew to Alesund, Norway from Bergen, a distance of about 200 miles. The 200 miles seemed to make a tremendous difference in temperature. In Bergen it was short-sleeve weather. In Alesund it felt like it was about fifty degrees – very brisk. Alesund is about the same latitude as Anchorage, Alaska, and I think we had truly reached the land of the midnight sun because it never did get dark that night. It was light twenty-four hours a day.

We rented a car and drove through the back country of Norway. We drove about 150 miles and went back among the fjords. The scenery was absolutely fantastic: the placid water, the ferry boats, the countryside, the picturesque fishing villages, the valleys. We climbed up through one pass, and the snow was higher than the car in places. Back in the states they use four or five foot poles to guide snow plows. Here along the sides of the roads they have twelve to fifteen foot poles to guide their plows. There were mountains with sheer walls, and the melting snow created literally hundreds of spectacular waterfalls that cascaded down the sides of the mountains. Most of the streams were overflowing with crystal-clear water gushing down toward the ocean.

At one point they'd built a road down the side of the mountain, all hairpin turns. It was like they'd built a road from Yosemite Valley right up Half Dome to the top of the mountain. I didn't believe they could build such a road. And it was a bit scary coming down.

Norway is a land of beauty. It is also a land of wonderful food. It seems like we had a smorgasbord for breakfast, lunch, and dinner while we were there. If I don't gain a lot of weight on this trip, I'll be amazed.

Yesterday we flew from Alesund over here to Helsinki, a distance of about 700 miles. It took us an hour and thirty minutes. It was a routine flight, no comments there. The big difference we noticed between Alesund and Helsinki was the temperature. When we left Alesund the temperature was about fifty-five degrees. The temperature here in Helsinki is eighty degrees and very humid.

The office had trouble finding us hotel space in Helsinki because there were so many touristsin town. The only thing they could find was a little hotel down by the railroad station. On a scale of one to ten, this rates about a two. The trucks and the trolleys seemed like they were going to come right through the room all night, which would be rather hard to do because I'm on the seventh floor.

I don't think any of us got much sleep last night due to all this traffic noise. Roy, who joined us in Oslo to make us a 3 man crew again, found us another hotel outside of town. We're going to move out there this afternoon and hope for some peace and quiet.

From a noisy hotel in Helsinki we moved about twenty miles outside of town to a brand-spanking-new hotel built by the government. It's called the Forest Lake Hotel, and it's built in a forest. There are pine trees, birch trees, a lake, swans, tennis courts, volleyball courts, a lighted trail through the woods, all absolutely beautiful. The only problem was, there were no people. It seemed ironic that all the hotels in Helsinki were booked solid, and here this big beautiful place twenty miles outside of town was absolutely empty. So we went from one extreme to another: lots of noise to extreme quiet. But it was a beautiful place, and we got a bit of rest.

While we were there our people took the boat from Helsinki across the Gulf of Finland to Leningrad in Russia. They spent the first night on the boat and arrived in Leningrad at about eight in the morning. They toured Leningrad all that day, spent another night in the boat, toured all the next day, and then on the boat and back to Helsinki. Their report on Leningrad was interesting. They said it was very shabby. There were no flowers, lawns were not cut, and no cars on big, empty streets. There were no shops – they never saw a food store. This was supposed to be one of the biggest and best cities in Russia. They said it was very demoralizing.

At any rate, the following morning we went to the Helsinki airport to pay the various fees and get ready to leave. The fees were like in all of the Scandinavian countries: very high, outrageous. For instance, the total bill at the airport, not counting fuel, was $480. The landing fee was reasonable, $67. Parking for three nights was $35. Finair Airlines handled us, and their bill was $258. Then catering was $30. We got some ice, a gallon of coffee, and 12 sweet rolls for $30. Transportation for eight passengers from the airplane to the terminal and from the terminal to the airplane was $44. Crew transportation from the airplane to the terminal and the terminal back to the airplane was $15, for only the two of us. All in all we figured it was a bit expensive.

The flight from Helsinki to Visby Island was very interesting. Helsinki is actually only about fifty miles from Russia. As a matter of fact, the Russian air boundary is only nineteen miles south of our airway. Consequently we were very careful about our navigation.

Visby Island is in the Baltic sea. It's southeast of Sweden, about 300 miles from Helsinki. It took us about fifty minutes to fly there. It was a gorgeous day when we landed, bright blue water, blue sky, a few puffy clouds, and green fields.

While we were there we took a cab into town to do a little sightseeing. It was a very interesting town, very old. I understand it was built first in the year 1000 AD. There was a monstrous wall around the whole town. The wall looked like it was maybe thirty feet high and fifty feet thick, and it surrounded all these beautiful churches, old buildings, and so forth. The houses were very old. Evidently the people were small, because the doorways were only about five feet high. There were cobblestone streets and that sort of thing.

That afternoon we flew from Visby to Vienna in Austria. Vienna is almost due south of Visby. When you go due south you fly straight over Poland, Czechoslovakia, and then into Vienna. We didn't have any overfly permissions for the communist countries, so we took a roundabout route. The direct route is about 600 miles, and the route we filed was about 1,000 miles. We took off southwest and went down over Copenhagen in Denmark, Hamburg, and south through West Germany – making sure we didn't cross the border into East Germany – then down over Munich, and finally almost due east into Vienna. Fortunately we had good winds, and it only took us about two hours and five minutes.

So at the moment we're in Vienna, and we spent the day sightseeing. I must have walked ten miles today. We went over to the Vienna Opera House and took a tour through that establishment. Absolutely stupendous. Horseshoe-shaped, with five tiers of balconies, beautiful acoustics, and beautiful workmanship. Then we went up to the Spanish Riding College and saw that. Of course we spent some time in the park and listened to the Strauss waltzes. They're always good.

At the moment we're standing by for a possible demo trip to Geneva. Our people are going to take a hydrofoil down the blue Danube. I don't know whether it's down the blue Danube or up the blue Danube, but they're going to take the hydrofoil from Vienna to Budapest. We're supposed to go over to Budapest in Hungary in two days to pick them up. We're hoping to be there two days early so we can do a little sightseeing ourselves.

It is now June tweny-fifth, and we're sitting in Strasbourg, France. To go back a little bit, the demo flight in Geneva fizzled out, so we ferried over to Budapest, a distance of 150 miles. It took us about thirty minutes to go over there.

That was the first Iron Curtain country we'd ever been in, and we didn't know what to expect. We were a bit leery of the conditions there. The air traffic control system was very good. The tower was very good. No hitch – we went over and landed and they parked us right in front of the terminal. A British Airlines agent handled us. I told him, “As soon as we clear customs and immigration I guess we'll move the airplane wherever they tell us to.”

And he said, "No, right here in front of the terminal will be fine."

I said, “We're going to be here for three days.”

He said, “This spot is great. This is for general aviation.”

It was just like going into Kennedy and parking right in front of the terminal and leaving the airplane there for three days. I couldn't believe it. They parked all the airliners farther out on the ramp. Most of the airliners were Russian airplanes. Of course there were lots of soldiers about. The agent gave us a ride into the city and got us to the hotel.

When we got there we changed our money into Hungarian currency. They would take the Hungarian currency every place except the State stores. They had state tourist stores and they wouldn't take their own money. They would only take foreign money. The theory was that they wanted money to come into the country, not go out. When you cashed your money going in they gave you a receipt for what you transferred. When you left you had to have your receipt, and they wouldn't trade more than 50 percent back into the original currency. Here again the principle was that they want the money to come in and not to go out.

We did quite a bit of sightseeing. Budapest is a very beautiful city. I didn't know it, but 'Buda' means hills, and that's on one side of the blue Danube. 'Pest' means plains and that's on the other side of the blue Danube. It's literally two cities, Buda and Pest. So they call it Budapest.

Our hotel was right on the blue Danube, and I had a room facing the river. It was really beautiful to sit there and watch the sunset, the boats flying up and down the river, the hydrofoils, the barges, the tour boats. We took one ride in a tour boat. This boat was steam-driven with paddle wheels, and it had been built in 1913. It was really fabulous to go down into the lower part of the ship and watch the big pistons going. You could watch all the machinery working.

Unfortunately, the people there were very unfriendly. Evidently back in about 1945 or 1946 when the revolution came along, the Hungarians expected the Americans to come in and help them or bail them out, and the Americans did nothing. So the Russians came in and in about three days they totally dominated Hungary. Consequently, the Hungarians are very unfriendly to Americans. It was really an uneasy feeling.

We left this morning. It was very interesting to have seen Budapest, but due to the uncomfortable feeling we were very glad to leave. So we flew today from Budapest to Strasbourg in France. That's only a distance of about 550 miles, and it took us about an hour and twenty minutes.

Today is June the twenty-sixth, and we're in Bangor, Maine. It sure does feel good to be back in the United States!

We left Strasbourg this morning. Originally our schedule was to spend two nights in Strasbourg, but I think the people had been gone so long that they were eager to get home. Instead of two nights we only spent one night there. As a matter of fact, we were scheduled to leave at two this afternoon, but everybody showed up about twelve thirty. We didn't quite have all the pieces together, but we managed to get going without any problems.

The flight from Strasbourg to Shannon is relatively short, 850 miles, and it took us two hours and ten minutes. The wind was about fifty knots on the nose, which isn't unusual for this time of year. The only interesting part of that flight was the fact that one of the VORs, the navigational fix, was given the name of Bray, B-R-A-Y. The two crew members accused me of going that route just so I could say that I flew over Bray.

At any rate, we were in and out of Shannon without any problems. From Shannon across the Atlantic to Gander is a distance of about 2000 miles. It took us four hours and thirty minutes. The wind component from Shannon to Gander was about -30, which is a moral victory for this time of year. Approaching the coast of Newfoundland, Art looked down and said, "Gee, look at that monstrous sail boat down there." We were cruising at 35000 feet, and that monstrous sailboat was in fact a monstrous iceberg. This is not too unusual to see the icebergs floating south.

We landed at Gander and refueled, cleared customs, and then flew on to Bangor. Gander to Bangor is 750 miles, an hour and forty-five minutes. So all in all it was a fairly long day. We flew a total of 3,600 miles, at eight hours and twenty-five minutes air time, and fourteen hours of on-duty time. Needless to say, we were a bit thrashed when we arrived here.

When we left Strasbourg it was raining, and it was raining pretty hard here in Bangor when we arrived. I had a shower and a cold beer. I had supper at eight p.m. local, but that was two a.m. Strasbourg or body clock time. En route we picked up six hours. So we're dead tired, and we'll probably go to sleep and wake up at four o'clock wide awake as a tree full of owls. It takes about four or five days to catch up to the jet lag.

But it sure does feel good to be back here. We can read the menus. We can understand the waitresses. The prices aren't in a foreign language. We're just back where everything feels very comfortable. Tomorrow, if we get all four engines started, it's on to Los Angeles. We can't make it non-stop from here, so we'll probably refuel in Grand Island or Lincoln. But with any luck we'll be home about two o'clock tomorrow afternoon.

It is now July fifteenth, and the body has long since become accustomed to the California time. It just seems like it's taken the last two weeks to catch up on the bills and the paperwork. Strangely enough, we've been extremely busy with the demo flights since we got back from Europe.

I did want to summarize the trip. It looks like we flew 20,000 miles and spent forty-six hours in the air. We were gone twenty-four days, and, of the twenty-four, we flew twelve days. For interest, on this trip we landed in nine different countries. The old saying goes, it's great to go on a trip but it's just as great to get back home.

1978 South America Flight

January, 1978

Today is January 21, 1978, and I'm sitting in Antigua, in the British West Indies. We're on the start of a two week business tour through South America.

To go back, about three months ago my boss, Lou Berger, called me in and gave me the itinerary for this two week business trip and requested that I do the legwork – the flight-planning, the overfly permits, the visas, the handling agents, the fuel allocations, the requirements for the stops, and the various things that are necessary to try to make a trip like this run smoothly. The trip would involve Antigua, then Brazil. We have five stops in Brazil: Belem, Rio de Janeiro, Sao Jose dos Campos, Sao Paulo, Foz do Iguacu. Then we're going down to Argentina. We'll be in Buenos Aires for three nights and then go down to San Carlos de Bariloche for a couple of nights. From there, we'll be overflying Chile, landing in Lima, Peru for fuel, overflying Colombia and going into Caracas, Venezuela to spend a night. From Caracas we need overfly permits for Panama, Costa Rica, Nicaragua, El Salvador, and then a landing permit and handling agent in Guatemala. We'll be in Guatamala City for three nights. From Antigua tomorrow, we'll be overflying Guyana, Suriname – which belongs to the Netherlands – French Guiana – which is on the northern coast of South America – and then into Belen where we'll enter Brazil and clear customs.

The crew on this flight is Lou Berger, the manager of the Aviation Department, as Captain. I'm the co-Captain. And then we have Alberto Martinez, who is the flight engineer, chief cook, bartender, and baggage handler. He's practically indispensable. He does everything except the flight planning, flying the airplane, and handling customs. He's a tremendous person. We had one backup pilot, so that if Lou or I got sick we'd have a full crew. Wouldn't you know it, but after three months of planning, two days before the flight came up I developed a rather nasty cold. I thought, what a time to come down with a cold. But the doctor gave me some medicine and I appear to be back in the ball game.

Yesterday we started our trip at seven o'clock local time, which is fairly early in the morning. We left Los Angeles at seven and flew non-stop into Miami. It's 2,400 miles. We had tremendous tail winds all across the country, up to 150 mph. This gave us a ground speed to close to 600 mph. It took us four hours and twelve minutes to go from Los Angeles to Miami. When you consider the time spent circling to climb up to altitude before we get on course and circling to land at Miami, it was a pretty fair time.

Then from Miami to Antigua was 1,350 statute miles. We had about a +30 tailwind on this leg. We flight-planned it at two hours and forty-five minutes, and it took us two hours and forty-three minutes, which is pretty good for this rough work. We landed here at three p.m. Los Angeles time, but we lost four hours traveling east to Antigua. It was dark when we arrived there, close to seven o'clock.

After we arrived at the airport in Antigua, we parked the airplane and put it to bed. We grabbed a cab for a thirteen mile ride to a hotel. I think this cab had two or three hundred thousand miles on it. It was barely running. We thought we were going to need to help push it up the hills. The carbon monoxide fumes were so horrible that all our eyes were watering. We were really glad to get to the hotel.

We had a couple of beers, and saw this steel band that they had at the hotel. They used steel drums to create music. I guess there were twenty players and maybe thirty steel drums. The music was beautiful. They evidently taper the tops of the drums and temper each section to a different degree, which gives them their different tones. The music was so beautiful that Lou swore there was an organ somewhere in the center of the band. It couldn't possibly sound that smooth and that good with only those steel drums. But it was just great.

We got up today and went out to the airport and did our chores, cleaned the airplane, preflighted it, ordered catering, customs, and flight plans, arranged for our fueling and that sort of thing. Then we toured the island. Antigua is a typical Caribbean island. Beautiful. Beautiful flowers, fleecy clouds, blue water, laughing people, everything just beautiful. Tomorrow the same cab driver will pick us up at five thirty in the morning and take us out to the airport for an eight o'clock departure for Belem and Rio de Janeiro.

It is now January 23, 1978, and I'm sitting in a hotel room in Rio de Janeiro in Brazil.

As we were climbing out after our takeoff from Antigua, again I was amazed at the beautiful sight of the water – the beautiful colors – the blues, the greens, the aquas. I've mentioned before that the water in the Caribbean has many shallow places with white coral bottoms. The sun shines down through the water and hits the white coral, and it reflects up through the water and gives you all of these beautiful shimmering colors.

From Antigua, things were routine until we started approaching the north coast of South America. With the land mass and all the heat, there were monstrous cumulus buildups with tops at 40,000 feet. However, they were widely scattered, so there was no problem circumnavigating them.

As we approached the equator, we could watch it on our inertial navigation display. It's a black box that knows the position of the airplane at all times and updates itself every two seconds. So we could actually see the airplane cross the equator. We were watching the dial, and it was counting down: point five north, point four, point three, point two, point one, zero, and then south point one, point two, point three, point four, and on. Just for interest, according to the map, it appears the equator is right at the mouth of the Amazon river. Through breaks in the clouds we could see the river. The delta reminds you of the Mississippi River, very muddy, emptying into the larger body of water.

We landed at Belem, which is just 100 miles south of the equator, on the north coast of South America. I'd expected a very small town, but we could see skyscrapers in the distance, so it was quite a large city. Once we got on the ground we had a communications problem. We couldn't understand the tower operator. We kept asking him to repeat but it didn't do any good. We still couldn't understand him. Even our flight engineer, Al, who speaks fluent Spanish, couldn't understand him. We pulled up in front of a building. I happened to look up into the tower, and the tower operator was pointing and gesturing around the corner. We kept taxiing, and sure enough there was the terminal building. We were in front of the wrong building and couldn't see the terminal on account of this big shed. So here with all this modern communication we're back to sign language.

It was very hot in Belem, about 87° and extremely humid. We had neckties on, but it didn't take long for us to shed those.

From Antigua to Belem was 1,550 statute miles, and it took us three hours and thirteen minutes – just a routine flight. Belem to Rio was the same distance, and that leg took us three hours and twenty minutes. As we climbed out across northern Brazil, we could look down and see dense jungle foliage. Then the land opened up and reminded us of Texas, with wide open spaces, but very little civilization.

Approaching Rio, the weather was horrible. It was a dark night with heavy rain and gusting winds, and we were cleared for an instrument landing. Here again, we couldn't understand what the controllers were trying to have us do. Fortunately, we were under radar control. After asking them to repeat four or five times, we finally said "ok," even though we didn't know what they wanted us to do. We just continued with the approach and figured if our route conflicted with another airplane, he would get excited. That was the big danger: if we weren't conforming with the normal flow of traffic, there was the possibility of a midair collision. Often at Los Angeles a foreign airplane will be coming in, and you can tell by the accent that he doesn't understand the instructions for going into Los Angeles. It horrifies me to think that pilots going into Los Angeles are as uneasy as we were going into Rio. A Most uncomfortable feeling.

All in all it was an extremely long day. We were up at five o'clock – out to the airport in the dark – and by the itme we got to the hotel at Rio it was eight p.m., pitch dark. So hotel to hotel, dark to dark, a long day.

We're in a hotel just south of Copcabana beach, and we can look out the window and see the gleaming white sand and the thousands of people and the pounding surf. It's quite a sight. This morning we rented a car and went sightseeing. I never knew Rio was a city of hills. The highways go through the hills. It almost makes San Francisco look flat, there's so many hills here.

The highlight of the trip was seeing the Christ the Redeemer, this huge statue on top of a hill 2,200 feet high. The statue itself is 125 feet high. There's a narrow road that leads most way up to it and then a couple hundred steps to get to the top. From there, being 2,200 feet up, you can overlook the whole city, the bay, the bridges, the airports, and the beaches. It's quite a sight.

This afternoon we spent some time on the beach. I just have to remark on the bikini bathing suits. It seems like 90 percent of the gals – whether they're three years old or ninety – wear bikinis. A good many wear what is known as string bathing suits. I think when they go to buy their bathing suits, the clerk just asks what color string they want, because there's not much more there. As a matter of fact, they wear these bikinis in the elevators, in the lobbies, in the streets – anywhere. For instance, a gal walked through the lobby at ten thirty at night in a bikini. We wondered, "Where is she going this time of night in a bikini?" I guess the answer was, anyplace she wants.

January twenty-fourth was our last day in Rio, and we made a full day of it. In the morning we took a cab and went out to Sugarloaf. I don't know where the mountain ever got it's name, but they have a famous cable car that goes to the top. It's just a container that hangs on a cable and goes pretty high across these vast distances. To me this little car swinging in the wind under this cable was a bit scary. You look down, and it appeared to me to be a couple thousand feet down. It wasn't very comfortable.

However, it was well worth the ride because at the top of this Sugarloaf you have a tremendous view. I could see the whole Bay of Rio, and I could look across and see the city and the harbor. On a ridge on the other side of the city the Christ the Redeemer was outlined in the skyline. Down below was the San Dumas airport, a 4,500 foot strip right on the edge of town that points right at Sugarloaf. Local airlines use Electras to go in and out of there. On the takeoff, the airplanes have to change their course, or they will go right through the cables leading up to Sugarloaf. So they take off, get the gear up, bend it a little bit to the left, and swing around the mountain and head on course. But it's quite spectacular to be on top of the mountain and look down at these airplanes taking off and coming at you and then turning. All in all quite a view.

In the afternoon we took a harbor cruise and saw the sights of Rio Harbor. Wouldn't you know it, on the way back the boat broke down. We drifted for thirty minutes before they got it fixed. By the time we got back it was dark. This was to some advantage because we saw all the lights of Rio come on, the bright lights along the shoreline.

A full moon came up as well. It was great, all in all a very interesting day. We had one flat tire in a cab, and we waited while he changed it. Then the boat broke down. But at least the cable didn't break going up to Sugarloaf.

The next day we left about noon, flew 200 miles to Sao Jose dos Campos. No problem – communications were much better than before. We had a six hour layover and then flew sixty miles to Sao Paulo. As we approached Sao Paulo, there was a thunderstorm right over the city. We were below it, but we went through some heavy rain. There was lightning from cloud to ground, and I thought, gee it sure would be ironic if we get zapped by lightning here in the only thunderstorm within 200 miles. But we didn't get hit and made a normal landing.

After we were on the ground and taxied in, it was quite confusing. A man with paddles or flags waved us one direction, a man with a clipboard motioned us another direction, and the tower insisted we go a third place. We opted to follow the man with the clipboard, as he was the agent who was meeting the flight and was going to handle us. He led us behind a hangar, and we opened the door and two cars drove up. We started unloading the baggage and our passengers.

A little Volkswagen came roaring around the corner, and a fat little customs man jumped out. He was waving his arms and irate and screaming. He was just absolutely livid. He insisted we should have been up front in the main terminal, and we should have gone through customs. Through the language barrier we tried to explain to him that we were an internal flight, a domestic flight, that we weren't entering the country, and that we didn't have to go through customs. He demanded to see our papers. Fortunately, when we had gone through customs up at Belem I had insisted that they give me an extra copy stamped and signed, proving that we had entered there. I showed him all these papers, and he calmed down quite a bit and allowed as if it was ok and left.

Today as we were loading, the same man came up in his car and sat watching us load the airplane, and as we taxied out he followed us out in his car, right to the end of the runway. I think he was firmly convinced that we were trying to smuggle something in or out, and, by golly, it wasn't going to happen on his station.

Today is the twenty-sixth. We flew from Sao Paulo down here to Foz do Iguaçu and circled the famous Iguazu Falls about five times. The people at the hotel had heard that there were some VIPs coming into Iguazu Falls in their private jet. While we were overcircling the falls everybody came out front to ooh and aah and say, "Here comes the VIPs."

We're in a rather old hotel here. I guess the hotel was built in the twenties – very old architecture, no air conditioning. It's about ninety degrees, very warm, very humid. But the view is spectacular.

On the veranda you can see these monstrous falls. The Parana River flows into the Iguazu River, and they create the cataracts. The falls are eight or nine times as wide as Niagara Falls. A camera just won't capture it; you'd have to have a wide-angle lens. They're unbelievably beautiful, so much water pouring down. They have walkways where you can go down along the water, and lookout points where you can take pictures.

At one of the falls, five or six birds would dart right into the water. I don't know whether the sheet of water was thin, and there were nests behind there, but to see these birds dart directly into the water was something else.

Where we're located, Iguazu is on the western side of Brazil. As a matter of fact you can call it three corners. Paraguay, Argentina, and Brazil all meet in one corner, and these falls are on the river that separates Argentina and Brazil. Argentina and Brazil have gone together and declared a national park of Iguazu Falls and preserved it for posterity. It is really spectacular.

The next day, we met a pilot who really brought us down to size. He was about fifty years old. He had his wife and two children with him, and he'd just flown his single engine airplane from Seattle all the way down to Iguazu.

He'd been flying for about two weeks through South America. He came down through Central America, Panama, down the coast, and across the Andes. He had weather problems where he'd have to land on dirt roads. He'd have to scrounge up fuel and run it through a chamois to put it in his tank. He didn't have any navigation gear that would compare to what we carried. All in all, he was really a pioneer. I would just hate to fly a single engine airplane down over all that water, all the jungles, in the kind of weather they have down around the equator. It's just mind boggling. But I guess there's still pioneers in the world. At least he brought us down to size. We thought we were doing a little something being out in the wilds with a jet, but it's nothing compared to what he's going through.

The flight from Iguazu to Buenos Aires was routine. It's about 875 miles and took us two hours. It was a beautiful day, hardly a cloud in the sky, so you could see all the country as we flew over. Letting down into Buenos Aires, we came in over the wide mouth of the Rio de la Plata, the river that separates Uruguay and Argentina. It is similar to the mouth of the Mississippi, a very muddy, wide delta area. We swung in over Beunos Aires, and this is just another monstrous big town like New York, Cleveland, or Chicago, a very large town on flat land. It was a routine landing, and we taxied in.

Then we started a three hour hassle. Nothing drastic, it just took time to do everything. We got our passengers through customs and immigration, and then there was a long delay while we located the people who were meeting our passengers. We finally got them in the cars and on the way to the hotel. Then I went with our handling agent up to operations and hassled over a landing fee for maybe half an hour. I went down to the bank to get the money converted, back up to operations, paid the fee, and returned to the airplane. We waited a while for a man to join us to park it. We had to take it across a field behind a hangar, lock it up, and get transportation back to the terminal to get our car to the hotel. All in all it took about three hours. When we got to the hotel it was beer time, and it really tasted wonderful.

The rate of exchange here in Argentina is most interesting. One dollar gets you 634 pesos. At the airport I cashed 300 dollars, and would you believe our landing fee was 130,850 pesos. That's about 210 dollars. You go out to dinner, and dinner might be 10,000 or 12000 pesos, sixteen to eighteen dollars. You walk down the street, and purses cost 38,000 pesos, shoes cost 50,000 pesos, and leather coats cost 200,000 pesos. So in my wallet I've got 10,000 peso notes and 5,000 peso notes. The 10,000 peso notes are worth sixteen dollars, 1,000 peso notes are worth one dollar and sixty cents, 500 peso notes are worth eighty cents, and 100 peso notes are worth sixteen cents. The lowest denomination are 50 peso notes, and they're worth eight cents. There are a few coins in circulation, but as a rule no one carries them because they're not worth anything. I also understand that the rate of inflation here is going up two pesos a day. The cost of living here is just as expensive as any other place.

Having Alberto along with us is really a joy. He speaks fluent Spanish, and when we go out to eat or for the taxis, he handles the various communication problems. Having Al along makes the flight very easy and comfortable.

It is now January thirty-first, and we are in Bariloche, Argentina. The flight from Buenos Aires to Bariloche was 850 miles, and it took us two hours. We started out across the flatlands of Argentina. It reminded me of the flatlands of Kansas and Nebraska, very clean and very flat.

When we approached Bariloche airport, the tower gave us the present weather and the wind. We couldn't really understand him, and we couldn't understand whether it was four knots or forty knots. Well, as we approached the ground we could see the wind was blowing like mad, so it was forty knots of wind. Forty knots is about forty-five miles per hour. So we had forty-five miles per hour of wind with a fifty-five degree temperature – the chill factor was very brisk. We all got off the airplane and the wind was blowing so strong that we had trouble standing up. Lou Berger pulled a funny. He said to the president, "Harry, ask the man over there if the wind always blows like this. If he says, 'what wind?' we're in big trouble."

Bariloche is on the western side of Argentina, right in the foothills of the Andes. On the other side of the Andes is Chile and the Pacific Ocean. Bariloche is a famous ski resort. During their snow season, literally thousands of people flock here for the skiing. It would be like our Aspen or Vail. The latitude here is 41° south, which compares to New York and Chicago in north latitude.

The thing we really couldn't comprehend is the temperatures here. Rio and Buenos Aires were ninety degrees, very humid. The temperatures here are about fifty-nine degrees in the day time and thirty-four degrees at night, just above freezing. It's just unbelievable, the relatively short distance we flew to get these extremely cold temperatures. I guess a lot of the rich people from Buenos Aires who can't stand the cold and the humidity come down here for their summer.

Bariloche reminds me very much of Lake Arrowhead or maybe Jackson Hole, with lots of evergreens and mountains, snow on the mountains, and lots of lakes. Our hotel is right on a lake. I can look out the window and see the beautiful water. Unfortunately there are whitecaps on the top of the water, and the whitecaps have whitecaps. It seems like there is always a strong wind blowing in this mountainous area. This is the third day we've been here, and the wind's been blowing this strong ever since we arrived. We've learned that this kind of wind blows 300 days out of the year here. It's gonna help us get off the ground, anyhow.

When we first planned this trip, we were concerned about going from Bariloche, to Lima, Peru, which is close to 2000 miles. The runway in Bariloche is relatively short. A jet engine hates heat, and it doesn't like high altitude. You lose power. We figured that, here at 3,000 feet, if the temperatures were warm we were going to have trouble getting off the ground. But with this kind of wind blowing and these kind of temperatures, I think we'll jump off the ground, so that takes a load off our mind.

Being this far south is rather strange. There is daylight until about nine thirty at night. Speaking of hours, another strange thing in Argentina is that their meal hours are entirely different than ours. They have breakfast at ten in the morning, lunch around two, tea at six, and they don't normally have dinner until ten o'clock at night. The restaurants don't even open until nine o'clock. We're not used to eating late and going to bed on a full stomach, especially if we have to get up early, but at any rate that's the custom here. Casinos and night clubs don't open up until eleven. So I guess folks normally play until three o'clock in the morning and sleep in late.

Today we went out to the airport, did our chores, and got everything ready for a seven o'clock departure tomorrow. I have one final word on these pesos. The fueling concern here wouldn't take any of our credit cards, so we had to pay cash. So I paid over half a million pesos for fuel today – 634,000 pesos. In US dollars it was still quite a lot of money – $1002.

It is now the second of February, and I'm sitting in a hotel in Caracas, Venezuela. I want to go back to yesterday, which was rather a full day. We got up at five o'clock in the morning in Bariloche, Argentina. The cab driver picked us up at five thirty and took us out to the airport.

The day before, we'd arranged for customs and the guards, catering, station agents, weather, flight plans, and all that sort of thing for seven o'clock. We arrived there about six and everything was dark, the buildings were closed. Bariloche is a military field, so we knew there were armed guards around. We knocked on doors, flashed the headlights, and blew the horn, but we couldn't raise anybody. We hesitated to drive across the ramp to the airplane because we didin't want to get shot. Instead, we drove around to the front of the terminal. We turned on the lights inside the cab, so if the guards did look out they would see who we were. We never could raise anybody, so we drove across the ramp and started our pre-flight in the pitch dark.

The sunrise came up around seven and people finally started to show up. It was sort of funny. The station agent must have been on a real toot because he looked horrible. He told Alberto in Spanish, "I don't know about you Americans." He said, "You mobilized half of Bariloche – we're not used to getting up at this time of day!"

But everything went smooth as a whistle. The catering was there, and the weather, and the flight plan. And when the cabs arrived we had permission for them to go right to the airplane. I collected the passports as they came by the terminal and got those stamped out. The passengers went right to the airplane, stepped aboard, closed the door, and away we went.

There were no problems getting off the ground at Bariloche. It was nice and cool, the wind was blowing, and the airplane popped off at gross weight. We climbed up over the lakes, over the Andes, and basically followed the coastline of Chile up into Lima. It was a long flight. From Bariloche to Lima is 2100 miles. It took us four hours and thirty-five minutes.

The only hiccup occurred as we were approaching Lima. We asked for the weather, and, as near as we could make out with the accent, Lima had sixty meters and four kilometers. Well, sixty meters is about a 180 feet ceiling, and that was below our minimum; four kilometers is about two and a half miles of visibility. We could look down and see it was low stratus, fog type conditions with holes in it. It was sort of an uneasy feeling, because if we shot the approach and had to pull up, where would we go? There are customs problems and fueling problems – we almost had to get in. We shot the approach and at 200 feet there was a runway right in front of us. No problem landing. When we departed about an hour later, a lot of the fog had burned off. Had we shot the approach and not seen the runway, we could have pulled up, circled a while, and shot another approach. But it was routine.

From there we climbed up out of Lima, flew across Colombia, and into Venezuala. Northbound looking down on the Andes, I had to think back thirty years to the time I took a load of cattle in a C-46 from the States down into Santiago, Chile, and then returned with a load of racehorses and no oxygen across the Andes and up the coast, making a stop every 800 miles. I'm certainly glad those days are gone. Now we are crossing the Andes at 35,000 feet in air conditioned comfort, with the cabins at about 6000 feet, with hot breakfast, and coffee. There have been a lot of changes, all for the better.

Letting down into Caracas was no problem. We're back to the hot and humid country. From Lima to Caracas was 1,800 miles. It took us three hours and forty-five minutes. The wind was blowing. I taxied up to the ramp and a whole mob of people came out to the airplane. Mack Truck has an assembly plant in Caracas, so we stopped to visit it. All the Mack VIPs were there to take care of our passengers and get them into the hotel. So no problems there whatsoever.

All in all yesterday was an extremely long day for us. We flew almost 4,000 miles at eight and a half hours flying time. We were, of course, extremely thrashed. We came in, had a couple of beers and dinner, and hit the sack. When I woke up this morning I realized that I'd slept for ten hours.

Today is February fourth, and we're in Guatemala city.

The whole trip has been running smooth as silk, so I suppose we were due for a hiccup, and the day before yesterday just wasn't our day. I got up in the morning in Caracas, stripped down to take a shower, and there was no water. No hot water, no cold water, no water to flush the john... no water whatsoever. I called the management, and the entire hotel was without water. I read later in the morning paper that a third of Caracas was without water. They were repairing one of their water mains, and they hoped to be finished "soon."

Fortunately, Lou Berger had an electric razor, so I managed to shave. It just felt funny, not being able to brush your teeth or wash your hands; here's a big modern hotel and not a drop of water.

Then we had a problem with the baggage. Some passengers requested that we go to their hotel and pick up their baggage to save a little time. We checked out early, and I rented a station wagon and went over to the other hotel. I managed to get the bags out of their rooms and into the car, but the management wouldn't let us leave because the rooms weren't paid for. That was reasonable. We didn't know whether Mack truck was going to pick up the rooms or what the situation was, so we thought we'd keep it simple. We knew they had to go back to the hotel, so we took all the bags back up to the rooms. We left messages with the checkout clerk, the desk clerk, the bell Captain, and the doorman. As a matter of fact there was another Garrett man there in the hotel, and we left a message in his box that we did not have the baggage and be sure to bring it out.

We went on out to the airport and did our preflight, got fuel, got our catering, and stood by. Well, sure enough the passengers showed up and the baggage was still in the hotel. Even the Garrett man got his message and assumed it was just his baggage that we didn't get. The worst part was that in the hotel lobby the president's wife said to her husband, "Hey, Harry, why don't you go up to the room and make sure the baggage is gone?"

He said, "No, no, I'll take my chances. I think it's gone."

Well, it was still in the room. The hotel is about an hour away from the airport. Five lanes narrow down to two lanes going through a tunnel, so the traffic is horrendous. It takes about an hour and a half. The Mack people who brought our passengers out got on the phone, and much screaming and arm-waving in Spanish ensued. I guess somebody from Mack finally went to the hotel and got the baggage. Two hours later it showed up. So we had a two hour delay, and that put a damper on everybody's spirits, but once the bags arrived everybody was so happy to see them again that they were back in good spirits.

The bad part was that we'd planned the flight so we'd arrive at Guatemala City in daylight. Guatemala City sits in mountainous terrain. It's 5,000 feet high, and it's in the bottom of a sort of bowl. So you shoot an approach into the airport with mountains all around. Not being familiar with the territory, we wanted to be able to see what we were doing when we arrived.

We took off from Caracas, a normal climb out, and flew over Baranquilla in Colombia, and then straight across the Caribbean. We were about 150 miles north of the Panama Canal. As we flew through the Panama control area, it was really a relief to hear an American voice and not have to wonder what he was saying and what he meant. As a matter of fact we were under radar contact. It made us feel like we were almost home.

From there it was across Managua, Nicaragua, and San Salvador. Fortunately the weather was crystal clear even though it was pitch dark by this time. At about 100 miles away we could see the lights of Guatemala City. Inasmuch as we were tired, it was really a relief to have good weather there.

So we landed at Guatemala City and taxied in, and the agent who met us – he'd been waiting about four hours for us – he whisked our passengers through customs and immigration and got them in the cab and on the way. So it was a rather frustrating day. But I suppose if that's the worst thing that happens on this trip, we have it made.

This is our last evening in Guatemala City. Tomorrow we go home – Guatemala City to Brownsville, where we clear customs and immigration. From there we go to Phoenix, drop a few folks, and then to Los Angeles. With any luck we should be in Los Angeles around five tomorrow afternoon.

We just finished two relaxing days here in Guatemala City. Yesterday we rented a car and drove about thirty-five miles outside of the city to a town called Antigua. I understand this used to be the capital of Central America, and it's all been restored. It reminds me of Williamsburg, Virginia, where they restored all the buildings and the streets and the atmosphere back to the way it was many years ago. The streets in Antigua were cobblestone, and they had a town square with a fountain. And of course there were all the buildings with the thick walls, the old university, and the old cathedrals. It was very picturesque.

A guide found us and tagged along, and he turned out to be so interesting that we hired him. He recommended this little hotel. We went through this doorway in the wall, and there was a huge inner court with trees, very attractive. They had a marimba band there. They had two long marimbas, and I think they had about eight players, and they got all kinds of music out of these two long marimbas.

From there we went about another five miles down this dirt road to a little village called San Antonio, where every household makes these beautiful embroidered shirts, jackets, skirts, wraparounds, and shawls. They had all these little stands along the side of the road. We stopped, and I bought six jackets. Every time a car went by these stands, layers of dust would fly up and cover everything. So I'm sure all of these jackets have to be washed and ironed. But the price was right. I bought these beautiful jackets for $7 a piece, and just this afternoon the identical jacket in town was $16. Of course, the one in town has been washed and ironed and is in a plastic bag. But I'm sure we can wash and iron the six that I bought.

Today was really the highlight of the trip. I got up at six a.m. The driver picked us up at a quarter to seven to take us to the airport. We'd signed up for a tour to go up to Tikal, about 200 miles of north of Guatemala City. Tikal is where the Mayan ruins that are famous throughout the world are located. Last night we went to a lecture to get a little preflight on what we would see there: the pyramids, royal palaces, and plateaus.

This morning there was a little weather up there. We were concerned about these foreign pilots going into this little strip. It was a low ceiling, but they came on in. Tikal is in a dense jungle, and they've hacked this little landing strip out of the jungle. It just seemed like the Convair wingtips were brushing the jungle on both sides as we landed. There was a turnaround spot, and we turned around and taxied back to the terminal.

It's hard to believe that this civilization started around 400 or 500 BC and lasted until 900 AD. I guess there were something like 50,000 people here. They did not have the wheel or metals, but they still managed to build all these beautiful buildings. It was spectacular.

We were supposed to leave there at three this afternoon, and we kept being told that we were going to board at three sharp. The airplane didn't get there until half past three. We talked to a charter pilot there and he said, "Well, three o'clock, more or less, *mas o menos* – the schedule's not really that important down here. That's just a general number."

While we were waiting at the Tikal airport, a DC-3 came in with a load of tourists. We were sitting out in front of what you'd call a terminal, just a tiny little building. I guess the DC-3 pilot didn't like tourists because he cranked up his engines and turned a tail in and blew dust over everybody. If that wasn't enough he did it a second time. I think if I'd been chief pilot I would have tried to impress upon him that, hey, these tourists are what's bringing in the money. Let's use a little public relations here and not dust them off.

It was really a fascinating day, so we're all set to head home tomorrow.

Today is February the sixth, and we're back in California.

To finish up this South American flight, we were in Guatemala, and three interesting things happened. Just as we were about to leave, one of the volcanoes started to spit smoke out. We could look off into the distance and see smoke rising from this volcano. It only lasted about ten minutes, and then it dissipated. Then one of the agents came running out and asked, "Hey, did you feel it?" We didn't know what he was talking about, but evidently there'd been an earthquake. I guess at the time we didn't feel it because we were walking across the ramp. The agent said it shook all the bottles in the terminal and gave them a bit of a scare considering the drastic earthquake they'd had there a short time ago.

The third thing was that single engine Bonanzas started to land one after another in Guatemala City. I talked to one of the pilots, and it was a Bonanza club from the United States. They take one trip a year. It was just like a whole flock of pigeons coming into the airport. I thought they were brave, flying across all that wilderness and jungle coming down there. I guess single engine airplanes go around the world – we're just spoiled.

At any rate we flew from Guatemala to Brownsville, Texas, where we cleared US Customs. The customs were very good to us there. We didn't know what to expect, because we had a planeload of suitcases, boxes, packages, gifts, and bags – just a complete conglomeration of containers. But customs took us at our word. We all made a declaration for what we'd purchased. Those of us who spent over $100 paid a duty on the excess, and they didn't look in a single suitcase or bag, so that made life easy for us.

From Brownsville we flew on into Phoenix, dropped a few folks, and then headed to Los Angeles. Strangely enough the worst weather the whole trip was in Los Angeles. They had a relatively low ceiling and rain.

To summarize the complete flight, we were gone sixteen days and flew 17,600 miles. The air time for the entire trip was thirty-eight hours. So our average speed was 463 mph, which isn't bad considering that includes climb out, cruise, let down, approach, circling for approach, and that sort of thing. We went over seventeen different countries. We landed in six countries. According to our passengers it was the most enjoyable trip they'd ever made. They told us how much they appreciated all the planning we'd put into it and how smoothly everything went. Of course we've got to give luck a lot of credit. The only real hiccup we had on the entire flight was the baggage mixup in Caracas. Considering the magnitude of the drill, things did go extremely well. As they say down south, "*adios, amigos,*" until next time.

1978 Europe-Kuwait Flight

May, 1978

We left on May the sixth, and we'll return on the twenty-fourth. We'll be gone about eighteen days, and we're going to be flying thirteen of those eighteen days, so it's going to be a rather busy trip. We're going from Los Angeles to Bangor, Gander, Dublin, Cork, Liverpool, London, Toulouse in France, Balboa in Spain, Madrid, back to London, Cork, back again to London, Edinburgh, Madrid, London, Edinburgh, London, Wick in Scotland, then Aberdeen, Frankfurt, Geneva, Athens, and down to Kuwait. We'll lay over in Kuwait about three days, our longest layover. Then it's back to Athens, Shannon, Gander, Newport News, and home to Los Angeles.

On this particular trip we only have a two man crew. Normally for a trip of this magnitude we carry three crew members. For this trip we will be in Europe most of the time, and we should have a lot of maintenance support. Also, we won't have room for a third man on two full legs. On other legs we only have a few people on board, and they are relatively self-sufficient.

On a couple of previous trips I tried to check out a younger pilot to replace me, but it was just too much for him. Everything was too new; it was too much to learn. It was a new airplane, new HF, new inertial, new overseas,

CHECK LIST	VISA	OVERFLY PERMIT	LANDING PERMIT	HANDLING AGENT	FUEL	SHOTS	REMARKS
BANGOR	—	—	—	—	YES	—	COMP FLT PLAN
GANDER	—	—	—	✓ YES	YES	—	COMP FLT PLAN
DUBLIN (EIDW)	—	—	—	✓ YES	YES	—	
CORK (EICK)	—	—	—	NO	YES	—	
LIVERPOOL (EGGP)	—	—	—	✓ YES	YES	—	
BILBAO (LEBB)	—	—	—	✓ YES	YES		
TOULOUSE (LFBO)	—	—	—	✓ YES	NO	—	
LONDON (EGGW)	—	—	—	NO	YES	—	HAVE LIMO AT ATHENAEUM INN (NEAR HILTON) 0400 FOR MR ASH
EDINBURGH (EGPH)	—	—	—	NO	YES	—	
MADRID (LEMD)	—	—	—	✓ YES	YES	—	
WICK (EGPC)	—	—	—	NO	?	—	BRITISH AIRWAYS TEL 2294 NO FUEL
FRANKFURT (EDDF)	—	—	—	✓ YES	NO	—	
GENEVA (LSGG)	—	—	—	NO	YES	—	COMP FLT PLAN
ATHENS (LGAT)	—	NO	NO	✓ YES	YES	—	COMP FLT PLAN
CYPRUS	—	NO	—	—	—	—	PRIOR PERMIT NOT REQUIRED
LEBANON	—	✓ YES	—	—	—	—	
SYRIA	—	✓ YES	—	—	—	—	
JORDAN	—	✓ YES	—	—	—	—	
SAUDI ARABIA	—	✓ YES	—	—	—	—	
KUWAIT (OKBK)	YES	✓ YES	YES	NO	YES	SMALL POX	COMP FLT PLAN ①
IRAQ	—	NO	—	—	—	—	IN BAGHDAD FIR BUT OVER SAUDI NOT REQ
BAHRAIN	—	NO	—	—	—	—	
SHANNON	—	—	—	✓ YES	YES	—	COMP FLT PLAN
GANDER	—	—	—	NO	YES	—	

① NOTE KUWAIT: IFIM SAYS ALL FLIGHTS MUST HAVE A FLIGHT PLAN ON FILE 24 HOURS BEFORE DEPARTURE. UNIVERSAL SAYS NO, YOUR PERMIT IS OK BUT [illegible] PERMIT [illegible] ON FLIGHT PLAN

Checklist for the 1978 flight to Europe and Kuwait

JET TRANSP[illegible]
FORM 10-3[illegible]

FRANK | April 12, 1978 | 6 | 8

AIRCRAFT MODEL AND NO.	TAS (KNOTS)	FLIGHT NO.	PREPARED BY
JETSTAR N731A	440		Frank Bray

AIRPORT	GMT DATE	GMT TIME	* TIME FACTOR	LOCAL TIME	LOCAL DATE	DISTANCE TO FLY	** BLOCK TIME	GROUND TIME	REMARKS
DEPART LOS ANGELES	5/6/78	1600Z	-7	0900	5/6/78	2400	5+45		SAT
ARRIVE BANGOR	"	2145Z	-4	1745	"			1 nite	
DEPART BANGOR	5/7/78	~~1200Z~~ 1100	-4	~~0800~~ 0700	5/7/78	640	1+45		SUN
ARRIVE GANDER	"	~~1345Z~~ 1245Z	-2½	1115	"			+45	
DEPART GANDER	"	~~1430Z~~ 1330Z	-2½	1200	"	1833	4+20		(Wind +20)
ARRIVE DUBLIN, IRELAND	"	~~1850~~ 1750	+1	~~1950~~ 1850	"			2 nites	
DEPART DUBLIN (EIDW)	5/9/78	1115Z	+1	1215	5/9/78	140	+45		Ferry TUES
ARRIVE CORK, IRELAND	"	1200Z	+1	1300	"			2+00	
DEPART CORK (FICK)	"	1400Z	+1	1500	"	240	1+00		
ARRIVE LIVERPOOL, U.K.	"	1500Z	+1	1600	"			1 nite	
DEPART LIVERPOOL (EGGP)	5/10/78	1100Z	+1	1200	5/10/78	165	+45		WED
ARRIVE LONDON, U.K.	"	1145Z	+1	1245	"			+45	Pick up Mr. Pattison
DEPART LONDON (EGGW)	"	1230Z	+1	1330	"	480	1+30		
ARRIVE TOULOUSE, FRANCE	"	1400Z	+2	1600	"			1 nite	
DEPART TOULOUSE (LFBO)	5/11/78	0930Z	+2	1130	5/11/78	190	1+00		Mr. Wetzel THURS.
ARRIVE BILBAO, SPAIN	"	1030Z	+2	1230	"			1+00	
DEPART BILBAO (LEBB)	"	1130Z	+2	1330	"	190	1+00		Mr. Pattison
ARRIVE MADRID, SPAIN	"	1230Z	+2	1430	"			1+00	
DEPART MADRID (LEMD)	"	1330Z	+2	1530	"	700	2+00		Ferry
ARRIVE LONDON, U.K.	"	1530Z	+1	1630	"			1 nite	
DEPART LONDON (EGGW)	5/12/78	0800Z	+1	0900	5/12/78	320 320	+1 +1		Mr. Teske FR[illegible]
ARRIVE LONDON	"	1500Z	+1	1600	"			1 nite	To Cork and return....

JET TRANSPORT FLIGHT ITINERARY
FORM 10-35 (R. 12-72)

DATE: April 12, 1978

PREPARED FOR	AIRCRAFT MODEL AND NO.	TAS (KNOTS)	FLIGHT NO.	PREPARED BY
	JETSTAR N731A		440	Frank Bray

AIRPORT	GMT DATE	GMT TIME	* TIME FACTOR	LOCAL TIME	LOCAL DATE	DISTANCE TO FLY	** BLOCK TIME	GROUND TIME	REMARKS
DEPART LONDON (EGGW)	5/13/78	0800Z	+1	0900	5/13/78	340	1+10		Mr. Azar SAT
ARRIVE EDINBURGH, SCOTLAND	"	0910Z	+1	1010	"			1 nite	
DEPART EDINBURGH (EGPH)	5/14/78	0700Z	+1	0800	5/14/78	970	2+45		Ferry SUN
ARRIVE MADRID, SPAIN	"	0945Z	+2	1145	"			2+15	
DEPART MADRID (LEMD)	"	1200Z	+2	1400	"	700	2+00		
ARRIVE LONDON	"	1400Z	+1	1500	"			1 hour	
DEPART LONDON (EGGW)	"	1500Z	+1	1600	"	340	1+10		
ARRIVE EDINBURGH	"	1610Z	+1	1710	"			+50	
DEPART EDINBURGH	"	1700Z	+1	1800	"	340	1+10		
ARRIVE LONDON	"	1810Z	+1	1910	"			2 nites	
DEPART LONDON (EGGW)	5/16/78	1300Z	+1	1400	5/16/78	475	1+30		TUES
ARRIVE WICK, SCOTLAND	"	1430Z	+1	1530	"			2 nites	
DEPART WICK (EGPC)	5/18/78	0900Z	+1	1000	5/18/78	700	2+00		May have to land Aberdeen to clear Customs
ARRIVE FRANKFURT, GERMANY	"	1100Z	+1	1200	"			1 nite	THURS
DEPART FRANKFURT (EDDF)	5/19/78	0900Z	+1	1000	5/19/78	275	1_00		Wind FRI
ARRIVE GENEVA, SWITZERLAND	"	1000Z	+1	1100	"			1 hour	
DEPART GENEVA (LSGC)	"	1100Z	+1	1200	"	970	2+30		Ferry- Wind +20
ARRIVE ATHENS, GREECE	"	1330Z	+3	1630	"			1 hour	
DEPART ATHENS (LGAT)	"	1430Z	+3	1730	"	1460	3+30		1851 long way/Wind +40
ARRIVE KUWAIT (OKBK)	"	1800Z	+3	2100	"			3 nites	Mr. Aza[illegible]

Flight itinerary for the Europe-Kuwait flight, Pages 1 and 2

JET TRANSPORT FLIGHT ITINERARY
FORM 19-35 (R. 12-72)

DATE ~~April 12,~~ MAY 3 1978

PREPARED FOR	AIRCRAFT MODEL AND NO.	TAS (KNOTS)	FLIGHT NO.	PREPARED BY
	JETSTAR N731A	440		Frank Bray

AIRPORT	GMT DATE	GMT TIME	* TIME FACTOR	LOCAL TIME	LOCAL DATE	DISTANCE TO FLY	** BLOCK TIME	GROUND TIME	REMARKS
DEPART KUWAIT	5/22/78	0700Z	+3	1000	5/22/78	1460	4+00		MON
ARRIVE ATHENS, GREECE	"	1100Z	+3	1400	"			1 hour	Mr. Azar
DEPART ATHENS (LGAT)	"	1200Z	+3	1500	"	1200	3+20		
ARRIVE PARIS, FRANCE	"	1520Z	+1	1620	"			1 nite	
DEPART PARIS (LFPB)	5/23/78	1400Z	+1	1500	5/23/78	500	1+40		TUES
ARRIVE SHANNON	"	1540Z	+1	1640	"			+50	
DEPART SHANNON	"	1630Z	+1	1730	"	1730	4+45		TUES
ARRIVE GANDER	"	2115Z	-2½	1845	"			+45	
DEPART GANDER	"	2200Z	-2½	1930	"	1200	3+30		
ARRIVE NEWPORT NEWS	5/24/78	0130Z	-4	2130	"				Customs Okay - 1½ hour notice MPE 10
DEPART									CALL WITH ETA OR CANCELLATION FROM GRANDE
ARRIVE									OFFICE 804 247 5836 OR AFTER 5 PM
DEPART									MR MILES HOME 804 868 7400
ARRIVE									IF NO ANSWER ESS 804 877 0209
DEPART									
ARRIVE									

Flight itinerary for the Europe-Kuwait flight, Page 3

JETSTAR N731A

Frank Bray   Bill Baxter

May 1978		Block Time
Saturday 6th	Los Angeles - Bangor	5 + 10
Sunday 7th	Bangor - Gander - Dublin	6 + 05
Monday 8th	Off	
Tuesday 9th	Dublin - Cork - Liverpool	1 + 30
Wednesday 10th	Liverpool - London - Toulouse	2 + 10
Thursday 11th	Toulouse - Bilbao - Madrid - London	3 + 45
Friday 12th	London - Cork - London	2 + 15
Saturday 13th	London - Edinburgh	1 + 05
Sunday 14th	Edinburgh - Madrid - London - Edinburgh - London	6 + 15
Monday 15th	Off	
Tuesday 16th	London - Wick - London	2 + 35
Wednesday 17th	London - Stuttgart - London	2 + 50
Thursday 18th	London - Inverness - Frankfurt	3 + 40
Friday 19th	Frankfurt - Geneva - Athens - Kuwait	6 + 45
Saturday 20th	Meeting at airport	
Sunday 21st	Kuwait - Kuwait - Kuwait - Kuwait	1 + 15
Monday 22nd	Kuwait - Athens - Paris	6 + 55
Tuesday 23rd	Paris - Shannon - Gander - Newport News	9 + 30
Wednesday 24th	Newport News - Los Angeles	5 + 20
		67 + 05 Total

35 Landings in 20 Cities in 11 Countries

* * * * * *

Abbreviated itinerary

new everything. So I have a crackerjack pilot by the name of Bill Baxter, who is considerably younger than I am, on this trip. He's been flying Captain for more years in this airplane than I have, and he's been flying test production work out of Los Angeles. He knows the maintenance end of the airplane backwards and forwards. He has never been to Europe before, but he has flown in South America, Canada, and Mexico. I think I'm training him to take over my job.

We left on a Saturday, and flew from Los Angeles to Bangor, Maine. The only thing of interest was a monster snowstorm over the Rockies. As we went by Denver, I checked in on the ATIS just out of curiosity. Denver gave 200 obscured half a mile in snow and 30°, which is rather unusual weather for the first of May.

Los Angeles to Bangor is about 2,800 miles. It took us a little over five hours, so that was a relatively easy day. We got up the next morning, May seventh, a Sunday, and flew from Bangor to Gander, New Foundland, about 750 miles. As we approached Gander, Allied Handling Service called us on the radio and said they had not received our computerized flight plan. We had received a copy in Bangor, so we gave it to them over the air, and they pre-filed for us. The weather was forecast to be good going into Gander. However, when we arrived they had about a thousand foot ceiling and three or four miles visibility with blowing snow. Here again, a bit unusual for the first of May. But there were no problems in and out of Gander. We climbed out through the snow and broke out on top and into the bright sun at about 16,000 feet. Just a beautiful day on top.

We were about halfway between Gander and Shannon when we heard a radio call asking for somebody to relay a position report. There were three single-engine airplanes flying from Gander to Shannon down at 9,000 feet. They were delivery flights. Here we were at 37,000 feet with four engines, and they were down at nine thousand feet with a single engine and dead reckoning. I did not want to trade with them.

We approached the coast of Ireland, went right over Shannon, and landed at Dublin. It was raining, but it was no major problem. Air Lingus handled us. They had been on strike for three weeks, but a supervisory person drove the bus, met the airplane, and got our passengers on their way. That was a good flight. Our computerized flight plan showed that it would take us four hours and twenty minutes. We had some good wind, so it actually took us four hours and sixteen minutes, not bad at all for 2,200 miles.

The next day, May eighth, was one of our few days off. We got up and it was very cold and dreary there in Dublin, fifty-three degrees, with a breeze blowing, drizzle, and fog – it was horrible. The cold went right through you. The time in Dublin is eight hours different from Los Angeles, so the body was all screwed up, not knowing whether to be awake or asleep.

We took a tour up the north coast of Ireland. I was interested by the thatched roofs on many of the houses. I'd seen a few of them before, but on this particular trip we must have seen about twenty of them. In this day and age it's really a problem to find anybody to repair these thatched roofs. I understand they have to be done over every three or four years.

All in all the tour was very interesting, when we were awake. The tour driver was an Irishman. He had a tremendous sense of humor and a fine voice. He kept telling Irish jokes and would sing us Irish tunes. He was very colorful and seemed to really enjoy his job.

Today is the ninth, and a beautiful day. At noon we flew down to Cork, only 140 miles, about a twenty-five minute run. We waited about six hours while the folks did some business, and then flew from Cork over to Liverpool. That was about a forty minute flight.

It is now Friday the twelfth, and Bill and I are sitting in the airplane in Cork. The wind's blowing – the airplane's buffeting a bit – and there are rainshowers on and off. The temperature must be fifty degrees, but with about a 20 knot wind blowing the chill factor feels like it's freezing.

Since we left Liverpool it really feels like we've been on a treadmill. On Wednesday the tenth, we flew from Liverpool to Luton, about fifty miles north of London, picked up a few folks, and then flew from there down to Toulouse, France. These were routine flights with beautiful weather, no problem whatsoever. When we arrived at the terminal in Toulouse, we had a bit of a language problem. Either the people there couldn't speak English or wouldn't speak English, but they were friendly, and we got along fine.

The following morning, we were supposed to depart Toulouse at eleven thirty, but the folks were three hours late. They said they were having such a successful meeting that they kept going.

We left Toulouse for Bilbao, Spain, crossing the Pyrenees Mountains on the border between France and Spain. It surprised me a bit, but there was considerable snow on top of the mountains. Bilbao is a seaport. It looked like a lot of shipping, like beautiful wine country, sort of mountainous. Very picturesque.

We saw that there were five or six acres of cemetery right at the end of the runway in Bilbao. There were some huge headstones, six or eight feet tall. I had to smile – here was a very densely populated part of town right under the approach to the airport. I guess none of the residents protested the noise level.

We landed there and dropped off two passengers. They rented a car to drive down to Madrid. After we got them in the car and on their way, it was back in the airplane. We flew down to Madrid and dropped off the rest of our passengers. Going into Madrid, we saw these fields of red poppies, just a sea of red. It was a beautiful day, the sun was out, and you could see the whole city of Madrid. I'd never seen it before. It was quite a spectacular sight.

After we got rid of the passengers in Madrid, we flew back to Luton in London. We arrived back about half past seven, just in time for a quick dinner, then get to bed, and back up again at seven this morning for a trip to Cork.

While we were waiting in Luton for a cab to our hotel we saw a strange sight. It was late afternoon and very foggy. There was a commotion out on the ramp, so I went out to see what was going on. Suddenly five World War II era B-25s came taxiing in out of the soup, nose to tail. These were twin-tail, twin-engine, American-made bombers. They taxied out of the murk like a ghost squadron coming back from a mission. They were in war paint. They had machine guns out the blisters and out the nose. Some of the windows were missing. They really looked beat up. The pilots had uniforms on, and they had their arms out the windows. The short stacks were barking. We found out later that they had been ferried in from the United States for a movie in England. It was a weird sensation to see those planes in the fog.

I can't believe the speeds they drive in the United Kingdom. When we took the cab from Luton to London, we were cruising between eighty and eight-five miles an hour, and many cars went by us like we were standing still. The motorways are just unbelievable.

I also want to mention a couple of experessions they use differently than us. For example, we say "take-out" service, and they say "take-away" service. Well, take-away sounds logical. The first thing on our menus is the appetizer. The English call them starters. "What would you like for a starter?" And then when it comes dessert time, they don't ask, "what do you want for dessert?" They ask instead, "Would you like a sweet?" They had lots and lots of sweets.

We brought one of our vice presidents from London for a meeting here in Cork today, and then in another hour we're due to go back to London. When the tower operator in Cork cleared us to land, he added, "Good luck." It reminded me of the time in Prestwyck when we were told that "the last chap didn't make it," which made me smile. Coming into Cork, we got below the cloud levels and saw all the green fields, the trees, and the shoreline.When they talk about the green of Ireland, it's certainly true. They have various bright and vivid shades of green, like a picture postcard. I guess one reason Ireland is so beautiful is because of all the rain they get.

While I sat in the cockpit of the airplane in Cork waiting for passengers I observed a very interesting sight. A monstrous four-engine turboprop was parked in front of me. It's called a Brittania. It's really a large aircraft. It has eight main tires and two nose-wheel tires. A large lorry or truck with an equally large trailer pulled up to this airplane with cattle in both the truck and the trailer. The driver was very clever. He pulled up to the front loading ramp in such a way that he could back up and jackknife the rig and unload the truck without disconnecting the trailer. If you can visualize it, it was like the truck and trailer were at right angles, with the rear of the truck against the loading ramp and the trailer parallel with the fusillage of the airplane. The tongue on the trailer was long enough that it swung under the rear of the truck and allowed him to do this. I don't know how many cattle he took out of the truck but it looked like fifty or seventy-five. Then he pulled ahead and backed the trailer up to the loading ramp. Next he unloaded the trailer, and I guess there's another seventy-five or hundred cattle in the trailer. These poor cows are going up the ramp into this big airplane, with five or six guys urging them on. Every once in a while a cow will hesitate, and the men will get frantic and zap it along. The plane looks large enough to hold 300 of these cows. I'd be interested to know where they're taking them.

It is now Sunday the twenty-first, and we are sitting in Kuwait. The last week has just been a mish mash of airports, countries, hotels, taxis, and flight plans. We've been in some seven different countries and fifteen different airports.

To go back to last Saturday, the thirteenth, we flew from London up to Edinburgh, a short, routine flight. We spent the night there. But Sunday was a bit of a busy day. We got up early in the morning, left Edinburgh, and ferried down to Madrid to pick up a group of our people. Then we flew them back to London, dropped them, went back up to Edinburgh to pick up the original group, and took them back to London as well. So all in all it was rather a long day.

Monday was the second day we've had off on this trip, and we spent it in London. We saw the usual tourist sights. We saw the changing of the guard at Buckingham Palace. While we were watching the changing of the guard, a beautiful mallard duck came winging over the crowd and splashed down in the huge fountain there at Buckingham Palace. It waded around and looked at everybody and wondered what all the commotion was about. We saw Big Ben, Westminster Abbey, #10 Downing Street, the Tower of London, Trafalgar Square, and Picadilly Circus. We took the boat trip up the Thames. That evening we went out to see the show, "No Sex, Please, We're British." It was about three days of sightseeing crammed into one day. The following day my legs told me that we had walked twenty or twenty-five miles. At least it seemed that far. But that was our last day off.

At the Park Lane London, our hotel, they frisked people at the door. Some years ago they had a bomb explode in the lobby, and they've been gun-shy ever since. So everytime we went in and out of that hotel it was just like entering an airport.

On Tuesday the sixteenth, we took our folks up to Wick on the northern coast of Scotland. They were to visit a castle up there. We dropped them and ferried back to London. As we were debriefing the airplane we noticed that three of our tires were rather thin. We knew we were going to have to make some twenty more landings. The tires wouldn't last until we got home, so we located four new tires in London and arranged to have them shipped up the following morning.

On Wednesday we flew from London down to Stuttgart, Germany. We dropped some people there, then ferried back to London. Tires were waiting for us, so we had the four new tires installed. Then we test-flew the airplane to make sure the antiskid brakes worked and the tires would hold pressure. Everything worked fine.

Thursday we got up early to ferry back up to Wick to pick up our people. We couldn't get a weather report up there, but the rest of the country was wide open. So it was a bit of a shock when letting down to call for the Wick weather and learn that they were 0/0 in fog, and not forecast to come up for the rest of the day. We asked the tower if he could get hold of our people and tell them to stand by. The closest airport to Wick was Inverness, about eighty miles south, and they were wide open. We landed there, and I called the boss. He arranged to drive down, so it was going to be a three hour delay.

The original plans were to fly people from Wick to Stuttgart for a meeting, and then back to Frankfurt. But inasmuch as this fog delayed us about three hours, it was too late for the meeting. I called the people in Stuttgart, and they said to fly the boss directly to Frankfurt, and they would meet them there. That afternoon, that's what we did.

We had a short night in Frankfurt, and then Friday the nineteenth was the real bear. The weather had been forecast to be good, but it was raining cats and dogs when we got up in the morning. It was really coming down in buckets. We got everybody in the airplane by noon, and there was an hour delay on the ground due to all this rain.

So we went from Frankfurt down to Geneva to drop these people. Then we flew down to Athens in Greece. The flight from Geneva was very interesting. We climbed up over the Alps. There was a lot of snow. We went right by Mt. Blanc, which is 15,780 feet. We flew down over Torino, Genoa, and across the boot of Italy. We flew over Florence, down the east side, up the heel, and over to Greece and into Athens. It was a beautiful day when we approached Athens. The water was sparkling, the city crystal clear. We came up the bay northbound and turned right over the city and landed. We met some more of our group there who were flying down to Kuwait.

We fueled up in Athens, filed a flight plan, loaded up this new group of people, and departed for Kuwait. By this time we were sort of thrashed. We'd already flown from Frankfurt to Geneva to Athens, which is a whole day's work, and now we were taking off on a 1,500 nautical mile flight to Kuwait. Out of Athens you fly over the Greek islands. I didn't realize there were so many of them. We flew over the island of Rhodes, over Cyprus, and then over the countries that are unfriendlies. We flew over Lebanon, Syria, Jordan, Saudi Arabia, Iraq, and then into the northwest corner of the Persian Gulf where Kuwait is situated. This huge body of water has always been known as the Persian Gulf, but now the Middle East knows it as the Arabian Gulf. It all depends on who makes up the map.

It was required that we get overfly permits for all those countries. We had them in hand. Lebanon's control area only involves about eighty nautical miles, so we were only in their territory ten minutes. We could look down and see the city of Beirut. There was hardly a cloud in the sky. There was about a quarter moon. So it was a very pretty sight to look down there and see the city. We looked further south and we didn't see any missiles or any gunfire, so that gave us a sigh of relief. It took us about sixteen minutes to cross Syria, about 130 nautical miles. Jordan's air control is also only about eighty nautical miles, so we spent about ten minutes over that country. However, we had a young lady on air traffic control who kept requesting information, and neither Bill nor I could quite understand what she wanted or why she wanted it. It was sort of an uncomfortable feeling not knowing exactly what the situation was. Finally, it seemed like they wanted us to go to 41,000 feet. We were at 37,000 feet. We were a little too heavy to be at 41,000, but we got up there and managed to hang in there for a while, and we passed down into Saudi Arabia. We didn't actually go over Iraq, but we did go through part of their control area. No problems there.

It was nearly eleven o'clock at night, and we were dead tired as we approached Kuwait. The weather down in the Middle East is beautiful. They have no weather, no rain, just lots of sand. We landed at Kuwait and entered into a madhouse. It seemed like thousands of people were all arriving at the same time. We'd made arrangements with Kuwait Airlines to handle us and take us through customs and get us into the hotel, but we couldn't raise them on the radio. When we arrived on the ground we never saw a soul. Fortunately our passengers had their friends meeting us, and they drove right up to the airplane and took us through customs and immigration, and got us on the way. Without these people helping us we might have been there yet.

Today we went out to the airport and demonstrated this airplane to the Kuwait Airlines people. They have a JetStar, and one of the reasons we're down here is to try to get them to convert their JetStar to our Garrett engines.

I took them for a ride, and the first man that flew was a Captain Nash. He's a British pilot who's down here flying the line for them. He's a highly qualified Jetstar pilot, so he flew it and did a touch and go landing. Then the manager of Kuwait Airlines, with his white robe and his white hat, got in the left seat and shot a full-stop landing. Then the chief pilot, who also had the white robe, white hat, and the sandals, climbed in the left seat. He was a 707 pilot and had never been in a JetStar. But he took it around the pattern once and landed.

The temperatures here in Kuwait got up to 115 today. This is only the end of May. They say in the summertime it gets up to 120 or 130. Fortunately it's a very dry heat. It's similar to Arizona, where the humidity is very very low so you really don't feel the heat all that bad.

To summarize this little flight, we left on May 6, 1978, and we returned to Los Angeles on Wednesday the twenty-fourth. In that period of time we made thirty-five landings in twenty cities in eleven different countries. We flew sixty-seven hours. I told Bill that he got three years of experience in three weeks. All in all it was a very interesting, fascinating, enjoyable flight.

1978 Around the World Flight

October, 1978

It is now the twenty-first of October, 1978, and I'm sitting in the beautiful Hotel Shangri-la in Singapore, wondering where to start this account of our second around-the-world flight.

To start at the beginning, I returned from vacation three or four weeks ago. The boss called me into the office and said, "Hey, Frank. Better start planning another trip around the world."

We had a very sketchy itinerary. All we knew for sure was that Singapore would be the first business stop. The logical route was San Francisco to Honolulu, to Majuro in the Marshall Islands, Biak in Indonesia, and finally Singapore. We figure a maximum range of 2,500 miles to have a safe reserve.

The word came back that we could not get a permit for Biak. The political situation was quite shaky out there. So we planned for Honolulu, Majuro, Guam, Manila, Singapore. They have Mobil Oil in Majuro, and I noticed that they require an international Mobil Oil card. We had a domestic one but not an international one. Our accounting department said it was impossible to get one in that short space of time.

A few days later I delivered an airplane to Vancouver. I talked to the chief pilot there and picked his brains on his world travels. I mentioned this Mobil Oil card, and he said, "That's no problem. Here's a man's name in New York. Give him a call, and he'll get it for you."

I called Mobil Oil in New York and talked to this man. He said, "Sure, I know Garrett AiResearch. No problem. Call this young lady in Los Angeles and tell her I said it was ok. Tell her if there's any question to call me in New York. She'll issue it on the spot." I called her, and sure enough she issued it, and we have it. It just seems strange that our department can't get us a credit card, but a phone call will do it.

Guam is a Navy base and requires a landing permit. I got the necessary forms, called the Washington office and had them hand carry it over to the Navy department. As it turned out, the schedule changed later and we never did go to Guam. So that was a wasted drill.

Out of Singapore we weren't sure what the schedule was going to be. I went over to the main Garrett office and talked to Nancy, Bill Pattison's secretary, and tried to get some information. She didn't have any information either, so she called her boss over in Rome and got him out of bed. He gave her the itinerary he wanted. I went back to my office and worked on the schedule.

I made out a check sheet for the itinerary he gave us. Down the left side of the sheet was a list of cities: Los Angeles, Honolulu, Majuro, Papua, Port Moresby, Bali, Bangdung, Jakarta, Singapore, Perth, Melbourne, Sydney, Canberra, Townsville, Darwin, Malaysia, Penang, Thailand, Burma, India, Delhi, Nepal, Kathmandu, Karachi, Tehran, Turkey, Ankara, Istanbul, Bulgaria, Yugoslavia, Shannon, Gander. Twenty-eight items in total. Then across the top of my sheet was: Visa, Overfly Permit, Landing Permit, Handling Agents, Fuel Allocations, Computerized Flight Plans, Shots, and Remarks. So that's eight columns. Twenty eight times eight is 224 little boxes to put "yes," "no," "check," or "pass." It's like that holiday commercial: we just don't want any surprises.

I worked out the schedules, typed out all the requests, and sent them down to Houston where our agent actually sends out these teletyped messages. Bill Pattison came back from Europe and called us over to the office and said, "Out of Majuro, can we go down to Port Moresby and do a little touring there and then head over to Bali to spend a couple of nights before going on to Singapore?" Checking the mileages, it seemed reasonable. So I called Houston, stopped the requests – stopped the presses – and reworked the itinerary.

A few days later there were more changes. Bill said, "Let's stop in Townsville. Also, the sales department's setting up a demonstration in Jakarta." He asked if we could pick up a passenger in Delhi on the way to Kathmandu. He said he had a meeting in Tehran now, and he wanted to drop a passenger in Ankara, and spend a couple nights in Istanbul.

Flying in the United States is very easy, but around the world the countries are not friendly with each other. They actually do not want airplanes flying over their borders, and you must have permits to do so. Most of the permits are good for the day requested, some plus or minus ten hours. India is plus or minus one hour. Thus changes in schedule can be a pure nightmare.

I'd like to say a little bit about the crew. We carry a three man crew. On this particular trip, I have Bill Baxter and Phil Laisney, both of them Captains and both crackerjack professional pilots. I can't say enough about them. They have never been out in this part of the world, but they're the type of guys who, when they see something that needs to be done, just go ahead and do it. It takes a tremendous load off my shoulders. So often we have pilots who just travel along for the ride, but they don't see things that have to be done. They don't question what I'm doing. They assume I know what I'm doing, and often that's a fallacy. These two professionals are checking on me all the way. Once we get back, they'll be experts on world travel because they've been around once. They're younger than I am, so they're in line to take my job away from me. They're really an excellent crew.

We rotate duties. One man's in the cabin, one man's in the right seat, and one man's in the left seat. On the next leg we just move counter-clockwise. Each pilot knows he is going to fly every third leg. This keeps him thinking and is good for the morale. In the final analysis, if things go right, we all get the credit. If things go wrong, I get the credit.

We departed Los Angeles on Friday the thirteenth. It seemed like an odd day to start, but we didn't have any trouble. After three weeks of paperwork, it was almost a relief to get started. It was also a relief to see that the wind factor between San Francisco and Honolulu was -20. This airplane can only live with a -50 on the way to Honolulu. We can't go to Honolulu every day on account of the winds, because there are no options between California and Honolulu. You either make it or you don't. You can go partway, and if your “how-goes-it” is falling behind, you have to turn around and come back, pure and simple. San Francisco to Honolulu is 2,400 miles, and that's right at our critical range.

We flew from Los Angeles to San Francisco in one hour. I had called ahead to have us parked nose up. With this particular airplane you can get more fuel in it in a nose-up attitude. The computerized flight plan said it was going to be five hours and eight minutes to Honolulu. The first half of the flight we were right on schedule and right on fuel burn. On the second half, the winds started picking up stronger than forecasted. At one point they were 100 mph on the nose, which was 50 mph stronger than forecasted. We were falling behind fuel burn and time, but it was nothing drastic. It actually took us five hours and thirty-two minutes, and we landed with fifty minutes of reserve fuel. For a pilot, if you have anything less than an hour's worth of reserve you start to worry that the gear won't go down or the airport will be closed or we'll be put in a holding pattern or whatever. It's just not comfortable to not have a good reserve. It was really a relief to see the islands, to come around Diamondhead, along Waikiki beach, over the harbor, and into the beautiful Honolulu airport. After flying over all that water, it's always quite a relief to see land.

We had a quick fuel stop in Honolulu, and then it was on to Majuro in the Marshall Islands group. This was another long leg – 2,300 miles. We flew by Johnson Island, about 800 miles southwest of Honolulu. That brought back memories. In the Navy, I used to land the four-engine flying boats in the lagoon at Johnson Island and taxi up to the wharf. It used to take us about five and a half hours to fly out there, and on this particular leg we were over there in about an hour and forty-five minutes.

We picked up the beacon at Majuro about 500 miles out, which was another relief. We navigate with this exotic electronic equipment, but the fact of life is that the more exotic it is, the more subject it is to failure. We could care less whether we had a failure now, because we had the beacon and could find the island. It was getting late in the afternoon, and it was just great to see the islands out there in front of us. After a long day, we'd reached our destination.

We crossed the International Date Line on the way to Majuro. We took off from Los Angeles on Friday and that same afternoon we landed in Majuro, but it was Saturday there. So in one instant in broad daylight wen went from a Friday to a Saturday.

Flying west you're chasing the sun, and it's easier on the body clock. We picked up five hours. We landed at Majuro at five forty-five local time, but body clock time was at ten forty-five. We'd been on duty eighteen hours. We were a bit thrashed of course. By the time we did the chores, it was dark, and we got a ride to the hotel. At least I think it was a hotel. It really wasn't much out there on the islands.

It's very hot and moist on the islands of course. There's no air conditioning. Lizards are running up and down the walls. In my room, there were no light bulbs. There was no lobby, just a lean-to. I went down to steal a light bulb. One of the guests saw me and said, "I've got an extra light bulb if you need one." But at any rate we got a night's sleep. We were up at five in the morning, still dark, and out to the airport in time to watch a beautiful sunrise. We loaded up the people and departed for Port Moresby in Papua New Guinea.

There's no ground communication between Majuro and the ATC center in Honolulu. We tried to raise Honolulu on our HF radio to get a clearance. We could hear them talking, but they couldn't hear us. So we went ahead and took off, expecting to get our clearance in the air. We kept calling Honolulu. We called Guam. We called Saipan. We could hear all these stations calling and other airplanes calling, but evidently no one could hear us. About twenty minutes after departure, the copilot wanted to circle for a while until we got our clearance. I said, "Nope, let's keep driving along. We'll get one sooner or later." That was the old non-sked mentality: press on. We flew at an odd altitude, so if there should be other airplanes in the air in our location, we'd have some sort of separation. We went almost 2,000 miles with no clearance, which was not good.

We sailed right over the island of Nauru, just south of the equator. Bill Pattison was in the cockpit. He said that the island was covered with bird fertilizer, and they were extremely rich because they had an unlimited supply. We tried to call them for a clearance, but we couldn't raise anybody down there. Then we sailed right by Bougainville in the Solomon Islands. It's north of Guadalcanal, and Bill had been stationed out there during the war, flying bombers and PBYs. He knew all the islands by heart. He'd bombed and sunk ships out there. He'd been shot at. He's quite a navigator. One of the main reasons we came this route was so he could see the territory that he'd spent so much time in. Listening to his war accounts out there was fabulous. Bill still claims that I was one of his check pilots down in Jacksonville, and as we're both ex-Navy, we have a pretty good rapport.

We finally got ahold of Port Moresby ATC and told them we'd had a bit of a communications problem. They said no problem, and they got us a clearance to let down over the

Stanley Range into Port Moresby. They didn't seem perturbed that we'd sailed into their area without a clearance. They said they'd expected us the day before and had the weather for us and flight plans.When we didn't show up, they did it again the following day.

That was rather a long leg. It was 2,000 miles from Majuro to Port Moresby, and it took us four and a half hours. It was extremely hot there – close to 100°. They are desperate for rain. The Stanley Range evidently catches all the moisture and keeps the rain on the other side of the island.

Bill Pattison and his guests toured Port Moresby. He'd been based down there as well as many other places. Then they came back to the airport, and away we went. With that hot temperature, we rolled and we rolled before we broke ground, but we finally did, and flew by Darwin in Northern Australia and on to Bali.

Port Moresby to Bali is 2,200 miles, five hours, and it was another long day. We picked up five hours from Majuro to Bali, so our on-duty time was fourteen hours – two long days in a row. It was a relief to have a day off in Bali to recharge the battery. Bali is beautiful. I'd been there before. It's very hot and very humid, but very pretty. Great fields covering the islands, oxen pulling plows. We saw the native dances and all these gals and women carrying the baskets and loads on their heads just like down in Haiti. It was a little nerve-wracking to be driving on the left side of the road. But the woodcarvings, the metal workings – all of it was very fascinating.

On the seventeenth of October we flew Bali to Jakarta. It's a relatively short leg, about 575 miles. It took us an hour and thirty minutes. Pilots hate Jakarta because it's such a hassle to get in and out – something always goes wrong there. There were 150 international pilots at our NBAA meeting in Washington, and the consensus of opinion was, if you can avoid Jakarta, avoid it. Don't ever land there. But our people had a business meeting there, so we had to land in Jakarta. We landed and were a little ahead of schedule, so naturally no one was there to meet us. We got a man on the ramp to help us out.

Things were going great until it came time to depart, and that was just pure disaster. Two of the people who had been there at the meeting wanted to ride up to Singapore with us. We'd arrived with six, and we were going to take eight out. When they saw that we were taking eight out, they grabbed our permit and said, "Your permit says six in and six out. You can't take eight out. You must offload two passengers. We don't care which two you offload, but you can only take six out." So there was a big argument.

The passports had already been stamped out, so nobody had a visa to leave by any other means. They said, "Well, sorry. If you take eight out, the airplane will be confiscated the next time you come in." We were due to come back there for a demo, so we couldn't leave with those conditions. We had to overfly the country twice more.

I went around and around until I finally got a man to say "I'll be responsible for this." I slipped him fifty bucks. I didn't know whether that was in fact true or not, but we put on eight people and departed and didn't hear anything more about it. But we sure did have an uncomfortable feeling about the whole thing.

From Jakarta to Singapore was another 575 miles or another hour and a half. This day we were only on duty ten hours. It was a short day. However, in Singapore it was a long, restless night because of lots of worry. We were supposed to return to Jakarta the next morning, but our Visa to Indonesia was cancelled. We'd gone in and out, and I hadn't realized at the time it was a one-shot deal. I thought it would at least be good for a week, but when they clear you out of the country they cancel your Visa. So I worried because we had no Visa.

Also, the landing permit for the demo was for Kemayoran Airport, and the demo was supposed to be at Hilam Airport. There was supposedly no fuel at Hilam. We didn't know what to expect when we got there. We got up in the morning, flew down there, and worried about the worst that could happen. In Indonesia they'd just as soon put you in jail and forget about you as much as anything.

I figured the best thing to do was to have only a three-man crew and no passengers, and Bill and Phil tossed a coin to see who would get to stay in Singapore. Phil won, so Bill and I flew it down there. Ken Goldsmith, who was a sales manager, put on Phil's uniform, so it looked like we had a three-man crew and no passengers, and away we went to Jakarta.

Well, would you believe everything went as smooth as silk? They were expecting us there at Hilam Airport and directed us to the military ramp. We demonstrated the airplane to the Indonesian Air Force. A lot of Indonesian bigwigs came out, and we flew them on a local demonstration and back to Hilam Airport. We'd given the immigration man our passports and explained that we were not leaving the airport. Therefore, we didn't need a Visa. I couldn't believe how smoothly it went. They had fuel there, too, so we put some fuel in and went back to Singapore. We breathed a sigh of relief at getting in and out of Jakarta again.

I had a day off in Singapore. Singapore is a beautiful city – clean as a whistle. It's hard to believe that a densely populated city can be so clean, but I know there are quite extensive fines for littering.

The Shangri-La Hotel was a beautiful place. I had a room on the back side overlooking the golf course, the tennis courts, and the swimming pool. One interesting thing was the rug in the elevator. They changed it every day, and, depending on the day of the week, it said, "This is Friday. Have a nice day."

We were in Singapore because Garrett was opening a new plant and a new foundry, so there were lots of ceremonies. There were about thirty-five Garrett people there. Bill Pattison was the ranking man. They had banquets, and about 150 guests attended. They also had displays, newspaper accounts, tours, and other entertainments. It's hard to imagine how much that whole shindig cost.

Then the shocker. Word came that they wanted another demo in Jakarta. There were some other bigwigs that had to see the airplane before they could approve conversion. I called Jakarta and didn't have much luck getting permits because of a language problem. I then called Houston to have them TWX Jakarta for the permits. At the same time, I changed the plans to depart from Singapore. Instead of leaving Saturday, we would leave Sunday. Instead of going to Perth, we would go to Port Hedland and then down to Melbourne.

Wouldn't you know it: Friday night, word came up from Indonesia that the wheels would be unavailable on Saturday and the demo was cancelled. For a few hours we didn't know what we were going to do, whether to go with plan one to leave Saturday morning for Perth or plan two to leave Sunday for Melbourne. We stuck with plan two, so I did not have to change all the permits back to plan one.

We were up early Sunday morning, the twenty-second of October. The runway at Seletar Airport is only 5,300 feet long. It wasn't long enough for our gross weight takeoff, so we had to ferry over to Singapore International. When the computerized flight plan arrived it was naturally for plan one and not plan two, as it should have been. The left hand didn't know what the right hand was doing. However, this wasn't anything drastic.

The taxi ride from the Shangri-La Hotel to the airport was a nightmare. We had some of the passengers' bags. One of the passengers went out with us, so we were in two cabs. Bill and I were in one cab, and it was a horrifying experience. There was a communications problem, and we were convinced that the cabdriver was taking us to the wrong airport. We thought he was headed for Singapore International, and we wanted to go to Seletar. We didn't recognize anything, and he didn't seem too friendly. If we ended up at the wrong airport, the whole flight would be delayed because we'd have to go back to the other one to get the airplane. However, we finally saw things we recognized, and we did end up at the correct airport.

It wasn't a very auspicious way to start the day, but we got to Seletar Airport, got our catering, fired up, and flew over to Singapore International, which was only about five minutes away by air. By ground it has to be at least an hour and a half.

We took off from Singapore, flew back down over Jakarta, and into Port Hedland, which is on the northwest coast of Australia. It's about 1,800 miles, and it took us about four hours.

On the way over we called the center and asked if we could do a little sightseeing. Bill Pattison had been stationed out there. We went down about 2,000 feet and circled the islands. We let him take pictures and relive his memories there, and then we flew on up to Port Hedland.

It was about ninety-six degrees, and there were all kinds of flies. It seems strange, but the quarantine officer came onto the airplane, closed the door, and sprayed the interior. He kept the airplane closed for five minutes to kill everything and then opened the door, and there's all these hundreds of thousands of flies outside. Bill made the remark that he ought to be spraying outside, not inside.

Anyway, we cleared customs immigration there. We were a speck concerned, because they had a relatively short runway, only 5,800 feet, there. These jet engines don't like hot air; they don't develop the power they need. They like cold air. We put on just enough fuel to get to Melbourne. It was my leg to fly. I got down to the very end of the runway, turned around, held the brakes, and put on full power. I let the engines spool-up and develop the power to make sure there'd be no hiccup, then I released the brakes and slowly accelerated. They had about a fifteen knot wind there, which helped us. It rotated in good shape, and away we went.

Port Hedland to Melbourne is a long leg: 2,000 miles. We had a good tail wind and were making a true air speed of 500 mph and a ground speed at some points of 580 mph. We flew right across Australia, over the Gibson Desert and the Great Victoria Desert. It seemed like we went a thousand miles with no sign of civilization whatsoever below. The desert is red sand, and you can see the waves in the sand almost like waves in the sea. It was just miles and miles of nothing.

It grew dark, and there wasn't a cloud in the sky. We could see forever. We could see the lights of Adelaide, 150 miles out. It was a beautiful sight to see that city over in the distance. We flew right over Adelaide, and we could look down and see the whole city.

We landed at Melbourne after having been on duty for thirteen hours, and we spent the night there. The passengers had business meetings in Melbourne.

Yesterday afternoon we flew from Melbourne up here to Sydney, and we're staying in a hotel room in Sydney at the moment. Today we had a short flight from Sydney to Canberra for meetings, and we returned to Sydney this afternoon. It's only 120 miles down to Canberra. I asked Bill and Phil if they would mind running the flight today while I stayed here in Sydney and did some paperwork and got caught up. They allowed as if they wouldn't mind, so I have a day off here today.

On October twenty-fifth we departed Sydney. A limousine picked us up at the hotel, drove us through security at the airport, and right up to the door of the airplane. Literally door-to-door service, furnished by Ansett Airlines. They're the national airline of Australia. The catering was good. They also had a nitrogen bottle there waiting. We had a slow leak in the #2 tire and had to top it off every couple of days. They also furnished a limo for the passengers at their hotel. They picked the passengers up and brought them right to the airplane. It was just excellent service.

We lifted off at seven thirty in the morning, took off right south of Sydney, and circled out over the ocean. It was a sparkling clear day. As we swung north, Sydney was off to our left, and we had a beautiful view of all the buildings, the opera house, and the harbor. It was really pretty. We flew about ninety miles west of Brisbane and on into Townsville, which is on the northeast coast of Australia. It's up there by the Great Barrier Reef, where they have the pretty water and all the marine life. It's great for scuba diving. Anyway, from Sydney to Townsville is about 1,100 miles, and it took us two and a half hours.

We picked up four passengers there who had left us in Singapore. It's sort of ironic. The one commercial flight they took on this trip was from from Singapore to Darwin to Townsville. When they changed planes in Darwin, part of their baggage went to Sydney and part of it went to Brisbane. So they really appreciate our service, because we at least don't lose their baggage.

We had a quick turnaround in Townsville. After taking off from there, we stayed down around 2,000 feet and tried to do a little sightseeing of the Great Barrier Reef. But it was a little bit stormy with a lot of showers, so the visibility wasn't too good. Consequently, we climbed up and headed for Darwin.

Darwin is on the north coast of Australia. From Townsville to Darwin is about 1,200 miles, and it took us three hours with headwinds. There was nothing of interest on that leg. Ansett airlines handled us there as well, and we had a quick turnaround. We took off from there and headed northwest toward Penang. We flew over Timor, Flores, Borneo, Singapore, up the Malaysian Peninsula, by Kuala Lumpur, and finally to the island of Penang.

On this tour we crossed the equator six times. It used to be a big deal to cross the equator, but this time we were going back and forth over it every few days.

It was a really a full day. This last leg from Darwin to Penang was 2,500 miles and took us five hours. We flew ten hours and twenty-three minutes in all – 4,800 miles – and were on duty fourteen hours. Needless to say, we were just a bit thrashed.

We had a very short night in Penang. We arrived at the hotel after dark in the evening and left the hotel at seven thirty the following morning, October twenty-sixth. When we arrived at the Penang Airport, we had a bit of a shock. The agent who was handling us billed us for $1,345, which seemed quite steep to us, and he wanted it in cash. That was for handling, maintenance, catering, and guarding the airplane overnight. We dug it up and paid the man.

We received two messages from the company. One of them didn't concern us at the moment, though it might in the future. It said that there was no fuel in Shannon due to a fuel strike and to plan a route that doesn't go through Ireland. The second message really did concern us. It was a message from the Rangoon ATC center asking if we had a permit to go through their airspace. We didn't have a permit, and we had been told that no permit was required due to the fact that we would not be over their land, just going through their airspace out over the ocean. I sent a message to Rangoon to this effect and proceeded on the flight plan.

We took off from Penang, and as we were reaching the top of the climb the Bangkok ATC center said that Rangoon refused us permission to fly through their airspace and that we should divert west to Port Blair on the Andaman Islands, then further west to the southern part of India and up into Delhi. Unfortunately that was so far out of the way that we wouldn't have had enough fuel to make Delhi.

We did divert to Port Blair and from there headed northwest to Calcutta. There's an airway going up there. We relayed to the various centers what we were doing and asked for clearance. The various centers acknowledged what we were doing, but they never did give us a hard-cut clearance. We weren't really sure we had a clearance to go that way, but we proceeded in that direction anyhow, giving routine position reports. We arrived over Calcutta, and they didn't seem to be too perturbed that we had come that way.

From Calcutta we were back on the original airway to Delhi. Between Calcutta and Delhi, we could look off to the right and see the whole row of the Himalayas. It was a very clear day. The sun was gleaming on the snow in the mountains, and even though the mountains were 150 to 200 miles away, it was a spectacular sight.

We landed at Delhi and ran into a real Chinese fire drill there. The agent that was supposed to handle us wasn't there. We finally dug him up. We were supposed to pick up a passenger there, and that was a real hassle. Fortunately we had a permit to pick up this passenger, because the authorities wanted to see it. There were all kinds of customs people there that couldn't understand a private airplane coming in to pick up one passenger. Immigration gave us a hard time. Fuel was in cash, and the cash had to be in the local currency. I didn't have a Visa, and they didn't want to let me through to the bank to get the currency, though they finally did. So I cashed $600 into local currency, paid for the fuel, went over to file the flight plan, checked the weather, and paid the landing fee. They didn't want local currency for the landing fee; they wanted US dollars. It took us two hours just to turn around and pick up one passenger.

From Delhi we headed back east to Kathmandu in Nepal. This was about 510 miles. We had a very good tailwind, so it only took us an hour and ten minutes. Kathmandu is down in a valley. Fortunately the weather was very good, because it's like letting down into the bottom of a bowl there. Farther to the east are the Himalayas and Mt Everest at 29,000 feet. Kathmandu Airport is at 4,300 feet. It was really a spectacular sight to see the tall mountains and the snow. I suppose it would be similar to the Continental Divide out in Colorado.

On our first day in Kathmandu the boss furnished four cars, and we drove for about an hour up to top of a ridge. The ride through the countryside and up the mountain was spectacular. All the hills there are terraced. They grow lots of rice. It reminded me of India, where they had little foot pedal threshing machines. A lot of the men were carrying wooden plows on their shoulders, and they had oxen to pull these wooden plows. We were probably up about 7,000 feet and could overlook the entire mountain range from there. It really was a pretty sight. On the other side, we could look down in the valley and see Kathmandu.

When we were going down the mountain, there were four cows in front of us. The cab driver just kept pushing them along, and the cows were running full speed. I thought for sure a cow was going to go over the cliff, but finally they found a place to turn off and one by one they did turn off.

I understand that Kathmandu is only about fifty miles from China. Maybe one of these days we'll get an opportunity to take our people into China.

Yesterday, October twenty-eighth, was a real bear. Bill Pattison and his party had taken a helicopter to a camp at the base of the Himalayas. This base camp was about 12,000 feet high. While they were there, a real nasty incident happened. Most of the party was inside a monastery when they heard screams. They ran out, and there was a large dog that almost looked part wolf attacking Bill Pattison. It had Bill by the ankle and was trying to take his leg off. The monk grabbed the dog, pulled him away, and put him on a big chain. Then, the people flew back to Kathmandu. I'll talk more on this later.

We're still having problems with our tire. It still won't hold air. For a partial weight takeoff, it's safe enough, but I wouldn't want to trust it for a gross weight takeoff. The legs we flew yesterday were short enough that we could depart about 5,000 pounds under gross weight.

The runway at Kathmandu is only 6,600 feet long and at an altitude of 4,300 feet. One potential problem with takeoff was the many hawks – beautiful birds – flying around the airport. Birds are a real danger for a jet, because if the engine sucks one in, the engine blows. If you lose one or two engines, the airplane might not stay in the air. Consequently, we did everything we could to scare them away from us. We had our navigation lights on, our landing lights on, our taxi lights on, strobes running, and beacon turning. It's been said that a radar will scare birds. Some way or another they sense the rays, and that scares them away. At any rate, we took off and didn't hit any of them. We went over India and into Pakistan and landed at Karachi.

Pakistan has unusual rules. It's impossible for an airplane to overfly Pakistan without landing. This is excluding scheduled airlines, of course. But all airplanes of our type must land in Pakistan, either at Karachi or Lahore. Pure and simple, this requirement is just so

Pakistan will get money from us for using their airspace. It is impossible to prepay, so you must land. We got in and out of Karachi without too much trouble, and then we went on to Tehran, Iran.

Our people had a meeting with an Iranian General and his group. The Shah of Iran has two JetStars, and we're trying to sell him on the possibility of converting his planes to our 731 engines. We were there about three hours. By this time it was pitch dark, but we went on to Istanbul.

For some reason or another, there was no communication between Iran and Turkey yesterday, so Turkey did not know we were coming. As we were going along the airway, we heard a position report of a British Speedbird, and he was going to arrive over a checkpoint within one minute of the time we were going to arrive over the same checkpoint. Both of us were at the same altitude. We called him and said, "Look's like there's a potential conflict. We're going to climb to 360, and if you'll stay at 350 we'll have some separation." We coordinated, and finally Turkey got the message that we were both there, and they provided positive separation. No big deal; it was just interesting that in this day and age there could be a communication failure and potential for midair collision.

We landed in Istanbul in heavy rain, and we were a bit tired. We flew three legs, each about 1,300 miles, which totaled almost 5,000 miles. Air time was close to nine hours, and our on-duty time was about sixteen hours. Consequently, we were really beat.

Today is October twenty-ninth, and we have a day off here in Istanbul. We're in the beautiful Hilton Hotel. My room is on the fifth floor and overlooks the very pretty Bosporus Strait, which separates Europe from Asia. Today it's just pouring cats and dogs. It's miserable weather outside.

We really have a problem now. The boss called the United States and got ahold of our company doctor, and they're very concerned that the dog that bit him back in the Himalayas was rabid. Bill has about ten days to find out if the dog has rabies or to start taking shots. I understand that if he takes the shots, it's possible that it could be fatal, and if he doesn't take the shots and it turns out the dog had rabies, that could be fatal also. So he's been trying to get in touch with people back in Kathmandu. He authorized payment – whatever expenses are necessary – for a veterinarian from Kathmandu to get on a helicopter, go back to the base, run the test, and find out for sure if the dog is rabid or not.

Unfortunately, the communications are very limited here. We can't get through, so we're leaving early tomorrow and flying to Geneva, which is a change of plans. Garrett Organization has a tremendous network of communications in Geneva. When we land there, Bill's going to try to get the Nepal embassy and the Swiss embassy and the US embassy together to ramrod this deal through. He figures that, between the embassies in Geneva and the communications network there, he can get a lot more done than by staying here. If he can accomplish what he needs to accomplish tomorrow, we'll continue on to Shannon, Gander, and back to the United States. If he can't accomplish this, I guess we'll spend the night in Geneva and play it by ear.

On October thirtieth we got up early in Istanbul for a flight to Geneva. It was a routine takeoff, and we headed west over the Turkey border and into Bulgaria. Sofia control in Bulgaria said that the next country, Yugoslavia, questioned our permit to fly over their country. We relayed our permit number and date to be sent to Belgrade control, to which Sofia replied, "I think it will probably be ok." That wasn't very encouraging. However, we sailed across the border between Bulgaria and Yugoslavia, and Belgrade didn't question it. It was really with a sigh of relief that we went through, because I'm not sure what we would have done if they had told us to turn back. I suppose the worst thing that could have happened would have been for them to demand that we land at Belgrade and pay fees and fines to straighten the situation out. However, we flew across their western border, glad to be back into Europe. We flew by the Alps and Mount Blanc and into Geneva. Geneva was fogged in that day, but fortunately they had minimum, so we shot an ILS approach and picked up the approach lights at about 200 feet. We were glad to see the runway, of course. Istanbul to Geneva is about 1,300 miles or two hours and forty-five minutes.

We spent the rest of the day at the airport waiting to see how Bill Pattison was making out. We received word late in the afternoon that we were going to spend the night in Geneva and that we needed to bring in some of the passengers' bags. It was the old baggage routine: sort out the bags they wanted, leave the bags that they didn't want on the airplane, and hire two cabs. With this mountain of baggage – and hoping we had the right ones – we proceeded to the hotel. The hotel was right on Lake Geneva, which was a very pretty sight.

The next day was the hardest drill of the entire flight. We flew from Geneva to Shannon to Gander to Milwaukee to Los Angeles. This is some 6,400 miles. Our block time was sixteen hours. Our on-duty time was about twenty-one hours.

We had been away from home for eighteen days. We did not fly on six of those days. Thus, in the twelve days that we flew, we flew 35,460 miles. That's an average of almost 3,000 miles of flying per day. We flew eighty-four total hours, or seven hours per day on average, so we were very glad to get home. But it wasn't quite as bad as it sounds.

We took off from Geneva around nine in the morning. We were chasing the sun, so we arrived in Los Angeles at seven that evening. Most of the flight was in the sunshine, which always makes life a little easier.

The sequel to this whole story is, first of all, the jet lag. The time difference between Geneva and Los Angeles is nine hours. Invariably, we'd wake up at two or three in the morning, as wide awake as a tree full of owls. Then we'd fall asleep in the afternoon between three and four. The old body clock was so screwed up; it didn't know whether to be asleep or awake. It was really backwards. Depending on the individual, it takes three to six days to get the body clock back to normal.

A day after we got home we had a shocker. This whole trip we'd had trouble keeping air in the #2 tire, and we thought it was a slow leak in the tire itself. In Los Angeles they filled the tire, and as they were towing the airplane to a new position, they heard this *psst psst psst* sound every time the wheel rotated. They could hear the air coming out, and they immediately suspected something more than a simple leak in the tire.

They jacked up the plane and took the wheel off. It was a split-rim, so they split the rims and took it apart. They found that the rim itself had a crack in it. As long as there was no weight on the crack, it would hold the 210 pounds of air pressure. But if there was weight on the crack, the weight would split the crack open just a speck, and a little bit of air would leak out. Consequently, as we were taxiing out and taking off, even though we'd filled it to 210 pounds, it was losing air. That was why, when we tried to put air in it in Kathmandu, it leaked out as fast as we put in it. The wheel had rotated so the crack was on the bottom. We'd put our hands all around the beads and valve stem and couldn't feel anything coming out, but we could sure hear it.

The consequences of that rim splitting all the way open and the wheel coming apart are just too horrible to think about. The tire would have blown, and then the other tire wouldn't have been able to hold the weight and would have blown as well. Then we would have been on the rims, and if we'd been up to a good speed, I doubt we could have held it on the runway. We would have swerved off the runway.

Anyway, nothing did happen, but we're thankful that we're home, and that they found out what was wrong. It's really amazing that we flew the airplane for over two weeks with a split rim. I guess it's one of those things where what you don't know won't hurt you.

The other sequel to this flight is that Bill Pattison is taking a series of shots to protect against the possibility that the dog in Nepal was rabid. The communications between the United States and Nepal were a bust, and the danger of the situation was too great to take a chance on. We're all keeping our fingers crossed over his condition.

1979 Around the World Flight

January, 1979

At the moment it is January 9, 1979, and I'm sitting in Seoul, Korea, trying to think of how to start this account of my third around-the-world flight.

I suppose most people would consider it very fortunate to go around the world once. I've already been around twice. So when this third flight came up my boss said, "Hey, Frank, you're the most experienced man we have. You've been around twice. You're nailed for the third time around." Frankly, I really wasn't in the mood for it. After a while enough's enough. On the other hand, there's something about it that appeals to my ego. If he wanted me, well, I wanted to be wanted.

Ever since the trip came up, it's really been a can of worms. First, Mr. Wetzel, the president of the company, wanted to go into Peshawar in Pakistan, and this is not a regular port of entry. It's on the northern border of Pakistan, just below China, and it's a military zone. They don't like civilian people in there. I talked to Kaiser, and they'd tried to get their people in there a year or so ago and weren't able to do so. So I didn't hold much hope for that. I decided to use Karachi as a backup.

In any event, the logical route from Pakistan to France is over Iran, Turkey, Bulgaria, and Yugoslavia. So that

CHECK LIST WORLD FLIGHT JETSTAR 3 EK JAN 1979	VISA	OVERFLY PERMIT	LANDING PERMIT	HANDLING AGENT	FUEL	COMPUTERIZED FLIGHT PLAN	SHOTS	REMARKS
LOS ANGELES	-	-	-	-	-	1	-	COMP F/P SFO - HNL
HONOLULU	-	-	-	NO	NO	3	-	COMP F/P HNL-WAKE-SAIPAN-SEOUL
WAKE	-	-	(OK) YES	(OK) YES	(OK) YES	-	-	
SAIPAN	-	-	(OK) YES	(OK) YES	(OK) YES	-	-	
SEOUL, KOREA	(OK) YES	YES	YES	(OK) YES	(OK) YES	-	SMALL POX	LANDING PERMIT NIL NV 6 OUT ? FUEL CASH HANGAR SPACE ?
TAIPEI, TAIWAN	(OK) YES	YES	(OK) YES	(OK) YES	(OK) YES	-	-	
HONG KONG	NO	YES	(OK) YES	(OK) YES	(OK) YES	1	-	COMP F/P HONG KONG - SINGAPORE UNIVERSAL SAYS WE DO NOT NEED INSURANCE BOND
BANGKOK								ATC ONLY. NO PERMIT REQUIRED
MALAYSIA	-	12 HR FLT PLAN YES		-	-	-	-	UNIVERSAL SAYS WE DON'T NEED. IN AND OUT OF SINGAPORE.
SINGAPORE	-	NO	(OK) YES	(OK) YES	(OK) YES	1	-	COMP F/P SINGAPORE - COLOMBO
INDONESIA	-	(OK) YES	-	-	-	-	-	PERMIT NO 17524/28/12/78
COLOMBO	NO	NO	NO	(OK) YES	NIL ~~YES~~	1	-	COMP F/P COLOMBO - KATHMANDU ALL CURRENCY DECLARED ON ARRIVAL.
INDIA MADRAS	-	(OK) YES	(OK) YES	(OK) YES	YES	-	-	TWO (OK) PERMITS, ~~OVER~~ MADRAS AND BACK.
KATHMANDU NEPAL	(OK) YES	YES	(OK) YES	(OK) YES	YES	-	-	FUEL CASH
PESHAWAR ~~KARACHI~~ > PAKISTAN	NO	YES	(OK) YES	(OK) YES	YES	2	-	PAKISTAN AIRLINES COMP F/P PAKISTAN - BAHRAIN - ATHENS
OMAN	-	NO	-	-	-	-	-	WE DO NOT OVERFLY THIS COUNTRY IFIM SAYS YES. UNIVERSAL SAYS NO.
UNITED ARAB EMIRATES	-	NO	-	-	-	-	-	FLIGHT PLAN ETA -2
QATAR	-	NO	-	-	-	-	-	" " "
BAHRAIN	NO	NO	YES	(OK) YES	YES	-	-	UNIVERSAL SAYS YES ~~FLIGHT PLAN~~
SAUDI ARABIA	-	(OK) YES	-	-	-	-	-	
JORDAN	-	YES	-	-	-	-	-	
SYRIA	-	YES	-	-	-	-	-	
LEBANON	-	NO ~~YES~~	-	-	-	-	-	UNIVERSAL SAYS NO
ATHENS	-	NO	NO	(OK) YES	YES	-	-	
STRASBURG	-	-	-	NO	-	-	-	
PAU	-	-	-	NO	-	-	-	
DUBLIN	-	-	-	YES	-	-	-	
CORK	-	-	-	NO	-	1	-	COMP F/P CORK - GANDER ATLANTIC TR
GANDER	-	-	-	NO	-	-	-	

Initial checklist for the 1979 flight around the world

was the second hiccup: after I'd planned the whole flight, the political situation in Iran blew up. The president called me and said, "No way do we want to fly over Iran."

Pakistan to Ankara, Turkey, where we planned on getting fuel, is near the edge of our range. So if the winds are too strong or the weather is bad in Ankara, we would have to land in Tehran. If they had a fuel strike there, we could be there forever. So I redid the flight plan to go south of Iran and over to Bahrain, and then up over Saudi Arabia, Syria, and Jordan.

Then the third hiccup was that one of the stops was Taipei in Taiwan. After the entire trip was planned the US government decided to recognize China, so Taipei was up in arms, bitter against the Americans. I'm really amazed our people still want to go in there, and we're going in there tomorrow.

To recount, the trip was going to involve Los Angeles, Honolulu, Wake, Saipan, Seoul, Taipei, Hong Kong, overfly Bangkok, Malaysia, Singapore, overflying Indonesia, into Colombo on Sri Lanka, Madras in India, Kathmandu in Nepal, and good old Peshawar, Pakistan. And now we're going south around Iran, so we need to consider Oman, United Arab Emirates, Qatar, Bahrain, Saudi Arabia, Jordan, Syria, Lebanon, Athens, Strasbourg, Paris, Dublin, Cork, and Gander. And eventually back home.

Our passengers were commercialing to Seoul. They took Korean Airlines and left Los Angeles at eight in the morning for Honolulu. Then they flew from Honolulu nonstop into Tokyo, and then on to Seoul. They crossed the international date line, but actually as far as the sun was concerned they took off at eight in the morning and landed in Seoul at eight that night. Technically it was eight o'clock the next night. So our first flight with the passengers was from Seoul to Taipei on the tenth.

I figured that, for us to make it comfortably, we'd have to leave Los Angeles on the fourth. And that would really only give us two days leeway in case of mechanical or weather problems. Complicating the situation, Lou Berger had some folks he wanted to take to Honolulu, so he definitely wanted us to go to Honolulu. I made up a little chart, and it was a real Chinese jigsaw puzz.e. To further compound this puzzle, Midway is closed on Saturday and Sunday. Wake Island is closed on Monday.

So plan #1 was to leave on Thursday the fourth and go Los Angeles, San Francisco, Honolulu, spend a day there, and then on Saturday the sixth fly from Honolulu, cross the International Date line, to Wake, and Saipan. Spend Sunday night there, and then Monday go Saipan to Seoul with Tuesday a free day, and be all ready for a Wednesday departure.

Plan #2 was Los Angeles, Seattle, and Cold Bay on Thursday the fourth. Then on Friday Cold Bay, Midway, across the International Date line, Wake, to Saipan on the sixth, and still get to Seoul on Monday.

Plan #3 was to leave on Friday.

Plan #4 was to leave on Saturday.

Plan #5 was to leave on Sunday.

Really the only sure way to make it was to leave on the fourth. On the third we decided we'd pack our bags and come to the airport and see how the winds were going to be. When we arrived at the airport in the morning we would decide what to do. GG said I didn't sleep much Wednesday night, the third. I was tossing and turning thinking about the various possibilities.

When we arrived at the Los Angeles Airport on the fourth, the forecast winds were too strong between California and Honolulu for Thursday, Friday, and Saturday, so that more or less dictated that we would leave and go via Cold Bay. The second factor that convinced us was the fact that Tropical Storm Alice was out in the Marshall Islands, and if we left on Thursday we could probably bypass the storm. If we waited until Friday or Saturday it might be right between us and our destination and delay us. So we loaded up the airplane at about ten and departed for Seattle and Cold Bay.

Cold Bay is in Alaska, on the Aleutian chain of islands. I think it's about 600 miles southwest of Anchorage, maybe a third of the way out on the Aleutian chain. Actually it's farther west than Honolulu. It's too far from

Los Angeles to Cold Bay to go nonstop, so the logical stop was Seattle. That's about a thousand miles away, two hours and ten minutes.

The flight to Seattle was routine. Seattle was crystal clear, just unbelievably clear, very beautiful. The temperature there was 43°, a little brisk. Then we headed on to Cold Bay. Seattle to Cold Bay is about 1,900 miles. It took us four hours and ten minutes.

By the time we got up there it was dark, rainy, and misty. The map showed a mountain called Frosty Peak just seven miles south of the airport. This peak is 6,700 feet high. It's hard to believe a mountain that tall is right next to an airport. Inasmuch as they did have a low ceiling and it was dark, we followed the approved procedures, took no shortcuts, and shot an approach into the airport. The temperature was about 40° with a twenty knot wind blowing, so the chill factor was very low.

There is not much at Cold Bay at all, just a barracks and a hotel with a small bar. We really felt out of place. We walked in with our coats and ties, and everybody else there was in wool jackets, stocking hats, and boots. We felt like people from outer space.

The mess hall was like Sloppy Joe's. The cook was in a longjohn top, sloppy pants, and unlaced shoes. I got a tray, and they just flopped the food onto the tray.

The rooms were sort of barren, but good enough for the crew. We were thankful we didn't have any passengers. I don't think it would have been sufficient. But we did get the last beds there. I guess another flight had gone in there before us. I think they only had thirty beds, and we got the last three. It was better than sleeping in the airplane.

We got up the next morning, and it was still dark, raining, and misty, but fortunately not freezing. So we took off in extreme darkness. Knowing that mountain is out there, after takeoff we started a left turn and climbed up through the overcast.

There was a big low pressure area between Cold Bay and Midway. Our inertial computer showed the winds were up to 175 miles per hour. Fortunately they weren't on our nose, so it didn't slow us up all that much. About 450 miles out of Midway we picked up the beacon and proceeded on. Cold Bay to Midway is about 2,000 miles, and it took us a little over four hours.

The amazing thing at Midway is the gooney birds. There are an estimated 400,000 gooney birds on Midway. I guess Midway is the gooney bird capital of the world. These are rather large birds. I guess the reason they're called gooney birds is because they're so gooney. They're very graceful in the air, but when they land they hit the ground, tumble over and come back up, shake their heads, and waddle off. The island is just loaded with them. There's a bird nesting on the ground every three feet or so. They're literally like acorns.

The problem is that the birds are a big danger to the airplane. While we were taxiing in, the tower asked if we'd had a bird strike, and fortunately we didn't. But there was a big military C-141 plane sitting there waiting for an engine change, with a gooney bird stuck in the engine; the bird bent it all up, so it was inoperative. We were really concerned because we were so heavy going out of there. We could just see us swallowing a bird and having the engine explode. If that happened we might be there a week or so waiting for an engine change.

We fueled up, got down to the end of the runway, and waited for a lull in the birds flying back and forth across the runway. Finally it seemed like a good lull, so we poured the coal to it and headed down the runway. Just as we were about to rotate three birds came across in front of us. We held it on the runway, hoping they would go over us, and they did. We must have missed them by about five feet. As soon as they went by we immediately rotated and headed for the sky. Strangely enough these birds don't seem to fly above 200 feet, so the big danger area is in those first 200 feet above the ground.

Again the tower asked if we'd had a bird strike. We said, "Fortunately not," and away we went. I don't believe I'll plan to stop in there again. It just appears to be too dangerous.

From Midway we proceeded on to Wake Island. We crossed the International Date Line, so we were suddenly in the following day. Landing on Wake Island brought back memories. We used to lay over in Wake on our trips to Tokyo during the Korean War. There was even a Trans-Ocean dispatcher who was there when we used to fly out there years ago. We were swapping lies, thinking back to the old times. It was really very interesting.

We departed Wake and headed further west to Saipan. We were about 500 miles north of Tropical Storm Alice. I guess they call it a typhoon out there. Of course it was so far away from us it didn't affect us a bit.

That day was sort of a bear. We went from Cold Bay to Midway to Wake to Saipan. As a man says, we were sort of island-hopping, but that was ridiculous. We flew 4,600 miles in about ten hours, and our on-duty time was fifteen hours. We departed Cold Bay at seven thirty in the morning and landed in Saipan at four in the afternoon, but we'd picked up four hours. So all in all it was quite a full day.

We had a day off in Saipan on Sunday the seventh to rest up and relax. It's a beautiful island. The temperature was in the eighties with a bright sun. The hotel was right on the beach. The water was crystal blue, good for swimming. We played tennis. Incidentally I got very sunburned. So it was probably lucky we weren't there for more than one day. The last time I'd been out to Saipan was some thirty-five years ago. In the Navy days I flew in the four-engine flying boats out there, taking out personnel and supplies. They were still bombing the island at that time. So coming back this time brought back memories.

I got a little pamphlet on Saipan, and it said that 3,000 American Marines and soldiers met their death there. Another 11,000 were wounded during the invasion on June 15, 1944. The amazing part is, it says that more than 30,000 Japanese defended Saipan on that day, and only a little more than 600 survived. It seemed to me a fantastic figure. Nearly a hundred US Navy ships, including sixteen carriers, stood off Saipan delivering three and a half days of softening-up blows in preparation for the invasion. A few days later just beyond the horizon Japanese and American aircraft carriers steamed head-to-head, and on June nineteenth engaged in the Marianas Turkey Shoot. The Marianas Turkey Shoot was a massacre. 402 Japanese and seventeen American planes were downed in one day, and three Japanese carriers sunk. As we toured the island, we saw many Japanese pillboxes, old tanks, caves - still memories of the conflict.

In the evening none of us got much sleep because we had not yet received our Seoul landing permit. We had most of our other permits in hand, but we'd sent three requests to Seoul for a landing permit and had not received it. We were in a quandary. If we didn't receive it, should we go ahead anyhow? Should we wait? We decided if it didn't arrive we'd proceed to Seoul and plead insanity. If they turned us back at the border, we could land in Japan and try to sort it out from there. But fortunately when we got up Monday morning and went out to the airport, there was a message there with our Seoul landing permit. So, that was really a sigh of relief.

The flight from Saipan to Seoul was routine, in beautiful weather. It was about 2,000 miles and took us about four hours and forty minutes due to strong winds. At times the winds were up to 150 miles per hour. We were at 35,000 feet and then climbed to 39,000 feet trying to get out of the winds, but they were just as strong up there. It wasn't exactly on the nose, so we struggled along and sailed right over the southern tip of Japan. It was sort of hazy down there. I couldn't really see much, and we were so high anyway. But we could see the island and then flew on into Korea.

As we approached the border there wasn't any problem with our permit, and we had many vectors. There seemed to be lots of fighters flying around South Korea. I'd like to tell you what they have down here in black and white on the approach charts. It says, "All air crews flying within the Republic of Korea should be aware of the possibility of encountering unreliable navigational signals and erroneous ATC instructions, especially in the Seoul area. Air crews receiving warning calls such as 'turn to such and such degrees or you will be fired upon' instructions to change course for no apparent reason should exercise extreme caution in reacting to the calls. Air crews should be positive of their position at all times to ensure that they do not inadvertently overfly national boundaries of prohibitive airspace." In other words, going into Seoul you're only twenty-five miles from the border, and I guess North Korea has been known to send up false signals or false instructions trying to entice the unwary airplanes across the border.

On the approach plates for Seoul itself, there's a warning area that you go by, and it says, "If an aircraft flies into this warning area without proper clearance a tracer shot will be fired. If the aircraft continues into this area it will be shot down without further warning." Well, that was enough to make us sit up and take notice and make sure that we were exactly on the airway and didn't stray.

We approached Seoul. The weather was good though it was very hazy, very smoggy. There was only about four miles visibility so we couldn't see much. When we touched down, we could see foxholes every four or five hundred yards along the runway with a man in each foxhole with a machine gun. Evidently they were guarding the runway and didn't want any strange airplanes to land there. So you can see our concern when we hadn't received our landing permit as to what we should or should not do.

Today we had a day off here in Seoul and took a city tour. It was very fascinating. I don't know what I expected of Seoul, but really not this. The hotel we're staying in is one of the most deluxe hotels that we've been in, just absolutely first class. The food is great. The tour guide said there were 7.8 million people in Seoul, and that makes it the eighth largest city in the world. I didn't realize it was that large.

My hotel room looks right out on the big square, and it's quite a sight. There's a sign by the window that says, "observation using telescopes and photographing from windows are strictly prohibited. Violators are punishable by law." So I guess they still have pretty tight security here. Anyway they don't want you taking pictures out your window.

One interesting thing I noticed, when the cars at night pull up to the stoplight, they all turn their headlights off and turn their parking lights on. Then, when the light changes, they turn their headlights on and go on through, and the people pulling up the other way to the now-red light turn their lights off and put on their parking lights. It's just a custom here, and I guess it's to keep the headlights from shining into the mirror of the car in front of you. It seems like a polite thing to do.

The women are very pretty here. It's odd to see the women carry their babies on their backs in these special garments they have. It's just like a knapsack on their back, and they go about their business with the baby asleep or looking around.

The rate of exchange here is $480 won to a dollar. So you just ballpark it 500 to 1. We go out to dinner, and that varies from 6,000 won to 7,500 won with food, drinks, tip, and so forth. 7,500 won is about fifteen bucks. We're carrying a whole pocketful of money with 1,000 won notes and 10,000 won notes and 5,000 won notes. It just seems like a whole pile of money.

On the tour today we went through various temples and saw the Buddhas and the pagodas. We traveled up to the top of a mountain. Behind the billboards along the roads they have built-in observation platforms with guards and a window in the billboard. So these billboards are actually doubling as the guard shack, and they're guarding all the roads. As I say we're only about twenty-five miles from the border with North Korea. It was also interesting to see the great wall that they'd built around the city. I think the wall was built in 1396 AD. There'd been so many invasions of this town that they built this wall, and it's still standing.

Another unusual thing that they have here is a curfew from midnight until four. It only applies to the citizens. Foreigners can be out and about, but if a Korean citizen is caught out between midnight and four, it's a fine of $30 or three days in jail. Needless to say, there are no taxis between midnight and four. The moral of the story is, don't get caught away from the hotel in Seoul after midnight.

We really lucked out on the weather here. The week before, the temperatures had been between sixteen and eighteen degrees Fahrenheit here – very cold. We anticipated everything in the airplane freezing. But today it's in the mid-forties, and it only gets down to the high-thirties at night, so we're very fortunate to hit it at this point in time.

Tomorrow morning we get up and head back to Seoul Airport for a scheduled two p.m. departure for Taipei. So we'll see what develops tomorrow.

The folks decided in Seoul that they wanted a three p.m. takeoff instead of a two p.m. takeoff. The security there at Seoul is so strong that once you go through customs and immigration it's impossible to get back into the main terminal. We'd anticipated this, so before we left Los Angeles we'd purchased a real fine set of walkie-talkies. The other two pilots went through security and out to the airplane and took care of fueling, cleaning, and parking the airplane up at the ramp. I stayed in the terminal to meet the passengers and help them through. I read in the paper that it was the warmest day in Seoul in seventy years, about forty-five degrees. Wouldn't you know it, the passengers were two hours late. So it got just a little bit cold standing there in the terminal for three hours.

I checked in with the crew about every thirty or forty-five minutes with the walkie-talkie, and it was really humorous to see the Koreans looking at me. At one point I had the walkie-talkie, and I was looking out the window toward the parking lot and talking to the crew in the airplane. The Koreans would look out in the parking lot, look at me, and look out at the parking lot to see who I was talking to out there. At any rate it worked like a charm. I could let them know about the baggage situation, when it left, when to expect it, and when to expect us with the passengers. These walkie-talkies were worth their weight in gold.

It was getting late when we finally got the passengers on the airplane. Korean Airlines and the Airport Operations got in a big hassle about whether we could take off or not. The sun was going down. I couldn't understand their language of course, but it appeared to be something about night and security. Finally our handling agent won the argument, and we jumped into the airplane, closed the door, fired it up, and away we went. We climbed up through the soup and into the fading sunlight, and proceeded on to Taipei.

It was a routine, smooth flight, about 950 miles, two hours and eleven minutes. We arrived over Taipei in good weather. We could see it sixty miles out.

We landed not knowing what to expect in the way of hospitality. But it turned out everybody was friendly, laughing and joking. It just went smooth as silk. One of the workers shouted, "Hey, stick with Barry Goldwater! He's the guy that likes Taiwan! Barry Goldwater's our man!" If you remember in the papers, Barry Goldwater was the one who frowned on our recognizing mainland China.

On the twelfth we left the hotel in Taipei and went out to the airport. We only had one little humorous incident there as we were clearing through immigration. The immigration man was very gruff and appeared to be unfriendly. As he was checking our papers, he said, "You know a lot of us here in Taiwan don't care much for Jimmy Carter."

He looked me right in the eye, and I replied, "Well, as a matter of fact a lot of us in the United States don't care for him either." That brought smiles. Everybody seemed to relax, as if to say, "maybe we're allies after all."

The passengers showed up, and away we went to Hong Kong. It was a short flight, about an hour and a half from Taipei to Hong Kong. The interesting thing approaching Hong Kong was the instrument approach itself. The Hong Kong Airport is situated right alongside these 2,000 feet high hills. As a matter of fact, at the end of one runway there are 400 foot hills with sheer walls. These sheer walls are painted white and orange in a checkered pattern to really make it stand out, so if the pilot doesn't know the territory he can look up and see these big squares and say, “Hey, make a turn!”

Fortunately when we came in the weather was about 2,000 foot broken, good visibility, so as we shot the approach we were able to see the territory. If you're landing to the northwest, then it's a straight-in ILS approach, but off the end of the runway you see these checkered cliffs. If you're landing the other way, the ILS is about forty-five degrees to the center line of the runway, which is the way we came in. You come down the localizer, and when you get to 700 feet you see the runway. They have lead-in lights in a slow curve, so you make a gentle right turn and land. If you don't see it of course you turn right and execute a missed approach. So you come down and off your left wing are these 2,000 foot sheer walls, and off to your right are apartment buildings right off the end of the runway. So it's a very fascinating approach.

Looking out the hotel window in the morning there were about 150 Chinese people out in the park exercising their kung fu, going through their drills and their motions. It was very interesting. We went on a tour, and the amazing thing in Hong Kong is the hills, with apartment buildings built right up the side of these sheer walls. At night you have no depth perception. The whole side of the 2,000 foot walls are solid lights, just a very spectacular picture. There is a lot of building going on here. The interesting part of that is the scaffolding. They use all bamboo pole scaffolding, just laced together with twine. It is said the Chinese don't trust steel scaffolding, so here you might see a fifteen story building with all bamboo scaffolding. It's absolutely amazing.

The highlight of the tour was going down to the harbor and taking a sampan out through the boat city. There are literally thousands of Chinese who live out on the water, and it just seems like thousands of sampans, junks, and fishing boats. We had this little old Chinese lady take us around in her sampan and up and down the channels. We saw all these sampans and junks with families living on board, chicken coops hanging over the sides, people on the top deck cleaning fish, on other decks with charcoal braisers cooking, and kids playing on top. I wondered about the kids falling overboard. I saw one about four-year-old youngster in a harness with a tether tied to the mast so he could only go so far.

The main channel is like a freeway, with boats flying up and down and in and out. Then there are little side channels where everybody's moored like the streets of a suburb, with sampans going up and down, delivering people, picking up people. And there are even sampans with take-out service, where they had big charcoal braisers and food. They were going up and down selling their wares to the people living on the boats. All in all it was just absolutely fascinating.

On January fourteenth we flew to Singapore. That day was very easy. We waited out at the airport, and the passengers actually showed up on time. It was sort of murky and foggy there in Hong Kong. The departure is rather interesting. You take off and go through a pass between two mountains, and radar monitors the departure to make sure you stay exactly on course and don't deviate. I guess they don't want anybody splashing into a hillside. From Hong Kong down to Singapore is about 1,700 miles, and it took us three and a half hours. We flew southwest down over the south side of the China Sea and skirted along the edge of Vietnam. As a matter of fact we went over a few of the outer islands off the coast of Vietnam. We could see it off to our right through the haze, not too clearly, but we could see it very sharp and clear on the radar set. The airway charts stress the fact that they think it's appropriate for you to be on the airways and not cross the buffer zone into Vietnam. Anyway, we approached Singapore. The sun had already set, but there was no cloud cover at Singapore, so it was very pretty coming in.

This was the third time we'd been in Singapore, so we didn't take a tour on our day off there. We just did a little shopping, lay around the pool, and took life easy.

Yesterday in Singapore was our day of frustration. We went out to the small airport, Seletar, where our airplane was parked to pick up our catering, and then flew over to Singapore International, which is only about five minutes away. We had to ferry over to the larger airport because of our gross weight takeoff for Colombo, Sri Lanka. The Seletar Airport was just too small for that heavy of a weight. We got the airplane fueled, the passengers showed up, and we closed the door and called the tower for clearance. Wouldn't you know, they'd lost our flight plan. After much searching, they finally located it and gave us a clearance. This took about twenty minutes.

They cleared us out to the runway. It's just a single runway at Singapore International. We couldn't believe our eyes. There in the middle of the runway were scrapers. There must have been at least fifty workers, trucks and steamrollers. They were repairing the center of the runway. There were only about 6,000 feet left to use for landings or takeoffs. With our heavy weight this wasn't near enough, so we were most unhappy. The tower said that the notice had been out that the airport was going to be closed. We came back and said that if they hadn't lost our flight plan then we'd have been out before they closed it. But pure and simple there was nothing to do but taxi back and shut down the engines. I went in and talked to the controller to see if there was any possibility of having them clear the runway just for a few minutes so we could get off the ground. Of course there wasn't.

So I said, "The taxiway is 10,000 feet long. How about letting us use the taxiway?"

Of course that horrified them. They'd never heard of such a thing, and they put their thumbs down on that. We had the chairman of the board, the president of the company, and the guests in the airplane, and the runway was going to be closed for another two and a half hours. I tried to talk the passengers into going into the terminal for a leisurely lunch, or at least into the VIP room where it's cool and comfortable. But they all had a good book and elected to sit it out on the airplane.

So we just stewed there for two and a half hours until they opened the runway. The runway was opened at three o'clock, so about ten minutes to three we fired up and taxied down to the end of the runway to be ready to go right on the dot of three. They gave us our clearance, the runway was clear at three, and away we went. I guess the only consolation is the fact that as we were taking off, we heard the tower talking to an airplane and telling him he was number eight to land. Evidently there were eight airliners circling, burning up fuel, waiting for the runway to open so that they could land.

From that point on things went fine. It was an easy flight from Singapore to Colombo, about 1,700 miles, three and a half hours. Coming in over the island was very pretty, with lots of palm trees and hills, strikingly green. The people at the airport were most friendly and cooperative.

We went on a tour today through the city of Colombo, and it looked like a setting out of the eighteenth century with teeming masses of people and hundreds of cattle-drawn carts. We went down through the markets along the streets with all the fruits and vegetables and meats. They were hawking fish along the streets. Just teeming humanity, a mass of people, and these old taxis honking. It seems like the only way they drive is with their horn. And people walk unconcerned back and forth across the street. It seemed amazing to me that people weren't being thrown left and right by the fenders of the cars.

The day before yesterday we flew from Sri Lanka to Kathmandu in Nepal. It was pretty warm in Colombo, about ninety degrees with about 80 percent humidity. But it was a beautiful day with hardly a cloud in the sky when we departed.

We were very fortunate. We'd heard that there was no fuel available in Colombo, so we'd put on enough in Singapore to go to Colombo and then up to Madras on the southern tip of India. We went to the time and trouble to get a landing permit for Madras so we could land there for fuel. But they did have fuel at Colombo. They not only had fuel, but it was Shell fuel, and they accepted our credit card so we didn't have to pay cash. So we skipped the Madras stop.

After departing Colombo we headed due north right over Madras and then northeast up over Calcutta. 150 miles out we could see the Himalaya range with Mt. Everest. We let down in the valley into Kathmandu. When we landed there were all sorts of VIPs waiting to meet our people. The hotel manager was out on the ramp. The manager of Royal Nepal Airlines was there with fifty or sixty baggage handlers. It was quite a shindig.

We had a bit of a shock. The airport manager said we'd just beat the deadline, that the airport would close in thirty minutes. Well, we had arrived about an hour early. We didn't know the airport would be closed, and it's just horrifying to think what would have happened if we had arrived after dark with the airport closed. I suppose we would have had to go back to Calcutta. But at least we beat the curfew, and everything was fine.

The first night here we sort of relaxed. After dinner we went down to the casino, and I had a marvelous string of luck. I won 650 rupees, which is about $51 US. I had a great time. I didn't get to bed until nearly three. But I tried it again last night, and I went through 300 rupees in about ten minutes, so I quit.

Today we had a good time. The boss chartered two helicopters for the day to the tune of a thousand dollars each. They took our party of eight people up to the base camp of Mt. Everest. From Kathmandu up to the base of the Himalayas was about sixty miles. It took us about an hour to get there.

Flying along seeing the countryside was very interesting. Like Ireland, there are many thatched roofs, brick buildings, mud huts, and dirt roads. A lot of the houses are way back in canyons. There appears to be no way to get to these houses except by footpath. I guess they have animals to carry in the goods, but there are no roads whatsoever going to many of the buildings. But the most amazing thing was that all these hundreds of square miles of mountainous areas and steep slopes are terraced for growing rice. It's just like somebody carved up the whole countryside and made terraces. And when you consider all this was done with hand labor, just a shovel, it's absolutely miraculous.

After about an hour's flying time in this rattling helicopter over this rather rough country, we landed at the first base, which is about 9,200 feet high. They unloaded some cargo and put a little more fuel on. Then from there we went on up to the base of Mt. Everest. The helicopters were flying at 15,500 feet. The mountains surrounded us and towered above us. It was a spectacular sight. It was always in the back of my mind that if that helicopter engine ever quit, we'd be in bad shape. However, the snow, the mountains, the streams, and the waterfalls were beautiful. There was even some civilization up there, houses with barnyards at the 14,000 foot level. It seems odd that people could live that high.

We landed at a monastery. This monastery was at 12,500 feet and had a tiny little helicopter pad with about a 5,000 foot sheer drop-off at the end of it. We saw the dog that bit Bill Patterson on the last trip, and would you believe he was roaming around loose. None of us wanted to get away from the helicopter to walk to the monastery because we didn't want to get bit. There seemed to be a language barrier. There were five or six natives up there, but we couldn't converse with them to say, "Put that dog on a chain," so we took quite a few pictures and departed.

On the way back we had an interesting experience. As we were going over this rugged country, the helicopter had a fuel filter blockage light come on, which means the fuel filter was blocking up and there was a danger of engine flameout. The pilot asked the mechanic if there were any spare filters on the airplane, and the mechanic said there were. He told us, "Well, we better sit down as a precautionary measure and change this filter. We don't want to lose the engine."

Up ahead there was a ridge on top of a mountain with just a little mud shack. He set it down beside this mud shack in the middle of nowhere and stopped the engine. It was just like ants coming out of the woodwork. People started running up the hills and down the paths. In the space of fifteen minutes, between 200 and 250 people must have surrounded this helicopter. We were fifty miles away from Kathmandu. These people came up and touched the airplane, looked at it, and looked at us. Obviously most of them had never seen a helicopter close up.

The mechanic changed the filter, and all the people were still standing around the helicopter. We tried to motion them away, but they didn't seem to realize what was going on. When the engine started and the rotor started turning, they backed up about six feet. The pilot poured the coal to it, and it blew up the dust and the dirt. Then the people started to scatter. But they obviously didn't realize the commotion this rotor was going to cause. So we returned to Kathmandu and were glad to be back. I'm not sure these helicopters are completely safe.

They have a siren both on the landing strip up at the camp and at the main airport here at Kathmandu. Every time a plane takes off or lands, they blow the siren. They do this because there's a constant stream of people, dogs, and other animals strolling across the runway. If they walked around the airport it'd be way out of their way, so they walk across the runway. When an airplane's coming in they blow this siren to warn everybody that an airplane's coming in and to clear the runway.

The flight from Kathmandu to Peshawar, Pakistan was interesting. To begin with, the takeoff from Kathmandu was fun. The airport is 4,400 feet high, and the runway is 6,000 feet long, which is relatively short for the weight of our airplane. We put on enough fuel to go nonstop over to Peshawar. It was the old drill of right to the end of the runway, shoulder straps on, hold the brakes, full power, spool up the engines, release the brakes, and slowly accelerate. But it was nice and cool in Kathmandu, and the airplane popped off the ground in good shape. We climbed on up and paralleled the Himalayas. They were beautiful, the snow gleaming in the sun, quite a spectacular sight. We proceeded westbound, entered India, and overflew Delhi. It was too hazy below to see much. And we sailed on into Pakistan.

There our problems started, though there weren't too many. The direct route from Kathmandu to Peshawar is about 900 miles. But inasmuch as India won't let you go direct from Delhi up across the border, the airways are about 1,450 miles. Karachi said we couldn't take the airway we wanted due to military restrictions, and they cleared us up over Lahore. That added another hundred miles. So the 900 mile flight was actually 1,550 miles, 650 miles out of the way.

Peshawar is an Air Force base. I was really amazed when we received permission to land there. The day we flew over there, I fully expected the military to cancel our permit and instruct us to land at Lahore. And particularly when they rerouted us over Lahore, I figured, here it comes, they're going to tell us to land at Lahore and that we cannot land at Peshawar. But we overflew Lahore and got our clearance. We had to circle Peshawar about ten minutes while some fighters took off. We finally landed, and it was just a beautiful day.

The airport there is very interesting. You usually think of airports as being in wide open fields, but this whole airport was covered with trees. It had a narrow groove down through the trees for the single runway and grooves in the trees for the taxiways and the terminal area. From the terminal you couldn't see the runway because of the trees. So it was really picturesque to see airplanes taxiing out through the trees and disappear, and then come up out of the trees. It was a very pretty airport. It was also interesting to see the MiGs and F-86s side by side.

Peshawar is on the northern border of Pakistan, and it's really off the beaten track. They don't see any tourists. The hotel was fine. We took a cab and toured the town a little bit. There were marketplaces, the teeming people, the little colored cabs, carts being pulled by animals, and lots of military. There were unbelievable amounts of military personnel, machine guns, soldiers drilling, soldier vehicles. The place was very military.

Yesterday we went out to the airport at Peshawar, and fueled the airplane. We received our bill and had a bit of a shock. Our bill at the airport was $4,728, and this had to be paid in cash. As it broke down, thc landing fee was $50, parking was $50, and the handling fee was $300. But the big cost was the fuel. The fuel bill was $4,300. We put on almost 2,300 gallons at $1.88 a gallon. That just about cleaned us out, but anyway I paid the bill.

The flight from Peshawar to Bahrain was about 1,800 miles. After we landed at Peshawar, I took our proposed flight plan over to the military to pre-file it. They told me that if we filed it six hours in advance, the military security would look it over, and if they approved it they would allow us to go the routing that we desired. So I left the flight plan with them. The next morning they assured me that the flight plan had been approved and that we could take the routing that we wanted.

We took off, and as soon as we got in the air, they rerouted us on a longer route than we'd planned. It didn't really make too much difference, but they routed us down over Karachi, which is on the south coast, a little out of the way. Then we turned due west and bypassed Iran. The shortest route to Strasbourg, France, would have been from Peshawar over Afghanistan, and then over Iran, Turkey, and across. But inasmuch as the political strife was going on in Iran, the boss did not want to fly over there. We must have gone 800 miles out of the way just to avoid flying over Iran.

Between Karachi and Bahrain, we were worried because we had not received our overfly permit yet. We have an HF radio, and we used it to call a radio up in Switzerland. We got ahold of them, and then they put a phone patch to Houston, Texas. So there we were way out in the Middle East talking to Houston, Texas. It came in loud and clear. Houston assured us that even though the permit had not come for Jordan, they'd been notified that it would be perfectly ok. They sent airplanes through there regularly without permits. I still didn't feel good about it, but we had no choice. We had to continue.

We went on and landed at Bahrain, nothing but sand and concrete there. Still, it was a beautiful day. We had a quick turnaround, about forty-five minutes, and then headed up to Athens. I was still on pins and needles about not having a Jordan overfly permit.

We were flying over Saudi Arabia, and as we approached the border of Jordan, we called for clearance across. The man on the ground wanted to know who the operator was and what our address was. I'm sure that was for billing purposes. But he didn't question us about our permit, so we sailed across there and really breathed a sigh of relief. I'd made up my mind that, if they didn't allow us to cross their country, I was going to divert and bypass Jordan and go up over Iraq. We didn't have a permit for Iraq either, but I figured we'd only be over their country about fifteen minutes, and by the time they noticed we were there, well, we'd be back out again. But it was no problem, so we proceeded over Jordan and over Syria, flying right over Damascus. We looked down, and that large city was a beautiful sight. From there we flew into Lebanon, right over Beirut, up to Cyprus, and then across the Mediterranean, over Rhodes, and landed at Athens. This was another 1,800 miles.

By the time we taxied out in Athens it was dark, but the weather was good. We climbed up to altitude and went up the boot of Italy. The weather was great into Strasbourg, France, at least up until the last fifty miles. We'd flown all the way from Pakistan into France and the weather was great up to the last fifty miles. They had freezing rain, a low ceiling, and very poor visibility at Strasbourg. As we were letting down, the airplane bounced like a cork in the rough weather. We shot the approach, and at about 300 feet we saw the lead-in approach lights and landed. The runway was very slippery. There was about a half inch of slush on the runway and on the taxiway. We taxied in and discharged our passengers, then moved the airplane and parked it.

We immediately hit the bar in the airplane and had a couple of cold beers. It had really been a long day. From Peshawar to Bahrain to Athens to Strasbourg all in one day was almost 5,000 miles, and it took us eleven hours and fifteen minutes of flying time. Our on-duty time was about sixteen hours. We'd picked up four hours, so it really wasn't as bad as it might seem, but when we got to the hotel we decided that it was time for bed rather than going down to the bar and having a nightcap.

We had a day off in Strasbourg. We tried to do a little sightseeing, but the temperature was about thirty-four degrees, with drizzling rain. It was so cold and raw that it really wasn't worthwhile going out of the hotel. When we got up the next morning, the temperature was still about thirty-three degrees. So it was out to the airport in a light rain mixed with snowflakes.

I filed two flight plans. We flew from Strasbourg over to Epinal, which is about seventy miles west, and when we landed there we were really in the middle of a heavy snowstorm. The snow was coming down pretty hard. They had about three inches of snow on the runway. The countryside that we could see looked just like Connecticut. Fortunately the airplane was really cold, and the snow was dry, so it didn't stick on the airplane. We picked up our passengers there. They'd driven over the day before for a meeting.

Then we flew from Epinal down to Pau, which is on the southern border about 100 miles east of Bilbao, Spain. It's down by the Pyrenees. The temperatures were in the fifties there, with the sun in and out. It was really a relief to get out of that snow and ice back in Epinal.

Yesterday morning we went out to the Pau airport. The airport there is a joint-use military-civilian airport, and while we were waiting for our passengers, I saw a very interesting sight. It's evidently a parachute-training base, because they had the military airplanes flying around, dropping sticks of parachutists. It looked to me like they were about 1,500 or 2,000 feet high. Twenty or thirty parachutists would come out at a time. We probably saw a hundred of them drop. As a matter of fact, as we taxied out for takeoff, we taxied right by their staging area. They were lined up waiting to board the next transport for their turn to drop.

There were maybe a hundred passengers waiting for a commercial airliner there. It's a rather small terminal. Our people showed up and cleared customs, and there were no porters to help us. So the other captain and myself grabbed a couple of baggage carts, loaded the baggage, and had to wheel this baggage right out through all these people. They were all staring at us. We went out the front door and down the ramp and up to our airplane. They must have thought, "This is a funny operation. Here's two four-stripe captains acting as porters." The other pilot told the chairman of the board a little later, "You know, another six months of this and I'm going to be qualified to be a porter at the Los Angeles Airport."

Well, he chuckled and laughed, and then his wife chimed in and said, "Yeah, you'd probably make more money too."

We flew from Pau up here to Dublin. It's only about 800 miles. When we landed here in Ireland it was clear, but very cold. It was one degree centigrade, just above freezing. We had a reservation in a hotel at the airport, checked in, and it was a barracks out in the country. There was no heat, and it was dirty, just absolutely filthy. So we looked at each other and said, "Hey, this will never do."

We asked around, "What is the best hotel in town?" We called them, and they had rooms. So we grabbed our bags, ran back down to the so-called lobby, made up a story and checked out of there. We got a cab and checked into this hotel here in Dublin. I guess there's a saying, going from the ridiculous to the sublime, because this is the newest and best hotel, and the comparison between what we were in and this is just unbelievable.

Tomorrow is the big day. Our people have driven down to Waterford, and they're going to drive up to Shannon. So we will ferry to Shannon, pick them up, cross the Atlantic, hopefully land at Gander, and then from there fly into Bangor, Maine. It's been an awfully long trip. All of us are getting restless, a little tired, a little cabin fever, so we're really looking forward to tomorrow.

We got up in Dublin at six o'clock on the morning of January twenty-seventh, went out to the airport, and the airplane was just a sheet of ice. We had Air Lingus come over with their hot alcohol truck and spray the whole airplane. Unfortunately, the ice was so clear and stuck to the wing that it didn't come off.

There's no way you can take off with that rough surface on the wing. It destroys the lift. They had to leave and go de-ice a couple of their own airplanes. We had a crash axe and went up on the wings and started scraping the ice off with the edge of the axe. We scraped most of it off. Air Lingus came back with their truck and put the hot alcohol on it and got the rest of it off. It was not a very auspicious way to start the day.

We ferried from Dublin into Shannon and met our people there and then had a very fine Atlantic crossing. Our computerized flight plan said we'd have a wind component of -23. Usually at this time of year you expect a headwind of 50 to 100 knots, so a -23 component was very acceptable.

As we were approaching the coast of Newfoundland, we called down for the Gander weather, and it was reported as 100 obscured and an eighth of a mile in fog. One end of the airport was zero-zero with fog. Of course that's below minimum, so we proceeded over Gander and on to Stephensville, which is another 200 miles down the road.

We had plenty of fuel to reach there, and the weather was relatively good there. The wind was blowing about thirty knots and gusting, just unbelievably strong, but we landed and got our fuel and proceeded on to Bangor.

We landed at Bangor and taxied up to Customs. When the customs man came on board, you could just see him shaking his head. This airplane's just come in from around the world, and it's been gone for three weeks. At each stop it's picked up packages, boxes, bottles, and dishes, and it looks like a Pier One store in the cabin. It just keeps accumulating things. I'd hate to have this airplane put on the scales to see what it weighs. We have lots of wrapped up rugs from the various countries, lamps, ladders – just name it and it's on the airplane. The customs man took everybody's word for what they bought. Of course most of the people were way over the allowable amount, so they paid the excess duty that was needed.

Then we went in to the hotel. It was rather a long day. Dublin to Shannon is only 120 miles, twenty minutes. Shannon into Stephensville is 2,200 miles, which took less than five hours. Then it was just a short hop from Stephensville down to Bangor, an hour and fifteen minutes. We flew approximately 3,000 miles, six and a half hours, but with all our problems I guess we were on duty about eleven hours.

It really feels great to be back in the United States. You can drink the water. You can eat the salads. To celebrate, we went to a Pilot House restaurant that specialized in Maine lobster. We had shrimp cocktails and fresh Maine lobster. I figured we might as well live it up, as it was the last day we were on the expense account.

It's just about freezing in Bangor tonight. The airplane is parked outside. We weren't able to get hangar space for it. We're hoping that when we get up in the morning it won't be another sheet of ice like it was in Dublin. We have an eight o'clock takeoff, which is five o'clock Los Angeles time, which will get us home around eleven tomorrow.

Well I'm back home in California now and very glad to be here.

Yesterday morning when I woke up in Bangor at six, I looked out the window and breathed a sigh of relief because it was raining. I guess it was about thirty-eight degrees. If it had been a little colder and all of that had been snow or ice, I think we would be there yet. We went out to the airplane and had no problems departing Bangor. We flew into Grand Island for a fast fuel stop. The winds were too strong for us to make it from Bangor to Los Angeles nonstop. So from Grand Island to Los Angeles. It really seemed great to be home.

To summarize, we flew approximately 28,000 miles in seventy hours of flying time. The boss said we ought to take the rest of the day off. It was a very interesting flight, but more than three weeks is just too long a time to be away.

1981 Around the World Flight

February 1981

It is now Sunday, the fifteenth of February, 1981. I'm sitting in a beautiful hotel, the Intercontinental, in Jakarta.

This is my fourth time around the world. It all started about three weeks ago when the President of the Garrett Corporation called my boss and requested somebody set up the trip. Since I was the senior man, I was given the opportunity to do the legwork.

Our folks would fly China Airlines from Los Angeles nonstop into Taipei on Friday the sixth. We were to ferry the JetStar from Los Angeles to Taipei and be ready to depart there on Wednesday the eleventh.

I started out with a checklist. And if you can imagine it, it's the old deal where you come down the left side of the page and you write Los Angeles, Honolulu, Wake, Saipan, Taipei, Hong Kong, Bangkok, Jakarta, Singapore, Malaysia, Thailand, Burma, Bombay, Oman, United Emirates, Qatar, Bahrain, Saudia Arabia, Egypt, Crete, Morocco, Cologne, Strasbourg, Epinal, Paris, London, and home. Then, across the top, you write Visa, landing permits, overfly permits, handling agents, fuel allocation, computerized flight plans, shots, and remarks. Down the left you have twenty-six items. Across the top you have nine items. And that's 234 little squares to fill in to make sure that nothing's forgotten.

After we picked the passengers up in Taipei on the eleventh, we flew them to Hong Kong. Yesterday, the fourteenth, we flew from Hong Kong to Jakarta. We're trying right now to get permission to fly into Bandung. It's only about eighty miles from Jakarta. The folks want to visit an aircraft factory there, then return to Jakarta. On Tuesday the seventeenth we head up to Singapore for lunch, visit our plant there, and then into Rangoon, Burma for two nights. Then from Rangoon to Bombay, India and spend three nights there. We'll have to make two fuel stops between Bombay and Fez, Morocco, so our plans are to go from Bombay, straight across the water to Bahrain for a fuel stop. Then we'll fly across Saudi Arabia and up through Egypt into Crete, refuel there, and cross Tunisia, Algeria, and Phoenicia, and finally into Morocco. After three nights there we'll leave Fez on the twenty-fifth for Cologne. Once we're back in Europe, it's almost like old home week, because it's relatively like operating in the United States and no problems there.

About two weeks ago, we had the first hiccup. A chairman of some company told our boss, "Don't take a corporate airplane into Rangoon, Burma. You're out of your mind!" Our boss wanted to know why, so I was assigned the job to find out whether it was feasible to take a plane into Rangoon or not.

Well, how in the world do you find out if it's feasible? I got on the phone and first called our handling agent, Universal Weather, in Houston, and they said they'd never booked an airplane into Rangoon. They'd received overfly permits, but they didn't know anything about landing there. I called the AOPA in Washington. Kitty Houser had never booked an airplane in there. I called Milwaukee, and they hadn't booked an airplane in there. I called WR Grace, Paul Stevens, over in New York. He does his own permit handling. He had not been there. I called Ed Black. They go all over the world in their G2, but they had never been to Rangoon.

Somebody suggested that I call the State Department in Washington. I called, got ahold of a Mr. Covey, and explained what we were doing. He said he didn't see anything wrong with it. He had no notes on Burma. He had heard it was hard to get a permit to land there, but if we had a permit, well, good luck. He said, "When you get back, let me know how it was."

We now have our permit, so as one last check I called Bill Stein at the NBAA – that's the National Business Aircraft Association – in Washington. He's the international man for our organization. I said, "Bill, we're going to Burma. Do you know anything about it?"

And he said, "Oh, yeah, Frank. As a matter of fact, I was expecting your phone call."

I said, "Bill, you're in Washington. I've never talked to you before in my life. I had to get your number from information. How could you possibly have known that I was going to call you?"

He said, "Well, I was just talking to the State Department, and they said that some guy would probably give me a call."

It just seems funny to me that I was in California, and the people on the East Coast could keep track of what I was trying to do.

There were two other contacts for Burma. I had found out that a Jerry Schroder had been through there, and one of the outfits located him in Paris. I called Paris and got ahold of him. He said, "Yeah, I've been there. The people are very friendly. The food is terrible. The hotels leave an awful lot to be desired." He even said you had to be out of the lobby before midnight, because that's when the rats come out. He said, "I don't know why anyone would want to go in there, but if you want to, then give it a go."

And then I found the name of Dave Sheenen, the aviation manager for Mobil Oil in Singapore. I figured surely the pilots in Singapore would be going into Burma now and then. They would have an idea of what was going on. So I converted the time so I could catch Dave in his office and picked up the phone. I called Singapore and got ahold of Dave. He said, "Well, there's really no problem. I'm amazed anybody would want to go there, but if you want to go there, have at it. However, I know a bunch of pilots that do go in and out of there and I'll check around and send you a cable if there's any problems." The next day I received a cable, and it said there were no problems in Burma. I related this to our management, so we're going into Rangoon, Burma.

Inasmuch as we were going to ferry the airplane from Los Angeles to Taipei, it was the perfect opportunity for GG to go along. The copilot has a girlfriend who elected to go along also. They flew with us as far as Taipei and then we bought them tickets from Taipei to Hong Kong. From there, they flew home.

The hardest part this time of year is getting from California to Honolulu on account of the strong winter winds. The airplane had flown on Tuesday the third, so on Wednesday they had it all day for maintenance. We could fly out either Thursday or Friday to arrive in Taipei on Sunday. We really only had a two-day leeway, and when we went to bed Wednesday night, it didn't seem feasible for us to leave Thursday morning with the strong winds. I told the gals, "We better be geared up to leave Thursday the fifth, and, if the winds are too strong, we'll try to leave the next day. If the winds are still too strong, we're going to have to do what we did two years ago: go up to Seattle, over to Cold Bay, down through Midway, Saipan, and across." Since it was twenty-three degrees in Cold Bay, we didn't want to go that route.

I called our weather service Thursday morning, and they ran a computerized flight plan that said the wind was only at -22, which is a moral victory for this time of year. I called everybody – maintenance, our office, the gals, the crew – and I said, "Be at the airport in two hours. We're heading for Honolulu."

We got to the airport, loaded up, and took off. The #2 generator light blinked, and it kept dropping off the line. I debated about going back and having them replace the generator. But I figured if we did that, we might not leave until the next day, and then we might not be able to make Honolulu. We'd have to go through Cold Bay in that case. On the other hand, maybe the generator would cure itself. So I elected to keep going.

We flew from Los Angeles up to San Francisco. We received a phone call from up there saying, "Stand by. Some of the passengers' baggage just arrived at the airport and will be there in an hour and twenty minutes to put on the airplane to take with you." So here we were back to the old baggage drill.

We had already filed our flight plan for Honolulu. We had to sit there on the ground an hour and twenty minutes and wait for the baggage to catch up with us, bags that the passengers didn't want to take with them commercially.

We flew to Honolulu. It was a routine flight. Fortunately the winds were as forecast, about a -22 component. It's 2,100 nautical miles from San Francisco to Honolulu. That's about 2,400 statute miles. It took us five hours and twenty minutes, right on the flight plan, and we arrived there in the evening. It was hot and humid.

The original plan was to go from Honolulu to Wake Island to Saipan to Taipei. Well, the military owns and operates Wake Island, and our agent sent word that the Island was closed due to their operations. So we could not go through there. The alternate is Majuro Island in the Marshall group, and the distance from Honolulu to Majuro is about the same as from Honolulu to Wake. It only adds about 150 more miles. Majuro is south of Wake, so it's a dogleg from Honolulu to Majuro to Saipan. We flew that leg, and the generator kept dropping off the line, so we knew we had a problem.

We had a day off in Saipan to rest up. The next morning we went out to the airport and started up. As we were taxiing out, the #4 generator hot light came on. There was no way that we could take off, so we taxied back and opened the cowl. Sure enough, you couldn't even put your hand on the generator because it was so hot. We had one spare starter generator, so we changed #4 and ran it up, and it worked fine. We departed from Saipan for Taipei with four starters and three generators. We shipped the old #4 generator from Saipan and sent word to Los Angeles to ship us another starter-generator to Hong Kong. We continued on to Taipei on three generators. We could get by with three generators from Saipan to Hong Kong and change the faulty one there.

Our stay in Taipei was very enjoyable. We were there three nights and did a lot of sightseeing. The weather was fine. One evening we went to a nightclub and saw a stage show similar to a Las Vegas stage show. It was dinner and a show. The whole time we were there I don't think we ever used a knife or fork. We used chopsticks. I became pretty proficient at it.

One lunch was very enjoyable. I think they called it dim sum. We were in a rather large restaurant, and the waiters and waitresses kept roaming around the room with little carts with all these different dishes. So as a cart came by, you would point to a dish or pick a dish off the cart. You could spend hours there nibbling, and your dishes would pile up. When it came time to settle up the check, the waiter or maitre d' came over with his pad and counted all the empty dishes. He would come up with a total from the number of dishes you had multiplied by the size of the dish. It was very good and seemed to work like a charm.

We put the gals on a commercial airline in Taipei and sent them on to Hong Kong. Our folks showed up and were glad to see their airplane. The flight from Taipei to Hong Kong only took an hour and twenty-six minutes. It was a very beautiful day. We arrived in Hong Kong around noon. The air was perfectly clear. I could look down and see the whole city, the harbor, the boats bustling back and forth, the hydrofoils. It was a spectacular sight.

We spent three nights in Hong Kong and took the tour. We went down to Aberdeen and saw the boat city where all the people live on their boats. One day we took the evening cruise in the harbor and watched the folks fish. The island of Hong Kong is very hilly. They have these apartments built up and down the sides of the hills, and at night it almost appears as if the whole side of the mountain is lit up. We took the ferry two or three times across the bay to Kowloon, a major shopping area. It was very enjoyable. We were disappointed that the gals couldn't continue on with us. But we had to say goodbye, and they flew commercial back to the States.

The flight from Hong Kong down to Jakarta took us four hours and twenty-six minutes. I think it was about 1,800 nautical miles, or about 2,100 statute miles. The weather was good when we arrived in Jakarta.

Our major piece of navigation gear is the INS, the Inertial Navigation System. On the last two legs it has quit on us about an hour into the flight. We have a backup VLF, Very Low Frequency, Long Range Navigation System, and that is also very accurate. However, it's not too comfortable a feeling when you have all your eggs in one basket. We can get by without the Inertial until we get to Europe, but we're going to need it to cross the Atlantic. We'll send a message to Los Angeles to see if we can get another black box either shipped into Paris or have somebody over there look at the box and try to repair it for us.

The starter-generator did arrive in Hong Kong. We thought there was going to be a problem getting it out of customs, but it went very smoothly. We located it and put it on the airplane, ran it up, and it worked like a charm. Now we're back to four generators and five starters - we have one spare starter. So that's a relief.

Today in Jakarta was a nice day. We went out to try to play tennis, but Jakarta is below the equator, and the temperature is somewhere in between 85° and 90°, and the humidity is the same. It's just so hot and humid that it's unbelievable. As we were playing tennis, the body would get warm, and there was just no way for the heat to dissipate. It only took about twenty minutes before we both almost collapsed and figured enough's enough.

From my room here in Jakarta I have quite an interesting view. I can look out across the city into the bay, where there are twenty or thirty freighters or oilers waiting for berth. This is a bustling seaport town. Ninety percent of the roofs are red tile, and it's quite picturesque. There's a park down below me with four soccer fields. It's very muddy. It's sprinkling out, but it doesn't seem to slow anybody down. Off to the right, there appears to be a bus interchange system. They have blue, red, and white buses with people getting off one and onto another. Everything is bustling. Like in many countries, they drive more with the horn than with the brakes here. And they also drive like the British, on the left side of the street, which is a little bit nerve wracking coming in from the hotel.

We're back in Jakarta. We just returned from Bandung. I think it's very interesting how things work out here in the Far East. We landed here in Jakarta Friday evening, and the boss said, "Monday we want to go to Bandung. I'm having dinner with some Indonesian dignitaries Sunday night, and they will get a permit."

I said, "Mr. Wetzel, as soon as you get that permit, would you please let us know?"

The next day I got together with our agent, and I said, "We are flying into Bandung."

Our agent said, "You do not have a permit. You may not go into Bandung." The reason they don't want private airplanes to fly internally in countries is that it takes business away from the local government airline.

When we went to the airport on Saturday, we couldn't get any fuel for the airplane. The main office had closed and the local fuel drivers refused to fuel us because they didn't have authorization. The same happened Sunday. We wanted to fuel the airplane on Sunday in case we went to Bandung. Here again, there was no permission, so no fuel. But they said we could fuel at seven thirty Monday morning, and there would be no problem.

Late Sunday night I received the message from the boss that we were going to Bandung. I called our agent. He said, "You don't have a permit. Those people Mr. Wetzel had dinner with have no authorization. Why don't you just stick around the hotel tomorrow morning, and I'll see if I can get you a permit."

This man's name was Gonzalez, and his nickname was Gus. I said, "Gus, we're going to be at the airport at seven. We're going to file a flight plan. You're going to call the fuel company and get fuel for us, and until somebody says, 'You may not go,' we've got to be geared up to go."

He said, "You don't have a permit."

I said, "Gus, that may or may not be true, but we are going to be geared up to go tomorrow morning."

There was dead silence, and he said, "Okay. I'll have a man out there tomorrow morning, and I'll call for fuel, and I'll go over to the aviation administration and see if I can get you a permit."

I said, "Great."

This morning we left for the airport at seven. I went in and filed a flight plan, and they didn't question it. I figured they would ask for a permit number, but they didn't. The agent was out there, and we finally got authorization to get fuel, but we couldn't get a fuel truck. We were due to take off at nine, and at eight thirty there was still no fuel in the airplane.

We have walkie talkies. We leave one set in the airplane. One of the three crewmembers stands out in front of the terminal with the agent to meet the passengers and take them through the maze to the airplane. It was my turn to be out front this morning. At about five minutes to nine the walkie talkie came on and the copilot said, "Hey, the fuel truck just drove up."

I said, "Great. As soon as they finish fueling give me another call."

Just as the passengers arrived, the copilot called on the walkie talkie and said, "We're completely fueled. The fuel truck is driving away right now, and we're set to go."

I said, "We'll be there in about three minutes."

So with the agent and the passengers, we went through the terminal, jumped into the little carry-all car, sped out to the airplane, stepped on, closed her up, and taxied out. The passengers never realized our problem. It seemed to them a smooth operation. They didn't see the fuel truck pull away. It was just luck that we didn't have a delay there. Even as we were taxiing out, we didn't really know whether we had a permit to go to Bandung. As I said, it's a military field, and the Indonesian people don't want you to fly internally.

Anyway, we flew over and landed. Our people got off. They asked for our permit number to land. I gave them our permit number for landing in Indonesia and hoped for the best. They were very friendly, and no one seemed to question it. About five hours later the passengers showed up, and we fired up and flew back to Jakarta.

Like with most governments, the bureaucracy is so big and unwieldy that they figure somebody's probably approved it, otherwise we wouldn't be doing this. If you ask somebody if you can do it, they're going to automatically say no just to be safe. So the moral of the story is never ask somebody if you can do something. Just go ahead and do it.

We're going out to the airport tomorrow morning at seven for a nine o'clock departure for Singapore, then Rangoon, and we'll see whether we got away with it or not. But, it was an interesting experience in Indonesia.

Another thing that's interesting about this traveling is the currency and the rate of exchange. It gets confusing. You've got rupees, you've got dinars, you've got pesos, and of course you've got dollars. As we started out, Saipan was easy. That was a ratio of 1:1. Then we headed to Taipei and that ratio was 35:1. Just to keep things simple, every country we'd go to, whatever currency they'd give us, we'd just call them disasters. So in Taipei, we got thirty-five disasters for one dollar. Hong Kong was 5:1, which was relatively simple. But here in Jakarta, the ratio is 615:1. For every dollar, you get 615 disasters. I cashed a hundred dollar bill and I literally had thousands of disasters in my pocket.

Tuesday was a very long – and interesting – day. We had learned that there was no fuel to be had in Rangoon.

That created a bit of a problem. I picked up the phone and called Houston to the tune of about $80. I called to see if they could get us an allocation for 5,000 liters of fuel in Rangoon, and, if not, I told them that we would need a landing permit and handling agent in Calcutta. We could fly from Singapore to Rangoon and have enough fuel to fly on to Calcutta, and then proceed to Bombay. Of course, we wanted to go direct from Rangoon to Bombay.

We got up very early, still dark. We got out to the airport and did our chores. Our people arrived on time at nine o'clock. I must say of the three times we've been in Indonesia, we had the least problems on this trip. It was a very delightful stay. The people were friendly – entirely different than the previous visits.

The flight from Jakarta up to Singapore was about 500 miles and only took an hour and twenty-two minutes. The weather was very good. We were only going to be in Singapore about five hours. We had requested permission to land at the International Airport because we needed the long runway for our next leg to Rangoon, but they refused to let us land there. We had to land at the smaller airport, Seletar. So we landed there, let our passengers off, and then had our agent get us permission to ferry over to the other airport, which he managed to do. It was like landing in LaGuardia, letting your passengers off, and then hurrying over to Kennedy to pick them back up again. It really didn't make any sense, but we were in their ballpark and had to do what they wanted us to do.

The flight from Seletar to Singapore International took all of two minutes and twenty seconds. You take off, swing a right turn, land on the other runway, and you're at the other airport. It was an extremely humid day. The temperatures were around 90°, but the humidity was 100 percent. We were all wringing wet. The folks arrived back on time, and from there we headed north over Thailand, into Burma, and landed at Rangoon.

Because we were one of the first corporate airplanes in Rangoon, we really didn't know what to expect. When we arrived, it was something like a Chinese fire drill. As soon as the door opened the fueling people wanted to fuel us.

We tried, in spite of language difficulties, to explain that we wanted to get our passengers on the way, and then would take care of all the chores. Everybody was very friendly.

I went in with the passengers, and they marched us all into the immigration office. There were about eight or ten immigration people in their uniforms, staring at us. One of them spoke fair English. He looked at me, and he said, “The first thing we want to know is why have you come to this country?” I tried to explain that we were tourists who just wanted to see their beautiful country. They had us fill out numerous forms and then passed the passengers on to customs. After the passengers left, they dragged me back into the office and said they wanted $72 for overtime. So I said, “Whatever's fair.” They wanted it on the QT before I went through customs and declared my currency. They didn't want local currency. They wanted US dollars.

I had to go through that old Charlton Heston deal all over again in Rangoon. One of the immigration officers asked in his very broken English if I was related to some movie star. I said, “Well, Charlton Heston was my distant cousin.” He screamed, “Charlie Heston!” Then everyone started pointing, laughing, and smiling. It seemed sort of humorous.

From there I went over to customs, and that was really involved. They have an extremely tight currency control in Burma. They don't want you bringing in items and selling them and taking out money. When you go in the country, you have to list everything of value you have with you - rings, watches, cassettes, cameras, lenses - you list everything. And when you leave, you have to show them these items again to prove that you didn't sell them while you were in the country. Not only that, but you have to list all your currency, no matter what it is - traveler's checks, dollars, even credit cards. Then they give you a long sheet of paper. You can only exchange money at a bank or a hotel, and every time you make a money transaction, it's recorded on the back of this sheet. So when you leave the country, the amount you converted and the amount you spent and the amount you have left have to line up pretty close. It's quite an involved thing.

Of course, I had to pay cash for the fuel, and that came to almost $2,000 dollars. They took me down to the bank to get the money. Everybody was extremely interested in this crazy American. There must have been about fifteen or twenty people standing around and watching me. I pulled out this wad of money and started peeling off hundreds. I think they were maybe a speck amazed.

We finally got out of the terminal and into the cab and headed for the hotel. We managed to get reservations at the India Lake Hotel, which is the best hotel in Rangoon. It compares to our fourth rate hotels. The paint was peeling off the walls. The carpet was threadbare. There were no springs in the bed, just wooden slats and a mattress. Wires were hanging out of the wall, going across the doorway and on floor: an electrician's nightmare. There was an old wooden cabinet, drapes that were half up, and a cracked window. All in all it was not quite what we're used to. If this is the best in Rangoon, I'm absolutely flabbergasted.

I had sort of a backhanded compliment from one of our crewmembers yesterday. He said, "You know, Frank, when we started this trip, you requested $20,000 cash to bring along, and I thought, 'Man, he's going way over board. No way will we need that much money.'" I had taken $10,000 for myself, and each of the crewmembers took five for a total of twenty. But you can see when you start paying two to three thousand dollars every time you fuel the airplane and five to six hundred dollars in handling fees, phone bills, and other incidentals, the twenty grand goes quite rapidly.

Checking out of Rangoon was the reverse of going in. It wasn't half as bad as we expected. Customs worked a little deal with us. They wanted some whiskey from a duty-free store. For a couple bottles, they put us right on through and didn't even go through our bags.

Immigration was a little bit more sticky. I had assumed when I checked in that the $72 was for in and out. But this was an entirely new crew, and I guess they had heard that the old crew got $72. So they figured they deserved $72. They brought me into the room and closed the door and explained to me in very strong terms that they would be unable to issue us a clearance from the country unless they had seventy-two US dollars. I figured what's fair is fair, so I said okay. But they said what they would like me to do is go down to the duty-free store and sign my name and passport number for this American cash. I had noticed the customs guy eyeing me, and I didn't know exactly what was going on.

When I went down to the duty-free store, I thought, “Hey, man, this is really a trap.” I turned around and walked back to immigrations with the immigration inspector following me, very mad. I said, “No way am I going to sign my name and passport number for a fictitious seventy-two bucks. If you want the $72, here it is. If you want to bring that book out to the airplane with the clearance, I'll sign it, and away we'll go. But until that happens, no way.” Then things got real sticky. He got mad and snatched the $72.

When our passengers came through, immigration got hold of one of them and explained to him that, as we were some of the first Americans in there, they would like some of our names and passport numbers as souvenirs. He took the passenger back to the store and had the passenger sign the book. I'm sure after we left, they put down some fictitious purchase for $72 or however they worked the deal.

At any rate we taxied out, and as we broke ground all the passengers clapped and cheered. I didn't know if they were happy we were able to get off the ground or happy to be leaving Burma.

The flight from Rangoon across the water to Bombay only took three and a half hours. We landed in Bombay and got the passengers through customs and immigration in fair shape. It only took us about three hours to get the airplane moved and cleaned and the toilet serviced. Then we finally went through customs and immigration.

The ride from the airport to the hotel in Bombay is pathetic. The area surrounding the airport is where the squatters and poor people live in bare shacks with dirt floors. There were thousands and thousands of people who just looked like they were starving. And the heartbreaking part was that when the cab for a red light, little kids and mothers holding babies would surround us, patting their bellies and pointing to their mouths. Obviously they were hungry. They hadn't had a bath possibly in years. You feel extremely sorry for them, but there were just so many that it was simply heart-rending.

And then we arrived at the hotel. We're in the Taj Mahal Intercontinental Hotel, and it's another world of massive luxury. The lobbies are filled with extremely wealthy people, yet I can look out my window here and see poverty. Shacks, lean-tos – side by-side wealth and poverty.

We have an eight o'clock takeoff tomorrow morning. We went out to the airport today to do the chores and get the airplane fueled. It's about an hour ride out to the airport, threading through the masses of humanity again, driving with the horn – no brakes, just horn. There are lots of fender benders. The person who sits in the front seat almost puts his feet through the floorboards.

Our agent picked up a customs agent and met us at the parking area so we could unseal the airplane and get in. We ordered up the fuel trucks and they said they would be there right away. They showed up an hour later. I wanted to file a flight plan. The ATC is up on the third floor. Naturally, the lift was out of service. So I climbed up three flights of stairs, and they informed me that I couldn't file a flight plan until we cleared customs and immigration the following day.

I found out what the charges were. 625 rupees for the ATC services, which is about $78. Landing and parking they would like to have in US dollars – $133. So I went back down the stairs and out to the airplane. By this time the fuel truck was there and had fueled the airplane. I found out the fuel bill was 27,935 rupees. You divide that by eight, and that comes out to 3,432 US dollars.

I went to a shop to exchange American dollars for rupees. As we were pulling into the parking area – the driver's on the right and I'm on the left because it's a right-hand drive – we were heading for a brick wall. He put on the brakes, and there were no brakes. We crashed. Bricks fell and cement flew. We were only doing about five miles per hour. I didn't hit the windshield. It just seemed miraculous.

Anyway, I changed American dollars to rupees. The driver had a walkie talkie, so he called his troops and said the brakes had failed and to send another jeep. After about an hour of transacting our business in the bank, we went back outside. There was an Indian underneath the jeep with some tape, and there was a man up front who had some hydraulic fluid, and he was pumping the brakes. They were putting the fix on the brakes.

It was back to the airplane with the rupees. I climbed the three flights of stairs again to pay the bills. This little drill took us about three hours at the airport, an hour both ways, so there's a five-hour day just to pay a couple of charges and put a little fuel in the airplane.

Tomorrow's going to be a very long day. We have a five o'clock pick-up at the hotel and an eight o'clock takeoff. We'll be flying to Fez, Morocco, which will require two fuel stops. The first leg will be from Bombay to Bahrain, and it's about 1500 miles, about four hours flying time. From there we'll go across Saudi Arabia and up through Egypt to Crete. It's about 1800 miles. It takes almost five hours on that one. And then from there, we'll fly across Tunisia and Algeria to Fes, Morocco. This is a long leg. It's about 2000 miles, over five hours. So our flying time's going to be approximately fifteen to sixteen hours, maybe seventeen depending on the winds. Our duty time's going to be about twenty hours tomorrow – a long day.

We are in a hotel in Luton, fifty miles north of London. It seems hard to believe that it was a week ago that we left Bombay. We left the hotel there at six o'clock to drive out to the airport. The most startling thing driving out was to see the hundreds and hundreds of people sleeping on the sidewalks. We drove through the suburbs, and people were huddled on the sidewalks and in the doorways in blankets, burlap bags, or any sort of covering. It was still pitch dark out. There's just so many people in Bombay that there is a lack of places to sleep.

We got ready to taxi at the airport in Bombay, and it was very foggy. It was a local ground fog: you could look up and see the sky, but the visibility was very poor. The ground controller said that they only had 500 meters of visibility, and what were our minimums? We didn't actually have minimums, but just to tell him something I told him our minimums were 400 meters. So he gave us engine start permissions, gave us taxi instructions, and told us to go down to runway twenty-seven for takeoff. He switched us over to the tower.

When we switched over to the tower, we could hear somebody at the other end of the runway getting ready to takeoff at runway nine, and here we were getting ready to takeoff on runway twenty-seven. We told the tower we were ready for takeoff, and he didn't even know we were out there! We told him we were down at the end of runway twenty-seven. Well, dead silence. The weather was below minimums for the other man at the end of the runway to takeoff, so we were cleared. But you can see how that horrible accident in Tenerife happened with the two 747's. The communications leave a lot to be desired.

Otherwise there were no problems departing Bombay. The people showed up on schedule. We took off and flew due west over the sea to Bahrain. It was a pretty day, and there were no problems in and out. We were there for about an hour, and then from Bahrain we crossed Saudi Arabia and up the Red Sea. We couldn't see the Suez Canal. We went a little east of Cairo, into the Mediterranean and landed on Crete for fuel.

We had a catering problem in Bombay, and it was going to be such a long day that I sent a cable ahead for catering at Crete. I didn't know whether the cable was going to arrive or not. But sure enough when we landed and taxied up to this rather small terminal, a car drove up with six hot meals that we put aboard. Well, the ironic thing was that I had gone through all this trouble of sending cables, trying to call on the telephone, and putting the food onboard, and the folks decided that as we were going to arrive in Fez around seven o'clock, they would hold off and have a nice dinner there. We had to throw out all these nice steaks, but that's just part of the game.

So it was a very long day. It was about fifteen hours of flying, two hours of fuel stops, and of course we were at airports two and a half hours before the flights, so we had close to a twenty-hour day.

By the time we arrived at Fez it was sunset, and we were so darned tired that we just put the engine covers on the airplane, locked it up, and left everything. We went to the hotel, had three or four stiff shots, something to eat, and slept for about twelve hours.

We were in Fez two days. The first day we were recovering from our previous twenty-hour day. But the second day we hired a guide. The big tourist attraction was a place called the Medina, a religious square with hundreds of little alleys and passageways and shops and people sitting in these little cubby holes. In one section they had the woodworking shops, and then there was the metal shop section. You had to have a guide because it could take you days to find your way out of this maze. There were donkeys up and down these passageways with huge packs on their backs carrying wool and hides. We went into the tannery there. It had quite a ferocious smell. They were dying all these various hides. We spent about two hours there. I was really glad to get back to the hotel and just sit there on the veranda that overlooked the countryside, the vineyards, and the hills. It was quite a picturesque sight.

On Wednesday the twenty-fifth, we flew from Fez to Stuttgart, Germany. It was only a three hour flight. We flew near Madrid and actually went right over Lake Geneva. Off to the right we could see Mont Blanc and into Stuttgart. It's a very easy place. They are set up for corporate aviation, so we didn't have to have a handling agent. I got the people through customs and immigration and into cabs and on the way.

From here on out the plans had changed. The boss had a meeting the next morning, but he wanted to leave in the afternoon for Paris. The cabs arrived, and the baggage went out to the airplane. Suddenly the boss discovered that one of his big suitcases was missing. Well, that's the old baggage drill. No matter how long we're in this game it seems like there is lost baggage. I went back to the little terminal, called the hotel, and sure enough, the bag was there. So I told the maitre d' to put it in a cab and send it out to general aviation at the Stuttgart airport. We'd pay for the cab. About forty-five minutes later the bag arrived. Then it was back in the airplane, close the door, and onto Paris.

One rather humorous thing happened in Stuttgart. I was filing a flight plan and just standing there looking at the weather sequence when this older British pilot came in. He's about my age, so obviously he'd been in World War II. He was talking to this German ATC controller, and they were having a little tiff. The controller was saying, “This flight plan said that you should've been off the ground twenty minutes ago.”

The British pilot said, “Look, mate, the company filed that flight plan, I didn't file that flight plan.”

The controller said, “Well, you're not off the ground.”

The Britisher said, “Well, mate, no big deal, just move it up ten minutes from now.”

The German said, “Ten minutes from now? You can't be off the ground in ten minutes!”

The Britisher almost blew his stack! He said, “Look, mate, if I can get a Spitfire off the ground in three minutes, I can bloody well get this transport off the ground in ten minutes! Now put the time down!” I wish I had had my recorder with me and been able to tape it first hand.

There was nothing special about Paris. We'd been to the Paris Air Show so many times that it seemed like old home week. We knew the people at the airport. They put us up at the Hilton Hotel. We'd been there before, and the people seemed glad to see us back. We had a full day there. We didn't do much sightseeing as it was barely above freezing. I spent most of the time in my room reading a book and trying to get over a cold.

Then on Saturday, which was yesterday, we flew from Paris to London. It's only 200 miles, but the problem was that the whole area was souped in with fog. We anticipated at the time of our arrival that the fog would've lifted enough to at least give us minimums. As we were approaching Luton, we were informed that it was still below minimums, and they asked what were our intentions. The other option was Stanstead, about sixty or seventy miles east of London.

We had limousines waiting in Luton, hotel reservations, and a spare computer that had been shipped over. Naturally we wanted to be in Luton. It was my leg for the right seat, Phil in the left seat, and Al in the jump seat. I told the controller that we would hold for thirty minutes, and if the weather didn't improve we'd go over to Stanstead.

In about twenty minutes he said they had bare minimums. It would involve a downwind landing, but it was still within our minimums. I elected that we'd shoot one approach, and if we saw the airport we'd land, and if not we'd pull up and go over to Stanstead. The normal procedure is that the man on the left will remain on the gauges and just fly the airplane, not try to fly the airplane and look out the window at the same time. The man in the right seat will look out the window. If you get down to minimums, which is 200 feet above ground, and you don't see anything, then you pour the coal to it, pull the flaps up, gear up, and climb on out of there.

It was really soupy. As we got down to 200 feet, Phil was just about to apply the power, and I could finally see the approach lights. All I could see was these dim lights through the fog, so I told him I had the approach lights and to keep coming. I guess we got down to about 100 feet before we could see the end of the runway, and then we were home free. So he plunked her on, pulled the reverse, put on the brakes, got us stopped, and taxied in. It was really a relief to be here. After all that struggle to make the landing, two hours later the sun came out. It would've been very ironic if we went off into the mud and a couple hours later the sun came out!

In any event, today was an off day, and tomorrow we're winding down the trip. We got word that there is a fueler's strike in Ireland. Normally we go from London to Shannon, which is only about 300 miles, fuel up, and then have plenty of fuel to fight the headwinds going across the Atlantic. Some operators are brave. Yhey go straight from London to Canada, but if they run into unexpected headwinds there are no options. You have to have enough fuel to make Newfoundland. With the fueler's strike in Ireland, that eliminated Shannon, Cork, and Dublin. We planned on going from here to Keflavik, Iceland. That's about 1,200 miles, and then we'd try to make it nonstop from Keflavik to Bangor, Maine, which is about 2,100 miles. So there's a good possibility that we can go from here to Bangor with only one fuel stop. Going north adds about 250 miles to the length of the trip, but due to the wind components there is a possibility that the flying time won't be any longer, and it will also eliminate a fuel stop. I hope this plan works out.

It is now Friday, the sixth of March, and I'm back in Los Angeles. I'm mighty glad to be here to wind up this account of the around-the-world trip.

We left London at about three o'clock in the afternoon and had tailwinds up to Keflavic. It only took about two and a half hours. Wecame down out of the sunshine, down into the cold, dreary Iceland weather. They had about 1,000 foot overcast, but the temperature was thirty-two degrees, and the wind was blowing at about thirty knots, so the chill factor was rather brisk. We had a quick turnaround there, got fuel and put on a little catering. We flew back up through the soup into the sunshine, and then headed nonstop into Bangor, Maine. The weather over the tip of Greenland was clear. Looking down into the sea, we could see the icebergs, the snowcapped peaks, and the inlets. It was really a gorgeous sight.

It was a long flight into Bangor. It took us four and a half hours. We landed there about six o'clock in the evening. I was a bit thrashed. I got up at six o'clock the next morning and noticed that everything outside was white. It was the first snow we had encountered on this flight. It was thirty degrees with a pretty good wind blowing.

We went out to the airplane and found it covered with snow. Fortunately the airplane had been cold, and the snow was so dry that it didn't stick. We got some brooms and cleaned off the wings and the top. Then I practically had heart failure because we couldn't get our little power unit started. That's what preheats the airplane. But we found that the micro switch was frozen in the tail of the airplane. One of the pilots went back in the boiler room with a broom handle and pounded on the micro switch while we worked the switch in the cockpit. Well, the APU fired off, and the man in the boiler room almost came up through the overhead. We got it started and preheated.

The plane went from Bangor to Minneapolis. We put on a little fuel and then on to San Diego to sort out the baggage and drop off four people. Then into Los Angeles.

On this trip, we were gone just about a complete month. We covered some 28,000 miles. We flew about sixty-three hours. All in all, this flight was far too long. We've decided that in the future we should set up a maximum of two weeks and arrange a crew change somewhere.

Anyway, I'm back at home and trying to get the old body clock readjusted so I'm not falling asleep at three in the afternoon and waking up at three in the morning. The next long flight coming up will be the Paris Air show, which is in June. I guess we're going to send three airplanes over there for that one. At the present time, I'm a little burned out on this international flying, so I don't know if I'll be going on that or not.

AIRESEARCH AVIATION COMPANY
OFFICE MEMO
"DON'T SAY IT—WRITE IT"

TO: Lou Berger

DATE: March 3, 1981

SUBJECT: Crew Report, February 1981
N731JS - Around The World Flight

COPIES TO:

This flight left LAX on February 4, and flew LAX/SFO/Honolulu/Majuro/Saipan/Taipei/Hong Kong/Singapore Seletar/Singapore International/Rangoon/Bombay/Bahrain/Iraklion/Fes/Stuttgart/Paris/London/Keflavick/Bangor/LAX. We returned LAX March 3.

Crew: Frank Bray, Al Rubke, Phil Laisney. Crew seats and duties were rotated each leg regardless of conditions. Left seat to jumpseat to right seat to left seat, etc.

At all times I attempted to stand clear on their flight legs, and I must admit they leaned over backward with a high degree of diplomacy not to step on my toes.

Both Al and Phil did a superb, highly professional job. Their drive, initiative, enthusiasm plus their many skills and talents made the whole complicated flight, with its hundreds of details, work.

The fact we were cooped up together for a month without a single bark or harsh word shows their maturity as well as their professionalism.

As far as the PAX were concerned, I believe the flight went without a single hiccup. Considering the tremendous number of possible "I got yas", this is amazing. For this, the credit is shared 3 ways. Should there be any complaints, I take full responsibility.

Phil happened to draw the two toughest approaches, Bombay and London. He did an excellent flying job on both. It wasn't fair but Phil did all the catering ordering. Also a super job!

Al is to be commended for his drive in getting parts for our sick bird. Tried in Bombay but managed to get a computer and tack out of Raunheim and brought to Stuttgart. Quite a feat considering the communication problems.

I consider both Al and Phil to be tremendous assets to Airesearch, and either one fully qualified to ramrod any international flight that comes up in the future.

Too often crew members are taken for granted. I have enjoyed flying with Al and Phil and consider them among the very top professional pilots I have known.

Please put a copy of this in their files for any future consideration.

Sincerely,
Frank
Frank Bray
"Honorary Skipper"

Crew report for the 1981 around-the-world flight

1981 Paris Air Show

June 1981

The Paris Air Show comes every two years. I guess the Garrett Corporation's been coming to it for at least twenty years, and I think this is my seventh show.

The crew on this particular trip is myself, the skipper, and co-Captain Phil Laisney, a highly qualified young pilot who is going to take over the operation one of these days. The third crewmember is Lou Berger, the manager of the flight department. He's over sixty-two and supposedly grounded, but he flies every chance he gets. I don't blame him a bit. If I were the manager, I would do the same. But in any event a three-man crew makes it very easy on me. Both of these guys are so highly qualified that I can be very relaxed. It takes a tremendous load off my shoulders.

We had lots of time to plan for this trip. About a month and a half before the flight, Lou Berger assigned a crew, and I was assigned to ramrod the deal. The tentative plans were that we'd leave on June first, a Monday, and fly straight through to Paris. It really doesn't pay to lay over. We would fly from Los Angeles to Milwaukee, then Gander, and arrive early in the morning in Paris. Then we would have a couple of days off.

The board of directors has a meeting in Epinal, down by Strasbourg, on Friday the fifth. It would be Paris to

Epinal, spend the whole day, and then back to Paris. Then we'd have quite a few days off. There was another board meeting in Epinal on the tenth. Same deal then: Paris, Epinal, back to Paris.

We're going to leave the Paris Air Show on Friday the twelfth, and that's going to be a long day. We fly from Paris to Marseilles, back to Paris to drop some folks, up to London, and then take the people up to Edinburgh. After we drop them in Edinburgh we'll ferry down to Marseilles.

Then on Saturday the thirteenth, we fly from Marseilles down to Ajaccio, which is on the French Island of Corsica out in the Mediterranean. We'll spend about five hours there, then up to Calvi on the northwest coast of the island. We'll spend two nights there and head back to the States on Monday the fifteenth. That's Calvi to Shannon to Gander to Bangor. The folks want to spend the night in Bangor. On the sixteenth it's Bangor, Lincoln, Los Angeles.

A trip to Paris is really a piece of cake compared to the round-the-world flights. Flying in Europe is not much more complicated than flying in the United States. So flying to Paris is not much different than flying to New York or Miami. The weather sequences and forecasts are a lot different and harder to interpret. For instance, they use octas for cloud cover, meters for visibility, and millibars for altimeter settings, but it's nothing drastic.

I suppose the biggest problem is the different accents on the radio. Everything's in English, but oh those accents. One time flying out of Scotland, a Scottish controller gave us a clearance, and we literally couldn't understand it. After asking him to repeat it about three times, we still couldn't understand it. Finally some American on another airplane in that part of the country came on the radio and said, "What's the matter, don't you guys understand the English language?" Obviously, we didn't. The similar expressions in aviation just don't mean anything to us because we don't understand the accent.

In Paris we had a French driver, and he couldn't speak English and we couldn't speak French. We indicated to him that it was time for lunch, and we'd like to stop and get something to eat. So he kept saying – we thought – "Magdonail's Restaurant, Magdonail's." We'd never heard of it. Finally it dawned on us that he was saying McDonald's.

We were going to depart Los Angeles at nine. I was sitting in the office at seven thirty in the morning, about to pick up the phone to file a flight plan to Milwaukee, when the phone rang. I was really surprised. It was Elizabeth Berger calling from Paris, France. She said, "What time are you going to arrive tomorrow, so I can have the cars at the airport to meet your passengers?"

I told her we'd be at Le Bourget Airport at nine o'clock the following morning. It was seven thirty in Los Angeles, but it was about four thirty in the afternoon in Paris.

From Los Angeles to Paris is about 6,000 miles and involves a ballpark of about thirteen hours of flying with four stops. In the end it turned out that we just missed our ETA in Paris by thirty minutes. I guess that's what's known as compensating errors.

We were mainly a freighter going out of Los Angeles. We had six minor dignitaries on board and tons of baggage. Of course the VIPs flew over commercial. They went nonstop. So we carried all the gear they didn't want to take with them on the airlines. We had six or seven bags of golf clubs, display kits, projectors, boxes of promotion literature, and luggage. As a matter of fact, we were so heavy we couldn't fill up the fuel tanks. Right away we figured that we'd probably have to stop in Shannon, because we won't be able to make Gander to Paris nonstop on account of our weight.

We had a bunch of baggage on for Bangor Maine, and that would involve an extra stop. However, it turned out that this baggage that we thought was for Bangor was actually for Paris. So that threw us right in a briar patch where we wanted to be as we didn't have to stop in Bangor. We could go from Los Angeles to Milwaukee, and from Milwaukee just overfly Bangor and head right into Gander.

Our director of maintenance, Dean Gregory, stocked the airplane. And when I say he stocked the airplane, boy, it was loaded. We had wine, liquors, cheeses, beef jerky, crackers – just name it, we were loaded. There was no way we were going to starve. And Dean's sense of humor shows what he thinks of the pilots. On each side of the cockpit, very prominently displayed, was a box of animal crackers. It showed what he thought of our mentality. We got a good laugh out of it.

We departed Los Angeles at nine o'clock and flew to Milwaukee, 1,700 miles, three hours and forty-five minutes. Then we flew on to Gander after a twenty minute fuel stop, another 1,700 miles and three hours and twelve minutes. We landed in Gander in the daylight. It was after eight at night, but by our body clock it was only four in the afternoon. It was cold and drab, fifty degrees and dropping. The agent there said it had been seventy degrees, but they expected to see thirty degrees that night.

There's no traffic to speak of in Gander anymore. It used to be a very busy airport when DC-4s and even Connies and DC-6s were crossing the Atlantic. Weather and winds were such that they'd have to stop there. But today's 747s and D-10s have no problem flying from New York to anyplace in Europe. So Gander has become sort of a ghost airport. But it's very convenient for airplanes like ours that can't make it.

From Gander we flew on to Shannon, and that's about 2,000 miles. It took us four hours and seven minutes. It was a very short night. We were going east, and the sun was going west. We were so far north that the sun just set a little below the horizon. We only had about three hours of darkness and still landed in Shannon in the daylight, at about six thirty in the morning.

Shortly out of Gander and over the Atlantic, we heard this voice on our VHF frequency asking if we'd relay a position report. We said of course we would, and we did so. After I relayed the position report I came back on his frequency and asked, "what kind of airplane?" He said it was a Piper Seneca. I asked what altitude, and he said he was at 11,000 feet, in the soup and picking up icing. I asked what his destination was. It turned out that he was going from Gander to Shannon just the same as we were, except his flight plan called for eleven hours and twenty-eight minutes versus our three hours and fifty-five minutes. He said, "Yeah, I'd like to trade with you guys because I'm going to have an awful sore butt by the time I get there!" I asked him what kind of navigation gear he had to go across the Atlantic, and he said, "Well I've got one of those old-fashioned gadgets on top of the glare shield. It's called a compass."

My lord. Here's a guy down in the soup icing up, taking a heading on deadk reckoning and crossing just like Lindbergh. I guess they're still doing it every day, but I sure wouldn't trade places with them.

From Shannon to Paris is only 600 miles, an hour and forty-five minutes. There were lots of thunderstorms over London, which was an unusual occurrence, but we swung around them and flew down over the cliffs of Dover. The dividing line halfway over the channel is the English and the French air traffic control point. I have yet to go across the line and call the French and they not say, "Bonjour, Monsieur," just as if they're glad to see you.

Paris was clear, so we had a good view coming in. We swung over Charles de Gaulle Airport and landed at Le Bourget. We landed there at eight thirty in the morning, and cars arrived at nine. Paris is a nine hour difference from Los Angeles, so that put our body clock time at almost midnight – a really long day.

The interesting part about France is that customs is so lax for private airplanes, it's almost unbelievable. We taxied up, and the operator there unloaded the baggage on the ramp. The cars drove right up to the airplane, we loaded the baggage in the car, the people got in, the doors closed, and away they went to the hotel. We never did see a customs man. When we went into the terminal, we let the operator know how many passengers arrived, but no names were ever given, and no baggage was ever checked. It is a pretty relaxed deal, like going from Los Angeles to

Cleveland. No one seems to care that you've come and gone.

We finally finished the chores, got in our car, and headed for the hotel. By the time we got to the hotel and in the sack it was noon, which is three a.m. Los Angeles time. At any rate we're in Paris, and it was a routine trip.

It is now Tuesday the ninth. We were off every day except last Friday, the fifth. We left Paris early that morning and took a group of the board of directors down to Epinal, about 200 miles east of Paris. Garrett has a manufacturing plant there. The folks held a board of directors meeting, so we were there all day.

They gave us a tour of the plant. It's sort of interesting. Evidently Garrett was looking for a place to set up a manufacturing plant in France, and the political folks made Garrett an offer they couldn't refuse to put it in Epinal. It seems like Epinal is a depressed area. The farming is decreasing and there is not much industry there. Unfortunately, the depressed people don't leave the area. Garrett erected a plant to manufacture turbochargers there, and at the moment we have 120 employees. They expect within the year to have 500 employees, and the ironic part is that now there's a housing shortage. It seems like a Catch-22 situation. In order to get employees, Garrett may have to build houses for them.

Except for that day, we spent our time at the Paris Air Show. It's a monstrous show. I was just figuring up how many people our company had over here. We had forty-six couples, which is ninety-two people, and sixty-six single people. That makes a total of 158 Garrett people. That's not counting the French Garrett people. In order to put up all these folks they're spread them out among nineteen different hotels. To provide transportation to these 158 folks, they hired two buses that make a daily round trip to the hotels and out to the air show. It leaves at eight fifteen every morning, makes the rounds to the big hotels, spends the day out at the show, and then drops them off at night. Of course the bigwigs have limousines. I think we have about ten limos with drivers. The minor dignitaries have Hertz rent-a-cars with French drivers.

We have two crews over here, and inasmuch as we're subject to call, the crews have two cars with drivers. In all the previous years we were fortunate to have the same driver who spoke English. But this year our two cars have French-speaking drivers, and they can't speak English, and we can't speak French. However, one of the pilots has a French to English, English to French dictionary, and the driver has the same, and they jabber and point back and forth and manage to get the job done.

On Sunday the Garrett Corporation gave a brunch for about 750 people at one of the big restaurants in the forest east of here. I think there were some sixty senators and fifty or sixty congressmen among all the other well-knowns throughout the industry at that brunch. It just makes you wonder who's minding the store back in the States.

Garrett has two stands in the show where they demonstrate their wares, but I guess most of the business is enacted in the chalet. There are hundreds of temporary chalets. They're put up every other year for the air show, and then they're torn down after the show. The corporations rent these chalets – they're like mobile homes – and that's where they do their entertaining. They have a catered lunch, they have a bar, and the back patio overlooks the runway where all the flight exhibitions are flown. The catering is just lavish. It's lunch only, but the lunch is unbelievable. Of course there's the open bar, and I don't know what it costs – I'd be afraid to ask. The overall cost of this thing is tacked onto the price of our product. It's coming to a point where I can't quite understand how anybody can afford our product.

The show itself is rather unbelievable. It's something like a war supermarket. They have all the fighter airplanes giving their exhibitions. The static area has tanks, radar, bombs, machine guns, infrared, everything to do with the military. There are movies in which a company will show

how their bomb can kill people more efficiently than Brand X. It almost seems ridiculous. You can just visualize a sheik walking through there with his clipboard and saying, "I'll take fifteen of those tanks, and I want 5,000 armor-piercing shells, and I'll need the radar. You better let me have umpteen thousand bombs, too," and on and on. And there's the businessmen in coats and ties taking orders just like in a supermarket.

I happened to be standing by some antiaircraft mobile tank units at one point. While the fighters were giving their exhibition, the tanks had their remote radar automatically tracking the fighters. As the fighters swished back and forth, the guns on these tanks were swishing back and forth following them. I just said to myself, "Man, I sure hope these things aren't loaded," or at least, "keep your finger off the trigger." It just doesn't seem reasonable in this day and age of civilization to work so hard to show that your weapons are bigger and better.

They've had so many crashes and deaths here in previous years that they've really cracked down on the ground rules for the local flying this year. There's a minimum altitude of 300 feet for non-acrobatic flights and 500 feet for acrobatics. They printed a little blurb in the local paper by the director, and it said, "You have to consider those altitudes as some kind of imaginary ground level. As far as I'm concerned, flying one foot under those heights means one thing: bang, you're dead. And of course if you're dead, you do not fly any more at the Paris Air Show this year." They have a radar and video cameras that record the program every day. One poor demonstration pilot for an Aerostar went too low, and he's grounded for the rest of the show.

The director remarked, "We do not want the demonstration pilots to demonstrate the airplanes to the limits of the envelope. This has never concluded a sales contract, which as you all know is a much more complex matter. We want a safe, sane, happy show, and we want you to enjoy it." Well, watching these pilots, they are clearly demonstrating the airplanes to the limit of the envelope. With some of the maneuvers that they perform in these heavy fighters at low altitude, you wonder how the thing stays in the air. Of course, it's just brute power thrust over drag. It's very interesting, but a bit nerve-wracking.

A few days ago we saw a very funny thing. We were sitting in a sidewalk cafe around the corner from the hotel. It was quite a large sidewalk cafe with a narrow sidewalk in front of it. This old drunk stopped by a lamppost in front of us, and he came up with a gimmick that I'd never seen before. He had a big rubber rat that he hid in his sleeve. He was looking over his shoulder. When he saw a couple of girls coming down the street, he'd wait till they were just abeam of him and then pop this rat right out in front of their faces. Of course they'd scream and jump back, and he'd raise his eyebrows with an expression like 'I gotcha!' Then he'd look at us and put this big rubber rat back in his sleeve and wait for the next victim.

He was a comic and really funny. I don't understand why somebody didn't belt him with a purse, or why somebody with a weak heart didn't keel over. But after about ten minutes of this, he had everybody really laughing at the tables. Then the payoff was that after he had everybody in a good mood, he put the rat away and brought out an old ashtray and walked up and down the tables for contributions. Well, it was better than a movie, and worth a contribution. I guess somebody in the hotel complained, because pretty soon a policeman came along and shooed him on his way. But in the space of about ten minutes it appeared to me that his contributions must have been at least $10, so he was probably one of these rich Parisians who had a chauffeur drive him to work in a Rolls Royce. But he was enjoying life, and obviously he had a sense of humor and would never starve.

Invariably there's an accident at the Paris Air Show, and, sure enough, one happened this year. But this year fortunately there were no fatalities. A pilot landed wheels-up in front of a couple million people. He swung around, put the flaps down, put the spoilers down, touched down, reversed the props, and screeched along the runway on his belly. And there the airplane sat.

I can imagine how the pilot felt. He got out of the airplane, and he's either still walking, or he headed for the nearest bar, and he's the drunkest pilot around. I can remember our incident when we ran off the runway down in Houston. There was no damage to the airplane, but there we were sitting in the mud. The chief pilot just got out of his seat, opened the door, and started walking. He left me there to face the passengers and explain what had happened, to get them to the terminal, and to send them home. So I know exactly how that pilot felt in the wheels-up landing. He just had to be crushed.

We made a second trip to Epinal. Another group went down there to visit our plant, and it was a real hassle. We had to ferry from Le Bourget to Orly. That's like ferrying from La Guardia to Kennedy, a very short hop. But the hassle of getting a slot out of Le Bourget on account of the air show, permission to land at Orly, the pogo routing, the language barrier, and when you get over there the parking all added up to a real pain. We were told that the reason we had to go to Orly was because the company had chartered a F-27, and they wanted both airplanes to leave at the same time and arrive at Epinal together so the buses could pick them up at both ends.

We flew down to Epinal. I guess it was mainly an eating deal down there. They showed the folks the plant, and they take them to lunch around one, and they were supposed to be back at the airport at five. Well, they returned to the airport about seven thirty, just up from the lunch table.

We flew them back to Orly, dropped them, and flew back to Le Bourget. The ironic part was that everybody came in their own cars. Our group could have come to Le Bourget and saved us all that hassle, but that's the way it goes. We didn't get back to Orly until eight that night, and a lot of the people had dinner engagements for six or seven. They were already absolutely stuffed, in addition to being late for dinner, just from one meal to another.

We had Thursday off. We went out to the airport, cleaned the airplane, fueled it, filed flight plans, and got ready for Friday.

Friday was a long day, and we were up early. We left at ten with one group for Marseilles, about 400 miles south of Paris. We dropped those folks and ferried back to good old Orly. We found out that there was an air controller's strike in England. We had to sit on the ramp for three hours until we could get a slot to go into England. We finally took off and took another group up to Luton, which is just north of London.

We dropped them, fueled the airplane, and then we really lucked out. We thought we were going to have another three hour wait to get out of there, but a slot became open. They said, "If you can be off the ground in fifteen minutes, we have a slot for you." We said, "we can," and we popped on out of there and back up on top and headed south to Marseilles again. Coming into Marseilles it was sunset and not a cloud in the sky, and it was just a really a beautiful sight with the sun off the side of the buildings and the water and the Mediterranean. We checked into a hotel right there at the Marseilles airport.

The French crews are really something. They dribble in there from six until midnight, and they get something to eat and then in full uniform they head for the bar. There are all these French crews in full uniform, stewardesses, captains, co-pilots, flight engineers, and they're laughing, joking, and drinking. I understand they stagger up to bed at two or three in the morning, and then the flights start out at six o'clock in the morning, and away they go again. I don't see how they do it.

We got up the next day, Friday the twelfth, and went to Ajaccio. It's on the southern coast of Corsica, only about 200 miles from Marseilles. There was another chartered airplane that went along with us for part of the group. We could only carry ten, and they had another ten. We went down to Ajaccio practically in formation, and we spent about five hours there while the hosts wined and dined our people.

Then we cranked up and flew up to Calvi on the northwest coast of Corsica, a distance of only about forty-five miles. The airport was very interesting. It's down in a valley opening up into the sea like a slot, so you normally land into the hills, uphill. If the wind is strong you can circle and slide down the side of the mountain and land downhill. We landed uphill and taxied off and parked.

Calvi is a beautiful little seaport town, very picturesque. We were in an old hotel with no air-conditioning. The town had rustic little curbed, cobblestone streets, with patio restaurants that are on a slope.

A corporate airplane from a German company arrived in Ajaccio at the same time as us. After we deplaned our passengers and while we were debriefing our airplane, we got acquainted with this German crew, including a very attractive stewardess. We went out to dinner with them that night. We were laying over there for two days, so they asked us if we were going to the beach the next day. I said, “Sure. We’ll meet you there at ten o’clock in the morning.”

The next morning after breakfast, we put on our bathing suits and went down to the beach. The German crew was already there. No one had warned us about the beach, so I was flabbergasted. It was a topless beach. All these beautiful young Dollys were prancing around, and every single one of them was topless. The stewardess from the night before was topless. It was just a little disconcerting. Where do you look when you talk to her? You look her right in the eye and continue the conversation. Walking down the beach you might see three young ladies walking toward you, bouncing merrily along. Do you look straight ahead? Do you look right? Do you look left? Farther down the beach ten topless women were playing volleyball. Now there is a memory.

The crew that we had befriended said, “If you're going to fool around with any girls in Corsica, make sure they're either Germans or Italians, and not from Corsica.” They said the families here are very clannish. They’re like the hillbillies: they all carry guns, and, if the girl complains, the uncles, the cousins, the brothers, and the whole clan will show up at your hotel and march into your room. The crew said, "It's just not worthwhile." They told us, for instance, that one of their pilots went down there to hunt, and, since he was an outsider, some local people from Corsica advised him that he better not hunt there, that there was liable to be an accident. They didn't like outsiders, and accidents happened to outsiders.

Bastia, a Corsican town, was in the soccer finals up in Paris, and this whole group of supporters went up there to cheer them on. They were blowing bugles, waving flags, and shooting fireworks. They were really spirited. That evening the soccer game was on TV. The town of Calvi literally came to a stop while everybody watched the game on TV. If they didn't have TV, it was on radio. You could walk down the street and listen to the game no matter where you were, because everybody had it on.

As it turned out, the Corsican team won the championship, and Calvi went absolutely berserk. It was the fourth of July, ten times over. Cars were roaring around the streets and blaring horns. There were a lot of sounds that sounded like backfires, but they were actually shooting shotguns in the air. They were throwing confetti. I thought the celebration would die out in about thirty minutes. Six hours later it was still going strong, and at six the following morning I still heard shots and fireworks. They were still celebrating. Walking down the streets the next day, we could see numerous shotgun shells literring the streets and in the gutters. It was like a war had passed through there. I could hardly believe it.

Tomorrow we head back to the States. We're hoping to get back to Bangor, Maine with just one stop. We want to go from here to Santa Maria in the Azores. It will be about a four hour and ten minute flight. Then the long flight is from Santa Maria to Bangor, which is five hours and fifteen minutes. If the winds are too strong we can always pop up to St. Johns, Gander, or Halifax – somewhere up there in Newfoundland.

We went out to the airport with our catering and ice and filed our flight plan. Our folks arrived at the airport at nine thirty. Then we had the shock of our life. The tower said the air traffic control computer at Marseilles had konked out, and there was no way to get an IFR flight plan. You have to go IFR at high altitude with a jet. They said we could come in and refile and go VFR (visual flight rules), but if we did that we'd have to stay below 17000 feet. But then we wouldn't have enough fuel to make Santa Maria. We could go to Marseilles, but we would be too heavy to land there. We didn't have anything set up for Lisbon, so we were sort of in a bind.

To compound our problem, the auxiliary power unit in the tail of the airplane had zonked out. We use that for ground power as well as ground cooling. It was about ninety degrees and the humidity was about 89 percent in Calvi, so it was like an oven in the cabin. In the back of the airplane it had to be 100 or 110 degrees.

We couldn't just sit there on the ground. We had to do something. I was just about to go in the little terminal and refile the flight plan for VFR and at least get off the ground, hoping that something would work out. The tower came in and said, "The computers are back online. do you want your IFR clearance now?" We said not only yes, but hell yes! They gave us our clearance, and we put our passengers into our sweltering airplane and took off. Once we were in the air it was all right, because then we had all kinds of cooling. When you get up to altitude the outside air temperature is about -50°, so it doesn't take too much to cool the airplane down.

Calvi to Santa Maria in the Azores was a routine flight. We went right over Lisbon and out over the water. It's about 1,950 miles, and we had a wind component of only about a -6, which was great. It took us three hours and fifty-five minutes to fly into Santa Maria, another island. The weather was sort of stinky out there. They had drizzle and rain and about an 800 foot ceiling. It was very cool, about sixty-nine degrees, with about a thirty knot wind blowing. But it was a good fuel stop. An agent met us. Due to the fact that we didn't have an auxiliary power unit, they hooked on an external power unit. We were only on the ground there about forty-five minutes.

From Santa Maria to Bangor turned out to be a routine flight, too. We climbed up through the soup, popped out on top at about 15,000 feet, and then flew in the sunshine all the way to Bangor. From Santa Maria to Bangor is 2,500 miles. Here again the wind component was only about a -16, which is a moral victory going westbound. It took us five hours and five minutes. It was raining in Bangor.

We spent the night in Bangor. The next day we flew from Bangor to Lincoln. The passengers lived in San Diego, so we dropped them in San Diego and then ferried home to Los Angeles. Bangor to Lincoln to San Diego was routine. The limos met us, and we unloaded tons of baggage and got rid of everything. We breathed a sigh of relief.

We only had eighty miles to go, and we were dead tired. We fired up our engines and just started to taxi when we had a hot generator light. We couldn't take off with that, because it indicated the possibility of a bearing out, and there's no way to stop a jet engine. In flight, we'd be windmilling, and it could catch fire with a bad bearing.

We had a spare one on board, so, as tired as we were, we taxied back and opened the cowl. Phil is a crackerjack mechanic as well as a crackerjack pilot. I was the gofer, and we got the spare out of the hell-hold, got the cowl open, and pulled the old starter out. It was so hot you could just barely touch it, and you couldn't turn it, so obviously a bearing was shot. We put the new starter-generator in, and it worked like a charm. It fired up, and we finally flew into Los Angeles really dead tired.

Then the crowning blow. I got into the office and found out that I was only to have one day off. I was to go to Denver for four days. I went and talked to the boss and said, “Hey I've been gone for two weeks, you know. Don't you have somebody else you can send to Denver?” I have the best boss in the world, and he apologized and said he would certainly send somebody else if he had somebody. Not only that, if it wasn't for the airline strike I could take the flight to Denver and then commercial home and commercial back up three days later to bring the flight back. But he didn't want to take a chance with the airline strike. I agreed with that.

I said, "Instead of buying me a ticket from Denver to Los Angeles to Denver, how about buying a ticket from Los Angeles to Denver to Los Angeles?"

He thought about that, and he said, "Well, that sounds reasonable. Let's do that."

We bought GG a commercial ticket from Los Angeles to Denver, and I flew the flight from Los Angeles down to Santa Anna, up to San Francisco to pick up some folks, and into Denver. I met GG there, and we had three wonderful days getting reacquainted. Then I put GG on an airline, and she flew back to Los Angeles.

I really had the scenic route flying home. The folks showed up at the airplane in Denver, and the boss gave me the schedule. It was Denver, San Francisco, Los Angeles, Santa Anna, San Diego, Los Angeles. So I was dropping people hither and yon. I still got back to Los Angeles a little ahead of GG's flight, so I picked her up and brought her on home.

That completes the two weeks in Europe and Corsica. The old time zone got us again – I had jet lag for the first five days. You're running out of steam about four in the afternoon, just can't keep your eyes open. And you wake up like a tree full of owls at about four in the morning. The old body clock was about eight hours off, but it's finally back on schedule, and I'm looking forward to the next flight.

1981 South Pacific Flight

September 1981

This last hurrah to the South Pacific all began a couple months ago. We had plenty of time to plan this flight. It's a Mack Truck trip - they called and requested the airplane. The tentative schedule was Honolulu, Majuro, Honiara in the Solomon Islands, which is Guadalcanal. Then Sydney, Melbourne, Brisbane, and Alice Springs in Australia, then on to Bali, Singapore, across Malaysia, Bangkok, Hong Kong, Taipei, Nagoya, and Tokyo. And home via Wake, Honolulu, and Los Angeles.

We're to have six passengers: the chairman of the board of Mack Truck and his wife, the vice president of international operations, a man by the name of Bob Sting, and his wife, and the president of the Signal Companies and his wife. Bob Sting was really ramrodding the whole itinerary.

They wanted to arrive in Sydney on Saturday, but with the international date line and inasmuch as a lot of the airports in the Pacific don't have night lighting, it was impossible for us to get there at that time. We recommended that they fly commercial to Sydney, and we would ferry over and pick them up there for the rest of the trip.

The four from Allentown elected to do that. They had no choice if they wanted to meet their schedule. But the president of Signal wasn't on that particular end of the safari, so he left a couple days early and flew commercial to Honolulu.

Our airplane was busy on Sunday the thirteenth, so the first day we could leave was Monday the fourteenth. We ferried from Los Angeles to Honolulu on the fourteenth with, would you believe, two crewmembers and zero passengers.

For this particular trip, we have a three-man crew. I'm the skipper, and I ramrodded the safari. We have a very sharp college graduate copilot by the name of Art Barth. He's the second in command. Then, Lou Berger, the boss of the aviation department – my boss – is along. He is now grounded age-wise as he is over sixty-two, but he still manages the department and still flies. He's never been out in the South Pacific, so he wanted to see what it's all about before he hangs it up. But he was busy on Monday with a golf tournament, so he commercialed over on Tuesday and met us in Honolulu.

As I've said before, due to winds you can't always make it from California to Honolulu. The airplane doesn't have enough range for it. We can live with about a -50 wind component. When we got up Monday morning, I checked the computerized flight plan. It said we only had a -9, which is a moral victory this time of year. I fueled up the airplane, loaded up, and flew from Los Angeles to San Francisco. As I mentioned before, we usually depart from San Francisco because it's about 170 miles closer to Honolulu.

We had a couple of hiccups going into San Francisco. The flight director's V. Bars jumped up. It was hooked to the autopilot. The autopilot tried to follow it, so the airplane pitched up rather violently. I disconnected the autopilot, and then the left gyro tumbled and a flag came up. After about four seconds it righted itself and acted normal.

On top of that, when we landed at San Francisco the inertial was acting up. I called maintenance in Los Angeles and told them our problems and told them that we were going to continue on to Honolulu. We would call them from there if we needed parts, and Lou Berger could bring them over the next day. Would you believe we've flown nearly thirty hours since then, and there hasn't been a single hiccup? I guess it was just a spike or temporary hang-up.

We had a routine flight from San Francisco to Honolulu. It's about 2,500 statute miles. The computerized flight plan said it would take five hours and three minutes. We pulled back on the power some to save fuel, so it actually took us five hours and eighteen minutes. We had considerable fuel left, so that was no problem whatsoever. It was the usual beautiful day all the way over; we didn't go through a single cloud. We could see the islands a couple hundred miles out – Diamondhead and the sparkling water and the white hotels. After going over that amount of water you always breathe a little sigh of relief being back on the ground, but all in all it was just a routine flight.

We spent one day in Honolulu, resting up. We rented a car and did the usual sightseeing. Driving out to the airport for our next flight, we saw two perfect rainbows. It was most startling. They were horizon to horizon with just vivid colors. It almost looked like a painting, but if anybody had painted that, people would say, "Hey, that's not realistic. It's impossible for a rainbow to be that bright." But it was.

On Wednesday the sixteenth we departed Honolulu at nine in the morning and headed west for Majuro. We flew right over the Johnson Islands, about 850 miles from Honolulu, where we used to land during the war with the flying boats. Then we flew over the international date line, and suddenly it went from Wednesday the sixteenth to Thursday the seventeenth in an instant. The distance from Honolulu to Majuro is about 2,300 miles, and I think that one took us about five hours and five minutes.

Air traffic control out there has no radar. There were a couple of planes taking off from Majuro just at the time of our arrival. Our clearance was to fly at 35,000 feet from Honolulu to Majuro and to pass over the top of Majuro at 35,000 feet, then commence our let down. So there we were at 35,000 feet right over our destination. As soon as we got over we pulled the plug, pulled the power off, put thespeed brakes out, and came down as fast as we could. But it still took at least ten minutes to get it on the ground.

We had our first 'I Gotcha' when we landed at Majuro. We knew it had Mobil gas, and we had a Mobil credit card, but it turned out that they required a Mobil international credit card, which we did not have. So out came the old billfold, and I think I paid a little over $4,000 cash for fuel.

Before we started on this trip we knew we were going to have to pay cash for fuel in Indonesia and possibly a couple of other spots. I got an advance of eight grand and the other pilots got an advance of five grand each. Filling the airplane up this once put four grand down the tube.

From Majuro we flew down to Haniara, to the old Henderson Field in the Solomon Islands. It wasn't too long a leg, about 1,400 statute miles and three hours flight time. We passed the equator into the southern latitudes. We landed at Honiara. It has a single rough asphalt runway that looks like it's had hard usage. It's hard to believe that we lost thousands of men taking that island just for that landing strip. But I guess that was the key to the whole area.

Guadalcanal was very interesting. The bridges are just one-way, with steel frames and wooden floors, just wide enough for one car. As one column of cars was going across the bridge, the people coming the other way would have to wait until a break in the line came, and then they'd go. On one of the bridges downtown they had a policeman right in the center of the bridge, and he was dividing up the traffic so the people could take turns. Even in the center of town there were one-way bridges andno traffic lights. The houses were on stilts, very primitive. It didn't appear like civilization had taken over at Guadalcanal yet. They must have been influenced by the English, because they were driving on the left side – or as we say, the wrong side – of the road, which was startling.

We passed a golf course that was seemed unusual. The fairways looked in good shape, nice and green, but the greens themselves were sand. We talked to one man there who was a golfer. He said, "Well it's real easy to one-putt these greens. You just take a rake and make a groove from your ball to the hole and give it a tap and the ball follows the groove into the hole. You can't miss."

We arrived at the hotel, and it was interesting. The lobby was wide open with no windows. Theredidn't appear to be any bugs. Fortunately the rooms were air-conditioned. There was lots of humidity there, of course. The ironic part was that the island was lush green, and it appeared that they had all kinds of tropical rains, but they had a sign up saying that, due to a water shortage, the water was only turned on for two hours in the morning and two hours in the evening. So you had to plan your shaving and your shower to the times that the water was on.

We spent the one night in Honiara and left at ten o'clock on the morning of Friday the eighteenth, a good, sociable hour. We flew on down to Sydney, 1,800 miles and four hours. They had beautiful weather in Sydney. We could see the bay, the opera house, the bridges, and the city. We spent two nights and one day in Sydney, took a harbor cruise and did the usual sightseeing. I didn't see anything really special, just the extreme contrast between Honiara and Sydney. Back in Guadalcanal, Honiara was so primitive, like it was still in the last century, and four hours later we were in the center of a bustling city with well-dressed people and mechanization. It was like stepping from one world to another.

On Sunday the twentieth we flew from Sydney up to Brisbane. It's only 400 miles. Our passengers had requested that we deviate and fly up what they call the Gold Coast here. They say it has the most beautiful beaches in the world. We asked the controllers if it would be possible to give us a radar vector over to the beach and let us down to about 1,000 feet so we could fly up the beach and let the people do a little sightseeing, then give us a vector into the Brisbane airport. They coordinated it with all the sections. They were most friendly, and they gave us the vector and let us down. There were quite a few clouds, but once we got below them the sight was rather interesting. To me, it was just another Miami beach with lots of buildings, but they did have gleaming white beaches.

In Sydney the question of sharks had come up. They have shark nets around the public beaches. These nets are supposed to be shark proof so people can go swimming and relax.

In Brisbane we took a boat trip about thirty miles up the Brisbane River to a place called Lone Pine. This is where they raise the Koalas. We call them Koala bears, but the Australians call them Koalas. There must have been at least a hundred of them there, just cute little rascals, eating and sleeping. I guess they sleep about eighteen hours a day, and six hours a day they look around and feed and nap. They were just tremendously cute.

We went out to the airport the next morning in Brisbane to do the chores, order catering, clean the airplane, and check the weather. It was a perfectly clear day, not a cloud in the sky. We had Texaco and Shell fighting over us to see who was going to fuel us. We normally use Shell, so Shell won out, and we tried to be diplomatic and state that we'd use Texaco on the next trip.

I had just a speck of a shock, nothing drastic. I found out we could not clear Australia at Alice Springs. We'd planned to go from Brisbane to Alice Springs to Bali tomorrow, taking off from Alice Springs and going down to circle Ayers Rock before heading on to Indonesia. The passengers wanted to see Ayers Rock, but the rules have changed and Alice Springs is no longer an airport of entry. We changed our fuel stop to Darwin. We'd just go Brisbane to Darwin, clear the country there, fuel up, pay our head tax, and proceed on to Bali.

In any event, we took off from Brisbane and headed northwest over the outback. Looking down at the ground from 35,000 feet, we made the remark that the ground looked more like West Texas than West Texas does. It was just miles and miles of nothing – no roads, fences, buildings, or civilization at all.

One of our women passengers looked down and saw all these black spots on the ground, and she asked one of the crewmembers what the black spots were.

He replied, "Those are the shadows of the clouds." We were flying above some fluffy clouds below us.

She wasn't convinced of that. She said, "The black spots aren't moving."

The crewmember replied, "Well, the clouds aren't moving. So if the clouds aren't moving then the shadows aren't moving and therefore the black spots aren't moving." She still wasn't convinced.

It was 1,800 miles from Brisbane to Darwin, and a beautiful day. It took us three hours and forty-five minutes. It just seems strange that in Sydney when people go toward warmer weather, they go north, toward the equator. Of course we always think of going to warmer weather as going south. But when we left Brisbane I guess it was in the low 70s and when we arrived in Darwin it was in the high 80s and humid.

When we landed in Darwin, we expected Anset Airlines to handle us. They'd handled us in Sydney and Brisbane. But when we opened the door there was Qantus Airlines to handle us, and as much as Anset wasn't in sight and we were in a hurry, we said, "have at it." So all the passengers went in and cleared customs and immigrations outbound, we paid our ten-dollars-per-head head tax, put some fuel on, and thirty-five minutes later we were on the way to Bali.

We popped out of Darwin and headed west for Bali. It seemed like a very short flight. It was only 1,100 miles, and we had a tailwind, strangely enough. So in about two hours and ten minutes we drifted on down and landed on a beautiful airport in Bali.

Here again, we had a communications problem with the airline that was supposed to handle us. We couldn't raise them on the radio, so we asked the tower to contact them. After we'd landed, they finally came out and said that this was the first they'd heard that they were supposed to handle us. But they took rapid care of the passengers and cleared everybody through customs and immigration, and there we were.

We're now in Singapore, and it seems hard to believe that just two days ago we were in Bali. We got up in the morning and went out to the airport to pay our landing fees and handling charges, fuel the airplane, dump the potty, and get our catering. The rate of exchange in Bali is 623 to 1. We had to pay cash for fuel, and it was over $2,000 US. So, multiplying that by 600, and you have 1,200,000 rupees. I've always wanted to pay over a million dollars for something.

As with most places, we had a language problem. I understood they wanted us to pay in rupees, so the agent took me down to the bank to cash in some traveler's checks. Well, it turned out they wanted US dollars. The trip into town was a waste because I had that amount in my pocket. The landing fee, I think, was 150 bucks. The handling agent was 250 bucks, and there were another 50 bucks for incidentals. We finally got all the chores taken care of there.

One of the air traffic control men whom I'd met on a previous trip was off that day, and he volunteered to take us on a tour of the island. One of the things that was very interesting to us was that he was on duty in 1974 when the Pan American 707 crashed on the other side of the island. He was a member of the investigating committee.

That flight was on the way from Hong Kong to Bali . The captain had been into Bali twice in daylight. He'd never been in at night before, but it was a clear night, and weather was not a factor. Evidently it was quite well lit by the moon. Anyway, he was talking to the tower and the tower cleared him to come over the airport at 12,000 feet, and to make sure he had the airport before he started his let down, because there's a 10,000 foot peak just northeast of the airport. That was back in the days before they had radar. They didn't have any DME; all they had was a homing beacon.

The captain had put in a long day, and he evidently saw the lights of this city and thought it was Bali or Denpasar on the south coast, but it was actually another city on the north coast. They got the tape recorder out of the airplane, and the tape recorder had the spiel by the captain of how beautiful Bali was and that they'd be on the ground in ten minutes and the folks were in for a tremendous treat. Then a little bit later it had the voice of the copilot questioning the captain, "Hey are you sure that's Denpasar? Things just don't look right. Are you sure that's it?" And the captain kept letting down and letting down, and he replied, "yeah, that's it, that's it. We're ok. Stop worrying."

It turned out that it was the wrong city, and when they realized it they poured the coal to it and ran into a hill on that dark night. I guess the moral of the story is, you can never be too careful.

We spent the afternoon touring Bali. Went up 5,000 feet up into the hills. Going through the countryside is just fascinating. It's almost like going back a thousand years. We saw all the people in their sarongs, women out in the fields with a hoe, many of them topless. Many of the women carried huge loads of rocks and gravel for repairing the roads on their heads. There were miles and miles of terraced rice fields.

We saw hundreds of kids coming and going to school, all in uniform. Some uniforms are gray. Some are green. We saw hundred and hundreds of white uniforms – sparkling white shorts and blouses – and I have no idea how they keep them that clean in their primitive conditions. They were all cute. Lou Berger made the remark that all the little girls and all the little boys looked like they were cut with the same cookie cutter. They all looked identical, all cute as buttons, and most attractive.

We went through the various centers where they had the weavers, the jewelry workers, and the wood carvers – very talented, very industrious people. But the competition's so strong that I don't see how they can make it.

We left Bali at nine in the morning for a very easy flight up into Singapore, only 900 miles, a little over two hours. We had beautiful weather until we arrived at Singapore, and then we started letting down through the clouds. We went into Selatar, a small airport. It's not the big international airport. There's no let down facility there, so the radar gave us a vector and we were still a little high. He asked if we could get down in time for a straight-in approach. We told him we could and pulled the nose up, dumped the flaps, put the speed brakes out, gear out, power off, and dropped down until we finally got below the clouds at about 1,800 feet. There three miles ahead of us was the runway. On the other end of the runway was a huge thunderstorm. We landed straight-in, and it started to rain. We'd just beaten the thunderstorm in, which gave us a sigh of relief.

Our agent there had everything extremely well organized, inasmuch as it was a very small airport. The limousines came right out to the airplane. The baggage went right in the limousines. He'd already pre-cleared everything with customs. He picked up everybody's passports, took them in and cleared them with immigration, came back out, gave them to the passengers, and within five minutes they were on their way to the hotel.

We did our chores, fueled it, cleaned it and so forth, and then we went into the Mandarin Hotel. Later we went over to the famous Raffles Hotel in Singapore. That's the hotel that made the Singapore Sling famous. We had dinner there.

The boss had business to conduct in Manila, and he asked us if we couldn't get clearance to go over to Manila on Monday the twenty-eighth and then back to Hong Kong on the twenty-ninth. Well, it takes a diplomatic clearance to fly into Manila. I called Houston, Texas to see if they could get the diplomatic clearance for Manila. Normally it takes seven working days to get a permit. Today is Friday, and nothing can be accomplished on Saturday or Sunday, but they're going to give it a go anyway. We probably won't get it until Monday. If we don't get clearance the airline will be the backup for the boss to go down there. It's only 700 miles from Hong Kong to Manila.

The boss is going down there to see the minister of energy. I think it's just a matter of prestige, taking his own airplane. But we're making every effort to get a clearance.

We had a very short stay here in Singapore. We're leaving in about an hour to go to the airport and fly up to Bangkok. I've never been there before, so I'm looking forward to it.

Now it is Saturday the twenty-sixth, and I'm sitting in Bangkok. We flew up from Singapore yesterday. I'd like to say the trip was uneventful, but it wasn't.

We went out to the airport early. It was about ninety degrees with about 95 percent humidity. We had the APU running for quite a while trying to cool down the airplane. The passengers showed up on time. It's a very short runway at Singapore, considering the weight we were trying to lift off. And wouldn't you know it, the wind died down, so there was no wind to help us get off. We taxied out, right to the end of the runway, stopped, set the brakes, brought the power up to max, and let the engines spool up, making sure we could get every ounce of thrust out of them. We released the brakes and flew on out of there.

As we were climbing out, our ears popped. We looked up at the instruments and could see that the cabin was climbing with the airplane. We weren't pressurizing. Naturally we were a little concerned. At a low altitude we couldn't make Bangkok. We suspected that the water cooler had frozen up. We tried high heat, and that didn't solve the problem. We went to manual on the heat controls, both in the cockpit and the cabin, and by going to full manual hot in both, we could partially pressurize. The water separator had frozen, and if you called for any cool air, there wouldn't be enough to come in to pressurize the airplane.

We originally filed for 35,000 feet, but we leveled off at 15,000 feet trying to get the cabin under control. Our big fear was that if the cabin went above 15,000 feet, all the oxygen masks would drop out. We have a couple of white-knuckle passengers, and I know that would have scared them to death.

We worked on it and managed to hold the cabin at 11,000, just a partial differential. So we went up to 31,000 feet with an 11,000 foot cabin, but just to maintain that pressure the cockpit was soon at 100° and the cabin was about 90°. We were pumping hot air in there trying to maintain pressure. We kept hoping the thing would pop loose so we could cool everything down.

We debated about going back to Singapore, but we knew VIPs were waiting for the folks in Bangkok. It was only a two hour flight. Our passengers said they could live with it, so we pressed on. Of course the valve let loose as we let down into Bangkok, so we had cool air, but by that time we were on the ground.

We had very good weather between Singapore and Bangkok, so we didn't have to worry about that. We could concentrate on our pressurization problem. Their radar was like Clevelend or Columbus: they picked us up a hundred miles out, had us identified, and gave us a vector – number four for approach. When we landed, it looked just like New York with all the 747s, the DC-10s, the airbuses, and the 1011s. It was a big city.

British Airways handled us, and they parked us out in the boondocks. As we spun around and parked and turned off the engines, a big bus pulled up with a photographer and the welcoming committee from the Mack Truck organization. They had women with flowers, and they took all kinds of pictures. We unloaded the baggage, put the people in the bus, and away they went.

This morning we set the alarm for six o'clock. We heard that one of the things we had to see in Bangkok was the floating market. It's a water tour. The buses picked us up at seven and took us to the river, where we boarded water taxis, about twelve people to each boat. As we went up the river we saw all the wharves, and then we turned down a little river or canal. All these people lived in little houses on stilts out on the water. It looked like wash day. Everybody was out there washing. They were very friendly people. They waved and didn't mind having their pictures taken. People were out in the muddy water, washing their babies, washing their hair.

As we neared the floating market, women would row up and hold onto the boat to sell their wares to the people in our boat. We tied up at the various docks and visited the markets. We went to a snake farm, where they were taking the venom from cobras, which was interesting. And of course you can't get in and out of any of these countries without visiting a few temples. We were on the water about three hours.

I couldn't believe it when we got back to the hotel. There was a telex from Houston with our Manila permit all in order and our revised permit back into Hong Kong. If the boss wants to go to Manila, we're all set. We won't know that until tomorrow, but I couldn't believe it was only yesterday that we requested it, and we have the permit already. I read in the paper that there's a typhoon out in the Philippines, and I'm not quite sure how that's going to affect our plans.

Sunday was a bad day in Bangkok. We were supposed to take our people from Bangkok to Hong Kong. They showed up at the airport at one in the afternoon, per schedule. We put them on the airplane and departed Bangkok for Hong Kong.

We thought we had solved our pressurization problem. We thought the system had iced up. But, just to be sure, we had opened up the rear belly hatch and crawled up in the tail and inspected the whole system. We couldn't find any leaks, so we figured the water separator had iced up and the problem was be solved. Well, we took off from Bangkok and had no pressurization whatsoever. The cabin was climbing with the airplane, so we leveled off at 9,000 feet, and of course the cabin was 9,000 feet, too. And there was no way we could continue on.

We had a little bit of foresight, and we had checked airline schedules just to see if there was some back-up transportation between Bangkok and Hong Kong. We didn't want to dump fuel, so we called the ground handling agent and told him to make reservations for six passengers, first class.

We were going to burn off some fuel and turn back to Bangkok. The reason no pilot particularly likes to dump fuel is because the fuel dump pipe goes back through the belly of the airplane and up the tail and out above the horizontal stabilizer. If that pipe happens to leak, then you're pumping kerosene into the belly, and of course it's flammable. If it catches fire, then the tail blows off and it just ruins your whole day. Everyone likes to just make a circle, burn it off with the engines and get down to a landing weight and come on in. We figured we could circle for about an hour and a half and burn down to landing weight and come back.

One of the passengers, a white-knuckler, one of the gals, was scared to death, fainting and gasping. We have a walk-around oxygen bottle, so we gave her oxygen. But she was panicking, and the boss said, "Get this thing on the ground." So there was nothing to do but dump fuel. We called British Airways and told them, "We're going to dump fuel, so if you don't hear from us again, you'll know what happened." We must've dumped over a thousand gallons of kerosene as we proceeded toward Bangkok, up the Bay of Siam. I guess it's called the Bay of Thailand now. We dumped, crossed our fingers, and obviously it worked all right because I'm writing about it now.

We left the speed brake door open. It's the door that opens up into the boiler room. We left it open to air everything out just in case kerosene had leaked out. There's so much electrical equipment that if you do get kerosene in the belly, there is always a danger of a spark setting it off. I know of one case where a JetStar pilot had to dump fuel and there was a leak in the line. The whole belly filled up with kerosene. He managed to land the airplane, and when he opened the hatch on the ground kerosene just poured out. He was lucky.

We flew back into Bangkok, unloaded the passengers, and called the airline to put them on a commercial flight to Hong Kong. We told the boss that we would solve the problem and catch up with them as soon as we could.

After they left the airplane, we made a federal case out of finding out what was wrong. We climbed up into the rear boiler room and stripped the insulation off the ducting of the air conditioning system. Sure enough, underneath the insulation where we couldn't see it, a couple of the mormon clamps had come loose. One of the pieces had slid back, allowing the bleed air to go from the engines into the boiler room, rather than coming into the cabin to pressurize it. It was just a matter of sliding the equipment back together and putting the mormon clamps back on. It was actually a fairly simple operation. We put the insulation back on and wrapped everything back up with duct tape.

The obvious next step was to take it for a test hop to see if it was fixed. Would you believe that running a test hop in Thailand is a major problem? We called the tower and told them that we just wanted a local test hop, just to pop up to 25,000 feet to check our pressurization and get back on the ground. We wouldn't be gone more than fifteen minutes. They said we had to file a flight plan. So I filed a flight plan, and the clearance official said, "Well, this is all well and good, but you don't have a permit for this. We've got to call downtown and get you a permit." It seemed like they were afraid we were going to bomb the capital there in Bangkok.

It took us two hours to get a permit to take the airplane off the ground to test fly it. But we finally got the permit, and we did test fly it. Everything worked out fine. By this time it was too late to proceed on to Hong Kong, because Hong Kong has a night noise curfew. So we buttoned up the airplane and went back to town for a short night.

The next day, Monday the twenty-eighth, we got up at four thirty for a five thirty pickup at the hotel for a seven o'clock take off. We had to leave that early to go to Hong Kong because they don't allow any supplemental traffic into Hong Kong between one and four p.m. local. That's a busy time, so we either had to land before or after. We elected to get an early start and get over to Hong Kong early in case the boss wanted to go to Manila that night.

The flight from Bangkok to Hong Kong was very interesting. We were just three crew and no passengers. On the direct line from Bangkok to Hong Kong, there's an airway that goes right across Thailand, Laos, Vietnam, and into Hong Kong. The airlines are allowed to fly it, but we are not allowed to fly it because it's an irregular flight. Those countries aren't all friendly with each other. So we had to go around the horn, southeast down over the gulf of Siam down by Cambodia, down the south end of Vietnam and along the coast, and turn back up northeast to Hong Kong. The direct course is about 1,200 miles. The way we had to go is about 1,800 miles. So it was 600 miles out of the way just because we couldn't fly across 100 miles of Laos and 70 miles of Vietnam.

We could look off the left wing and see the coastline. We were only about twenty-three miles off the coast of Vietnam and about 150 miles from Saigon. Of course, we couldn't see Saigon as there was a lot of cloud cover. But we knew people on the ground in Vietnam were watching us because our transponder was blinking. Our transponder picks up the ground radar, so when it blinks, you know that some ground radar is interrogating your image.

We arrived in Hong Kong. The weather was forecast as good, but when we arrived they had a low ceiling with rain. The ILS minimum is 700 feet, and it's a most unusual approach. They have mountains there, and the runway is built by the bay. So you come down the localizer and the glide slopes down to 700 feet, and then hopefully you see the runway. Then you have to turn 45° to the right and come down through the buildings and the town onto the single runway. If you land on the runway in the other direction, there's a solid granite wall with big white and black checkers painted on it. So you're landing on a runway with a wall at the end. It's a most unusual airport, but it's really fantastic to see these big 747s come in at a relatively low altitude and bend around so they can land on the runway.

On arriving at the hotel, we had a message, and we were disappointed. The message said, "The boss wants to go to Manila in the morning." Here we thought we were going to have a day off, and now it was down to Manila, spend five hours, and then back to Hong Kong. But in Hong Kong we checked into the Parameter Continental, right on the waterfront, and they gave us waterfront rooms. I could look out and see the whole harbor: the hustle and bustle, the Chinese junks, the ferry boats, the freighters, the tankers, all just teeming with activity. I could sit there in the window and watch it for hours. It was really interesting.

On Tuesday the twenty-ninth we got up early on our day off to fly the boss down to Manila. He had to go down there to see the Minister of Energy about a private matter. Evidently it was pretty important, because we only had the one passenger.

When we got up in Hong Kong it was raining cats and dogs. We went out to the airport. Our poor bird, the airplane, just doesn't like water. On the ground, it leaks quite a bit. Of course, in the air, when it's pressurized, no water can get in. But on the ground, the windows aren't really that good, and moisture gets in everything.

The first problem was that the right speakers didn't work. The earphones didn't work on that side, so now all our eggs were in one basket. Pilots hate it when they lose communication – it's almost disastrous. It took us three shots to get the APU started. It was full of water and moisture and didn't want to run, but it finally took hold and started. We finally got the boss on board, and then we could not get the #1 engine started. We turned the computer off and started it manually. The computer was full of water and wouldn't work. By this time we were starting to think, “What can possibly happen next?”

We got all four engines started. Then we hopped on out of there and up on top into the sunshine, and everything seemed a lot better. The interesting part was that the president of the company, our one passenger, was up front in the jump seat. It was almost like having a check pilot riding along, watching every move. It was just a speck disconcerting.

We flew on down to Manila. It's only about 700 miles, and it took us an hour and a half. We had real good weather on the way down there. The only problem was that the Manila radar gave us the vectors to the airport, and then they got busy talking to a British speedbird and forgot all about us. So we sailed right through the localizer and kept going south. Finally we got a word in and said, “Do you want us to head back to the airport?” He seemed a little embarrassed and vectored us back in. We had the airport in sight the whole time, but it makes you wonder if there were mountains around and you weren't checking and double checking, where you would be.

We landed in Manila and had the VIP treatment. A big Mercedes Benz limo pulled right up to the airplane, picked up the boss and whisked him on his way. There was a big hotel on the airport, right beside the terminal. As we taxied into the terminal, the whole top floor of this hotel was burning merrily, with smoke pouring out of the windows, ladders up against the walls and water being poured into it. The agent said it had been burning for three hours. Later, when it subsided, I could see that the whole top floor was gutted.

Then our chores started. which took us about four hours. They parked us, then we had to move the airplane to get it fueled, and then we had to pay for the fuel. Then we had to move it back to the cargo area. Then we had to pay a handling fee. That was $350 US dollars cash. Immigration wanted $50. The clearance people wanted $80. But the funniest part was – I say it's funny now – the customs wanted $450. Our agent whispered to me and said, "Hey, that's way too much money." The customs handed me a typewritten bill with all these things itemized on it up to $450.

I smiled at them and said, "I'd like to have $450 myself, but that's not reasonable. We have to come to something far less than that, or I've got to do a little telephoning. 450 bucks is a little much."

They raised their eyebrows and gave a little grin, and I said, "How about $150?" Well, they didn't think that was very appropriate, so we compromised on $220. Two hundred and twenty dollars! They were very happy, and I considered it a moral victory. Possibly, if I had been a better bargainer, it would've been less than that.

It seemed to me very similar to Mexico, where they'll just charge what the traffic will bear. I can't imagine bargaining with the US Customs on their fee. It's almost like they're killing the goose that's laying the golden egg, because they didn't do a thing for us. We were only there for five hours.

I figured that little journey down to Manila, with fuel, fees, engine maintenance and so forth, cost us about $8,000. I sure hope that it was important.

We returned to Hong Kong, and it was nighttime when we approached. Fortunately the weather was a little better. In the United States on a straight-in approach you have flashing high intensity lights that are in sequence on the runway. It looks like running rabbits. We always say, "Hey, follow the rabbit." In Hong Kong, they've got the flashing sequence of lights, but it's in a curve. You come down and hit the end of the strobe lights, and it curves 45° to the right, right to the runway, right across the city. So they had these high-intensity lights on top of buildings in a perfect curve from where you would see it leading into the runway. Also, landing at night, all the boats in the harbor and all the high-rise apartments on the side of the hill were lit up. All in all it's really a fabulous sight.

We went back to the hotel, got a few beers and something to eat, and hit the sack.

On Wednesday, the last day of September, we went back to the airport for a flight to Taipei in Taiwan. We were supposed to have a ten o'clock departure, but we got word when we got to the airport that it would actually be an eleven o'clock departure. It's only about 550 miles from Singapore to Taipei, an hour and fifteen minutes. That was another short night. We left the hotel at Hong Kong at eight o'clock and got to the hotel bar in Taipei at a quarter after four in the afternoon. So that's eight hours and fifteen minutes for a one hour and fifteen minute flight. It just takes a long time to get everything accomplished. We have to get to bed early because they want to leave tomorrow at eight o'clock in the morning.

We had a five o'clock pick-up at the hotel in Taipei. It's a long cab ride from the hotel to the airport. It cost us 1,000 NT, the New Taiwan dollar that converts to about twenty-seven US dollars. We arrived at the terminal, and it was so early in the morning that everything was locked up. We were a little concerned that we weren't going to be able to get in, but there were some military guards there who unlocked the door and let us in. They went back and woke up the agent. China Airlines handled us, and the agent was asleep behind the counter. He woke up and got the paperwork in good shape and took us out to the airplane.

The only hiccup was with the catered breakfast. I had ordered a hot breakfast of scrambled eggs with ham, rolls, and juice. When the caterer came with the breakfast, the scrambled eggs and ham were ice cold. The casseroles had been in the ice box all night. And not only that, there was dry ice in the tray carrier to make sure that the hot breakfast stayed good and cold. I don't know how the Taiwanese have their breakfast, but when they order a hot breakfast, it seems to me that it should be delivered hot. Here it was again, the communications problem.

Taipei to Nagoya, Japan is a relatively short flight, 1,200 miles and 2¾ hours. The interesting part about this flight was that typhoon Elsie was out in the same area. When we went to bed the night before, we knew its position but we didn't know whether it was going to go northwest, northeast, or north. If it went northwest, it would've been on our course to Nagoya. Fortunately it turned northeast. As we were cruising along at 35,000 feet, we could see the whole system off to our right. We were 300 miles away and could see lots of clouds but nothing drastic.

The forecast for Nagoya was excellent, just a few scattered clouds, but like most forecasts it wasn't as predicted. When we arrived there, they had a 500 foot overcast, poor visibility, and a mist. We taxied in, and we were on Japanese soil.

The Japanese people were most interesting. A good many – I'd say about 25 percent of the women there – were dressed in the traditional Japanese dress, the kimono with the sash and the ornamental board on the back, and the white stockings with the notched-toe sandals. The women puttered along, walking the respectful three paces behind the husband wherever they went. I don't know where we men went wrong in the United States, but I guess that's the way it goes.

That night it was raining very hard from typhoon Elsie. We had elected that we would go out to the airport the next day and check the weather. If the typhoon was heading toward Tokyo, we'd stay in Nagoya another day, but if it stayed out at sea, we'd head on to Tokyo. We'd tried to get hangar space for the bird to keep it out of the wind and the rain.

I was really amazed the next morning. I woke up, threw the curtain back, and there wasn't a cloud in the sky. It was just a beautiful, sparkling day. It was breezy – I guess there was about a thirty knot wind blowing – but there was no weather whatsoever. Typhoon Elsie had veered a little bit more northeast, and all that was affecting the island of Japan was the wind. There wasn't any rain associated with it.

So, we cranked up and flew 200 miles to Tokyo. We flew right by Mt. Fiji, a beautiful sight though there was no snow on the peak, and into the Narita Airport at Tokyo. That's the brand new airport that all the demonstrators tried to keep from opening because the government had confiscated the farmers' land to build this huge complex. It was very quiet, no airplanes moving. We were the only airplane!

When they directed us onto the ramp, what I saw was amazing. There must have been five cars and twenty people waiting there for us: the airline representatives, catering people, mechanics, field service people, ATC people, the toilet servicing group. They were all lined up just as if the President of the United States was arriving. It was quite a sight.

We did all our chores and hopped in the cab for the city. Narita Airport is about forty miles from the city of Tokyo, so depending on the traffic, it's an hour and a half or two hours into town. Last night we went down to the Ginza with all the bright, colorful lights and the people and the action. I was really amazed at the price of things there. It was the first time I'd ever seen a $50 tie or $320 pair of shoes or a $200 shirt. The three of us went out to dinner. It was nothing spectacular, but the bill was $90. So it was $30 each for dinner. I think our hotel bill was about $110 each. I'm not sure a person could afford to live in Tokyo unless he was on an expense account.

Today was a leisurely day, one of our few days off. We took a sightseeing tour. We went out and did some shopping. We have to get to bed early tonight, because we have another five o'clock pick-up tomorrow and an eight a.m. takeoff. If all goes well, we'll go from Tokyo to Wake Island in about four hours. And then from Wake Island to Honolulu is about a five hour flight. The problem is that we lose five hours. We pick up a day, but we lose five hours. We take off here on a Sunday, cross the International Date Line, and land in Honolulu on a Saturday. But by the time we get to Honolulu, it'll be eleven o'clock Saturday night.

The flight to Wake Island was routine with good weather. It's about 2,000 miles or four hours. It was a pretty island, a little atoll, beautiful water around the island, and a single landing strip, water to water. The strip covers the entire southern part of the atoll. We refueled, and then onto Honolulu.

Due to the fact that we were flying east and the sun was going west, it got dark shortly after we reached altitude. About an hour and a half before arriving in Honolulu, we were sailing along, tired and waiting for the time to pass, when a light came on on the overhead panel in the cockpit. We looked up, and it indicated that our windshield heat inverter had failed. We tried to transfer one of the other inverters to the windshield panels, but they wouldn't transfer. There was no way to get heat to the windshields.

There was nothing drastic about that, except that when we let down into moist air, the windshield would be inclined to fog up. So as we let down, it started to fog up and we wiped and wiped, and I was able to see the runway all right. It's impossible to wipe it clean. We landed with no difficulty, but as soon as we turned off the runway the ice cold windshields immediately fogged up on both sides. It was so thick that it was impossible to wipe any of it off. We taxied very slowly and opened the side DV, or direct view, windows. I could see out to the left, and the other pilot could see out to the right, but neither of us could see straight ahead. So I sort of zigzagged and taxied in very slowly. Of course the tower wondered what our problem was and why we were taxiing so slow. As we were coming to the ramp, our agent was there waiting and waving violently, and he finally shook his head in disgust. He couldn't understand why we were just creeping in. Well, we didn't want to taxi into anything. It was almost like taxiing blind. It was like trying to see through a pinhole. It was dark, and the whole inside of the cockpit was fogged up.

As soon as we opened the door, the agent popped up, and we said, "Take a look."

And he said, "Oh, no wonder you were taxiing so slow."

"Sorry about that." But it was no big deal.

The leg from Wake to Honolulu was 2,300 miles, four hours and forty minutes. It was rather a long day with a total of 4,300 miles, nine hours of flight time, and twelve hours on duty time. We were just a bit tired. I had made up the schedule a month in advance. I said we would be in Honolulu at ten forty-five p.m, and on the way I told the agent, "Hey, we'll be back at ten forty-five. Have customs ready, have your baggage handlers ready and, we'll be here at ten forty-five on Saturday night." Well, as luck would have it, we taxied up to the ramp at ten forty-five, which I guess is quite a coincidence.

US customs was there to meet us. Around the world, the US customs is the toughest to get through and the most unfriendly. They met the airplane and said, "Everything comes off." Meaning, of course, all the baggage, gifts, boxes, and so forth – the crew included. Usually we send the passengers in, they clear, and then we clear later. But customs wanted to see everybody. Of course it was late at night at this time, after eleven o'clock. We took all the baggage off and the bundles and the gifts and locked the airplane and went into customs. They went through our baggage with a fine-tooth comb. They wanted to see our declarations, the gifts we'd bought. Then they wanted to see the receipts for the gifts. Of course the receipts were made up in local currency, so I'm not really sure what that meant to them. They even checked the labels on the suits to see if they had a foreign label. And of course they checked cameras, watches, and jewelry. It was as if they didn't believe you.

We had another slight delay there. As a rule, customs can handle immigration duties also if everyone is a US citizen. Due to communications errors, it failed to get through that we had two Canadians on board. So we had to hang around while they could locate an immigrations man, get him out there, look at the Canadian passports, and say, "Hey, that's great," and pass them on through.

The next day, after we got a good night's sleep, we went back to the airport to do the chores. We pulled out the power shield on the front of the electrical panel. It's a huge panel that covers all your electrical units. We pulled it out, did our research, and found a blown fuse for the windshield heat. We put a new one in, put power back in the airplane, and everything worked perfectly.

We spent the rest of the day in Honolulu, got another good night's sleep, and then made a routine flight to San Francisco. It turned out there was a board meeting Tuesday morning in San Francisco, so we flew into San Francisco on Monday and spent the night. Tuesday afternoon, we flew nine board members from San Francisco to San Diego. We dropped all of them and tons of baggage and then ferried back to Los Angeles. It sure was great to finally get home.

For the last two weeks we've been flying around the South Pacific with one of our electronic fuel computers inoperative. We've been flying with that one on manual. Just for interest, the day after we returned, our maintenance pulled the computer and took it apart, and they dumped a whole glass of water out of it. Evidently rain had gotten into the computer and filled it up while we were sitting in Hong Kong. A full glass of water in a little black box – no wonder the darn thing wouldn't work.

To summarize the last three and a half weeks, we visited thirteen places and about ten countries. We flew 26,000 miles in about sixty hours of block time.

Without any further ado, I'll sign off. So, everybody back to the bar.